Combat Reporter

Combat Reporter

DON WHITEHEAD'S
WORLD WAR II DIARY AND MEMOIRS

Edited by John B. Romeiser

FORDHAM UNIVERSITY PRESS
NEW YORK 2006

World War II: The Global, Human, and Ethical Dimension
ISSN 1541-0293

Library of Congress Cataloging-in-Publication Data
Whitehead, Don, 1908–
Combat reporter : Don Whitehead's World War II diary and memoirs / edited by
John B. Romeiser.—1st ed.
p. cm.—(World War II—the global, human, and ethical dimension; 12)
Includes bibliographical references and index.
ISBN-13: 978-0-8232-2675-7
ISBN-10: 0-8232-2675-1
1. Whitehead, Don, 1908– 2. World War, 1939–1945—Campaigns—Africa, North
3. World War, 1939–1945—Campaigns—Italy—Sicily. 4. World War, 1939–1945—
Journalists—Diaries. 5. World War, 1939–1945—Personal narratives, American
6. War correspondents—United States—Diaries. I. Romeiser, John Beals, 1948– II. Title.
D766.82.W48 2006
940.54′1373092—dc22
2006021330

Printed in the United States of America
08 07 06 5 4 3 2 1
First edition

Contents

Editor's Note and Acknowledgments

THE Donald F. Whitehead war diary covers an eight-month span, from September 1942 to April 1943, and provides the primary source material for this book. My transcription has retained the original spelling and punctuation. Interpolated or clarifying material is bracketed immediately following. The second source for this project is an unfinished typescript of a book that Whitehead was clearly planning to write on his World War II experiences. The text covers only his assignments in North Africa and Sicily and omits his coverage of the fierce combat on the Italian peninsula, the Normandy invasion and battle for France, and the subsequent liberation of Nazi Germany. In the case of the unpublished book, I have done some modest editing to correct misspellings and make the text more consistent.

Home once again and able to verify his AP stories and other sources, Whitehead had the time to check the accuracy of his spelling of certain place names and individuals, as well as to shed additional light on his diary's material, which might not have been apparent to him at the time he wrote it. It is not clear why he never finished what would have been a magnificent contribution to the understanding of the press during wartime. I suspect that being called to Korea to report the war for AP diverted his attention. By the time he returned from Korea, he had been assigned to Washington, where he began working on a book on J. Edgar Hoover and the FBI, a topic made much more relevant and marketable by Cold War fears.

The Whitehead war diary was found in his personal possessions in Tulsa, Oklahoma, where his only child, Ruth Whitehead, had moved near the end of her life. I am grateful to her daughter, Marie Weidus, Don Whitehead's granddaughter, for making this precious journal available to me so that I could complete this project. Moreover, she was patient in allowing its use for almost two years as I moved forward on this book, a privilege that permitted me to verify the accuracy of each word on multiple occasions. That is not to say that Don Whitehead's handwriting was not clear and legible, especially considering the precarious circumstances under which he wrote. When a fountain pen was not available, he would sometimes record his entries in pencil, then go back and retrace the words in black ink. As he points out, German bombers were all too often plying the skies above him and his fellow correspondents, dropping their deadly payloads and shaking the ground for hundreds of yards just as he was sitting down to write.[1] On other occasions, he had to contend with the bitter cold of the Libyan winter or sudden deluges that penetrated his shelter and left inky splotches on the ruled pages of his leather-bound diary.

For those who are interested, the bulk of the Whitehead papers, letters, and photographs, spanning a five-decade-long career that included two Pulitzer prizes, can be found in the Special Collections of the University of Tennessee's Hoskins Library.

In conclusion, I would like thank Kurt Piehler, director of the University's Center for the Study of War and Society, for his steadfast support and encouragement. I would also like to thank Command Sgt. Major Ben Franklin (First Infantry Division, Sixteenth Regiment), who helped me understand many of the abbreviations and terms found in the diary. His effervescent and eternally hospitable wife, Ute, deciphered some of the more troublesome words. Even though born and educated in Germany, she said that the handwriting was not that different between German and English. She and Ben have been my constant inspiration throughout my research on Don Whitehead.

Foreword

RICK ATKINSON

No one bore witness better than Don Whitehead. Among World War II combat correspondents, he was one of the few whose powers of observation and literary sensibilities remain vibrant generations later. A self-effacing former advertising manager for a newspaper in Harlan, Kentucky, Whitehead possessed the priceless impulse to go to the sound of the guns. As a reporter for the Associated Press, he covered the invasions of Italy and Normandy and the campaigns across France and Germany through the end of the European war. He distinguished himself further in Korea, and he won the Pulitzer Prize twice.

When Whitehead went off to war, the professional and independent combat correspondent had been in existence less than a century. Until the Crimean War in the 1850s, those who wrote about battle tended to be either participants, like Julius Caesar and Thucydides, or fiction writers, like Stephen Crane and Leo Tolstoy. It was up to Ernie Pyle, Edward R. Murrow, John Hersey, Whitehead, and other great reporters to disprove or at least mitigate Senator Hiram Johnson's grim 1917 aphorism that "the first casualty when war comes is truth." The professionalism, skepticism, and courage of those World War II correspondents set the bar very high for the journalists following in their footsteps, such as David Halberstam and Neil Sheehan in Vietnam.

Whitehead put himself in harm's way for months and then years at a time. He had an ear for irony and an eye for the telling detail—the first American gun to fire across the Messina Straits from Sicily into mainland Italy in August 1943, he tells us, was dubbed *Draftee*. He also possessed a knack for metaphor, describing how a battered seaside villa "trembled like a palsied old gentleman" during a heavy shelling at Anzio in 1944. We see Whitehead homesick and weary, poignantly pining for his wife, yet pressing on to do what had to be done. If at times he could be cynical and appalled by war's waste, he had earned those moments of disgust as surely as had any GI with a sleeve full of chevrons and years of overseas service. This volume, deftly combining his diary and a previously unpublished memoir, brings Whitehead and his reporting back to life, and twenty-first-century readers are the richer for it.

Introduction

THROUGHOUT his distinguished career as a journalist, Donald Ford Whitehead always aspired to be where the action was. From the time he was a young boy growing up in Harlan, Kentucky, where he once witnessed a murder between feuding families, Whitehead not only understood the necessity but relished the opportunity to witness the breaking news he was charged with reporting. Like his friend and fellow journalist Ernie Pyle, whom he first met during the Sicily campaign, Whitehead assumed the considerable risks of frontline reporting, so that he could get a more authentic story for his readers back home. Years later, he explained that the reason he wanted to leave the safety and security of reporting out of the Associated Press headquarters in New York City was that he "wanted to be up front where the fighting men were."

Born in Inman, Virginia, on April 8, 1908, newsman and author Don Whitehead became city editor of the *Harlan Daily Enterprise* in 1929 and covered the labor wars of the early 1930s in Harlan County, Kentucky. Whitehead's affiliation with the Associated Press began when he joined the wire service in 1935 as night editor in Memphis, Tennessee, and then became an AP correspondent in Knoxville from 1937 to 1940. In early 1941, Whitehead was transferred to New York as a feature writer. His pay increased from $65 to $85 per week, but only after he informed his boss in New York that he could not make ends meet on his Knoxville salary.

After the attack on Pearl Harbor in December 1941, Whitehead increasingly saw his assignments shift, as he began to cover the preparations for war stateside, including the Lend-Lease shipments of bombers to England via Newfoundland and military maneuvers in the Carolinas, where recruits trained with logs on wheels in place of artillery and shouldered pieces of wood instead of rifles. Like many, he knew that the army had a long way to go before it would be ready to tackle the disciplined, well-equipped troops of Nazi Germany and Imperial Japan. In August

1942, he was notified that he would be going overseas and began the process to be accredited as a war correspondent.

Upon his arrival in the Middle East to cover the British Eighth Army's pursuit of General Erwin Rommel for the Associated Press, Whitehead quickly learned the difference between the war correspondent and the combat correspondent. As he wrote in his unpublished autobiography in the early 1950s, the text of which is incorporated in this book: "Here was the opportunity I had been seeking, the chance to become a combat correspondent. Those of us in the trade developed a snobbish pride in drawing a distinction between a 'war' correspondent and a 'combat' correspondent. WE righteously considered our combat status a step higher in the correspondents' caste system and, consequently, we had the same clannish feeling that bound combat troops against the rear echelons who had never heard a shot fired in the war."

On a personal level, staying in Manhattan to work for the largest and most prestigious wire service in the world surely must have made good sense to Whitehead. He was thirty-four, and he, his beloved wife Marie, and their young daughter Ruth had moved to a nice home on Long Island. At a time when many women did not normally pursue careers, Marie Whitehead had taken a job with a Manhattan advertising agency. Don Whitehead's career path looked bright as well. But there was a war that needed to be covered, and Don was convinced that he was just the man to do it. Despite warnings of the considerable personal risk he would undergo and the uncertainties as to when he could return home to his family, Whitehead did not blanch. In his usual gung-ho manner, he acknowledged these pitfalls and challenged his cautious higher-ups, "Time's a-wastin. When and where do I go?"

While Whitehead referred to the supportive role that his wife played in his switch to the hazards of frontline war reporting, it is abundantly clear from her letters to him in North Africa that she missed him deeply, just as he so profoundly missed her. Some of his most poignant entries relate to their separation. On December 4, 1942, Whitehead wrote from Cairo, a city that he found both enticing and maddeningly frustrating: "I found seven letters from Marie waiting for me at the office. It was wonderful to hear even though hearing has made me blue." Just under two weeks later, he marked their anniversary while writing from Marble Arch, Libya: "Fourteen years ago Marie and I were married—our fourteenth anniversary and I'm sitting in a tent in the desert 10,000 miles from home." In Médenine, Tunisia, in March 1943, he wrote in a similar vein: "There was a letter from Marie, too. She was feeling so blue when she wrote it. And I can do nothing to help her. It's such a helpless feeling. All I can do is pray that this goddamned war will be over before many more months have passed." Later that same month, still wandering in the desert and pursuing Rommel in what seemed an endless "fox and hound" chase, Whitehead wrote despairingly: "Most of my thoughts of the future revolve around one person—and that is Marie. God, how I want her—how I long to hold her in my arms—that will do it. But I can see us in each others arms without actually feeling ourselves together—but we'll be in a heaven of our own—a timeless boundless space beyond understanding. That time will come because of our love—and then there can be no loneliness or heartaches or pain."

The narrative that follows chronicles Don Whitehead's journalistic trek from New York City through Sicily. The diary itself focuses solely on his time in North Africa. It is unclear why Whitehead stopped writing his impressions and reflections one month before Allied troops captured Tunis and expelled the Germans and Italians. Perhaps once he had been assigned to Sicily to cover the U.S. military operations there in July 1943, the Associated Press expected him to devote all his attention to reporting the American side, leaving him less time to keep his journal current.

The Sicily portion of this narrative is drawn from his unfinished book typescript, written almost a decade later. The source for some of the Sicily narrative can be found in the dispatches Whitehead wrote for the Associated Press. Both the diary and his unpublished war memoirs are relatively short, so I decided that it would make more sense to combine them, with the diary serving as the primary source. The alternating voices of the frontline reporter and the more seasoned correspondent, writing six years after the war has ended, are woven together in such a way that the reader will, I hope, gain from the richness of their complementary perspectives. In order to distinguish these two narratives in the North Africa section, I have chosen to italicize the nondiary sections. While a certain amount of duplication can be found in several entries covering similar events, they are, for the most part, written from entirely different viewpoints.

The diary records the heartaches, triumphs, and tribulations of a frontline reporter coming of age and acquiring the skills needed to compete against rival journalists and to please the higher-ups at the Associated Press, while always keeping the scoop in mind. It also provides graphic slices of life in a combat zone, including the daily battles with thirst, the cold, the heat, fleas, sandstorms, and bland rations. Cognizant of the dangers of war reporting, Whitehead and his colleagues speak openly of their fears but shake them off with a great deal of stoicism and good humor. The shared cigarette, unearthed cache of red wine, or swig of smooth Kentucky bourbon from a flask in a buddy's knapsack often give them the necessary courage to face another day of fatigue, discomfort, and pervasive boredom.

In many ways, Whitehead's unfinished World War II memoirs offer a gloss on the earlier diary, by providing a retrospective historical view that would have been lacking in the journal. One of the most striking examples can be found in reference to Benghazi, Libya, on November 22, 1942, where Whitehead records: "We toured the ruins of Bengasi today, poking about in dark, silent buildings lettered with trash and discarded clothing and household odds and ends. In the Jewish quarter the rabbi said the Germans had hung four Jews as a warning not to be friendly to the English. The word 'Jew' was printed on the doors of their homes and the little stalls in which they had their shops." Several months later after the British entered Tripoli, Whitehead gained a greater sense of how the Jewish population had suffered under German and Italian rule:

> In the afternoon Tucker, Zinder Lloyd Williams of Reuters and I went down to the Ghetto. Never have I had such an experience—it was embarrassing and shocking. As soon as the Jews learned we were American and English, they mobbed us. Men threw their arms around us and kissed our faces. Women patted us. Children clung to our legs and kissed our shoes. Everyone wanted to shake hands. A husky fellow grabbed us by the arms and pulled us through the crowds down a dark stairway into a room where a patriarch in a white robe sat at a bare table. Dozens crowded into the room. The doors were barred. They gave us wine, nuts, candy. We were given a royal welcome as though we personally had liberated them. They told us the Italians had treated them worse than the Germans.

Writing almost a decade later, he offers an expanded and more poignant account of the Tripoli experience:

> The torrent of people flowed after us until the room was jammed and no others could squeeze their way inside. Women brought us wine and bread and cheese. Everyone, who could, reached out to touch us or to

grasp our hands as though we were Messiahs and a touch would heal the wounds they had suffered in body and spirit.

They were laughing and crying and shouting. We were the symbols of liberation to these people. We represented the hope that had burned in their hearts for so long. We were freedom come at last.

And suddenly I felt humble and ashamed . . . ashamed that any human being could suffer the indignities these people had suffered. Ashamed that they should have reason for such gratitude.

I felt like weeping. And I did.

Having witnessed the horrors of the Nazi death camp Buchenwald later in the war, Whitehead was perhaps better able to articulate more explicitly the joy and gladness of an oppressed people and to share in their emotions.[1]

Unlike his wire dispatches for the Associated Press, the writing in the diary and war autobiography is more personal and less dispassionate. Whitehead is able to vent his frustrations with the petty politics of the command structure or with the bureaucratic hurdles he often had to clear just to be able to report. His complaints are more numerous in the diary, which he probably never expected to see the light of day. Cooped up in Cairo for weeks before he is able to join the Eighth Army in the desert, he grouses: "Cairo becomes more nerve-racking as the days go by. This place gets on your nerves, in your hair and rasps like a file. It's the politics, the gossip and the petty problems, which only hamper any effort to get a job done. I'm still waiting for the British to come through with my credentials."

Moreover, he expresses the horror of combat and its attendant destruction of innocent lives and property in graphic terms, using language that would most likely have never made it past the censors at Associated Press headquarters in New York. At Mersa Brega, on December 16, 1943, Whitehead writes: "The bodies of Scotsmen lie in the minefields where they were caught by exploding traps, growing black in the sun. Mines are everywhere. I saw a desert burial of a young Scot beside the road, while the bagpipes played in the distance. The padre said a few words and the soldiers stood silent with their heads bared. On the road a few yards away rolled the tanks, guns and trucks. Planes roared overhead— but the group at the grave seemed oblivious to all the noise and uproar." The terseness of this brief entry in the diary contrasts sharply with the more lyrical yet darker description from his unfinished war memoirs.

Again, the perspective of ten years and much more dying along the way transforms the event into a compelling vignette of war:

> The bodies of Highlanders lay in the minefields growing black under the sun. Sappers were busy clearing the roads for the advance and could not take the time to recover the bodies. The stench of death lay heavily over the desert.
>
> Once we stopped and watched the burial of a young Scot beside the road. Across the sands rolled the high, reedy wailing of the bagpipes, a thin and mournful dirge in the roar of planes overhead and the rumbling of tanks and trucks along the road. Soldiers stood with heads bared while the chaplain intoned a prayer. The body was lowered into a shallow grave and covered with sand. The white cross looked lonely and incongruous marking the mound already being rippled by the wind.

While in Sicily covering the battle for Mount Brolo, Whitehead takes aim at General George Patton, a man who, though a brilliant tactician, epitomized for him the vanity and arrogance of an individual with no empathy for the sacrifices of the common soldier:

> A short time later General Patton came riding up in his command car. His varnished helmet shone in the sun and the famous pearl-handled revolver glinted at his side. He was accompanied by young Senator Lodge of Massachusetts.
>
> The command car stopped at the base of the hill where the tired, filthy infantrymen were filing down from fire-blackened Mount Brolo, dragging their feet like gaunt zombies. Along the roadway and on the sides of the mountain lay the bodies of scores of Americans cut down in the bloody twenty-four-hour battle. There were more bodies in the lemon grove below the road but we couldn't see them.
>
> "All you men from Massachusetts fall out over here!" Patton ordered.
>
> A few weary doughboys trudged over to the roadside and stood listlessly waiting. The senator from Massachusetts walked over to them and made a little speech. Lodge may have delivered an excellent talk there among the dead on the slopes of Brolo. But for the life of me I cannot remember what he said. All I recall now is Patton standing tall and straight in his command car.
>
> "The American soldier is the greatest soldier in all the world," the general said. And then he pointed to the mountains. "Only American soldiers can climb mountains like those."

All at once the whole little tableau sickened me. I wanted to get away from the voices of the general and the senator. The dead scattered on the hillside and in the lemon grove spoke eloquently enough.

On a less somber note, Don Whitehead often enjoys regaling his readers with amusing anecdotes and yarns. Sometimes the joke is on Whitehead himself as, for example, the time he met an officer who shared his enthusiasm for the Bluegrass State and for horse racing. Writing in his diary, he recalls: "I hadn't heard his name when we were introduced. We were sitting on a cot in the semi-darkness and I poured him a slug [of Canadian Club] into his canteen cup. The talk turned to horses. I began giving him pointers on racing and sharing my knowledge of the turf." As it turns out, the unknown officer is none other than Lieut. Col. C. V. "Sonny" Whitney, a famous and wealthy horse breeder. As Whitehead remembers: "Even in the darkness, Lieut. Col. Whitney probably could see the blush that suffused my burning face. But he was a gentleman. He didn't laugh."

After the campaigns in North Africa and Sicily drew to a close, Don Whitehead went on to cover the invasion of Italy, the landings in Normandy on D-Day, the race across France (getting a well-deserved scoop on the liberation of Paris), and, finally, the arduous slog across Germany as the Allies moved toward Berlin and V-E Day, May 8, 1945. The bulk of his World War II reporting for the Associated Press can now be found in *Beachhead Don: Reporting the War from the European Theater, 1942–1945*. He was fortunate enough to have survived almost three years of harrowing reporting and countless close calls with no more than a few scratches. Soon thereafter, he was on the trail of the big story once again, and in 1946, he covered the explosion of an atomic bomb at Bikini Atoll. A few short years later, he joined American forces in Korea, where he provided distinguished coverage of that conflict for the AP. His efforts were rewarded, at long last, by the awarding of two Pulitzer prizes for distinguished journalism.

During the 1950s, Whitehead served as Washington bureau chief for the *New York Herald Tribune* and wrote the first of his five books, the best-selling *The FBI Story*, which was later made into a popular movie starring James Stewart. He returned to Knoxville in 1959 to begin writing a column for the *News Sentinel*, a pleasant change of pace from the grueling war reporting and working in Washington. Whitehead died in Knoxville on January 12, 1981, at age 72.

One

FROM MANHATTAN TO CAIRO,
SEPTEMBER–OCTOBER 1942

September 19, 1942
New York

Actually, I don't believe I ever thought I'd be chosen as a war correspondent for the A.P. It was one of those vague and incredible jobs about which you read with a great deal of envy for those who were helping write the history of World War II. When I read the stories of Bob St. John and Larry Allen and Quentin Reynolds and Drew Middleton I felt so restless and dissatisfied that my work became a burden of trivia. It seemed slightly absurd to be writing of movie stars, Harlem and front page celebrities when there was a war to write about—the raw material of death and agony and heroism.

More and more I knew I could never be happy until I had a chance to report this war from a sideline seat. There would have been a gnawing frustration that would have poisoned me for years to come.

I suppose Marie[1] has sensed the feeling. It's something that can hardly be explained. God knows it's going to be hard for both of us and yet it has to be.

It's strange how little things can change the course of your life—or at least you see the turning point as the result of some trifling event.

In my case, the change came one day last month when Charlie Honce happened to remark that Drew Middleton was resigning A.P. to go with the *Times*.

"I wish I could get his job," I remarked casually.

"Well we're needing new overseas," Charlie said. "Why don't you see what you can do about it?"

A few weeks before, Alan Jones had discouraged me when I asked about the chances for a foreign assignment. It was the usual old brush-off—"You're more valuable where you are." So I just forgot about the whole thing and said to myself that it wasn't in the books for me to get a foreign assignment.

I went to Gould.[2]

"I'd like to have Drew Middleton's job," I told him. "I've felt as though I were marking time and I want to get overseas. I'd like to have your support and blessing."

Gould said: "We can't promise you Middleton's job. We can't make any commitments on what a man will do if he is given a foreign assignment. But I think you could do a good job for us. I'll be glad to give you my approval."

And so the wheels began turning upstairs.

Vic Hackler sent down a letter "for the record":

"Before we send you on an assignment outside this country . . . it is only fair that I outline to you the other side of what may appear now to be a picture of a glamorous experience.

"There is great danger involved. Two of our foreign staff members are now missing and we fear they may be dead. Others have been injured or have had very narrow escapes. Many have become ill.

"There is no telling where a man in foreign service may be sent. In many countries the living conditions are terrible, drinking water is dangerous, and none of the ordinary comforts of home are available.

"All such assignments now have to be 'for the duration,' because of the uncertainties of transportation. Former provisions for home leave cannot apply in war time . . ."

I understood all those things. I replied, "Time's a-wastin. When and where do I go?"

John Evans gave me instructions about passport, inoculations, and the other matters of routine necessary to prepare for the assignment. I got a draft board release.

But to this day I don't know where I'm going except it will be in the Middle East. My passport instructions came for India, Turkey, Iran, Iraq, Palestine, Egypt—and other countries en route.

It looks like Toby Wiant[3] and I will go together with George Tucker and Clyde Farnsworth to follow soon. Evans says we will go to Cairo for training under Ed Kennedy[4] and then be sent to various places from there. We'll get our uniforms and other equipment in Cairo.

Today there came a letter from Col. Francis V. Fitzgerald, Chief of the Security Control Division of the War Department's Bureau of Public Relations.

"Concerning your request for priority in air travel to India, this priority has been granted.

"The company which will carry you will contact you to arrange final details. This contact may come at a short notice. Therefore, it is desirable that you get your passport and other affairs in order, so that you can leave on short notice."

Evans says Cairo—the war department says India. Somebody has got to decide and soon. And my passport hasn't arrived yet—and I have not gotten visas—and there are still several inoculations to take for typhus, cholera, yellow fever, and tetanus.

Fortunately I'm accredited by the War Department to the U.S. Army and don't have that to worry about. But there's always the fear that the transportation order will come through before I clear the passport and visas. I'm not worried about the serums, I can get those on the other side.

In all this rush, I can't help but feel there's a slight quality of the absurd to my assignment.

I suppose this is what a great many newspapermen consider as a big-shot assignment—you are chosen because you have "arrived" as a big-time reporter.

At least that's how I would have felt a few years ago as the city editor and advertising manager of the *Harlan Daily Enterprise*.[5] Such an assignment would have seemed fantastic.

But I don't feel like a "big shot"—just a little scared and awed by what has happened and amazed that it has happened to me.

September 23, 1942
New York

It looks as though India is going to be my stamping ground if and when I get across.

My God, this business of trying to be a foreign correspondent is just one great mass of red tape, delay, nervous tension, and more delay. As for work, I'm about as useful in the office as a keyless typewriter.

My passport came today and Toby Wiant and I started on that great adventure of trying to get visas. Our passage may come through at any time—and both of us without visas.

The British were polite but nothing could be done until they have had a reply from a cable to India approving our entry.

"Perhaps we'll hear in three or four days," a Mr. Robinson said. "Then we can give you the necessary visas."

Three or four days!

"Can't you give us visas for Iraq, Trinidad and the other countries en route to India? If we have those then if necessary we could get the visa for India in Cairo."

"Oh dear me no," Mr. Robinson said. "We must do these things in an orderly manner. After we hear from India, we'll give you all the visas at once."

No use beating our brains out here. So we headed for the Egyptian consulate. The consul general was out but would be back in an hour.

Finally we entered his office.

"I cannot give you visas," he said. "I have nothing against you personally, but some of the newspaper men have abused our hospitality. They write gossip that is none of their business and say things about the Royal family that embarrass us.

"No, I cannot give you a visa. However, if the minister in Washington wants to give you a visa, that is all right. I cannot take the responsibility.

"I could give you a transit visa—but that would not permit you to stay in the country."

Since we might have to stay in Cairo, we requested he call the minister and ask his approval.

That was that.

The consul general of Liberia was next. Good old Liberia—a land that hasn't yet learned how to use red tape.

At 25 Beaver Street we entered a small office where a large, intelligent looking Negro man sat behind a desk.

We stated our business. He reached into the desk and pulled out a battered old ledger that looked like a cash book in the cross roads general store. He entered our names, the number of the passport and other necessary information, and stamped our passports. At least we could now pass through Liberia.

"Is there any fee?" I asked.

"Oh, no," the Liberian government representative said.

"But I have a little book I sell for 25 cents telling something about Liberia."

The least we could do was buy a book. Even Gene Talwadyn would have appreciated that visa stamp had he been in our place.

Next on the schedule was the Iranian consulate, a luxurious suite of rooms in an apartment hotel on upper Fifth Ave.

A beauteous French girl escorted us from the elevator into the reception room. The consul general was out but later we found him in.

The country of Iran rates ace high in my books. Quickly and courteously they prepared our visas and the lovely young French girl led us to the elevator, chattering all the while.

"I am so cold," she said with a coquettish look at Toby.

"Yeah, this coal and oil shortage is terrible," said Toby. And right there I began to have my doubts about Toby.

September 25, 1942
New York

The Indian visa cable hasn't come through yet! It may be we'll have to pick it up in Cairo if transportation beats the cable. There's no way to hurry the process—just be patient and wait. I suppose we're getting good training for future visa jitters.

We'll know at noon tomorrow whether our passage is booked this weekend. The agent at Pan-American Airlines said the list of passengers would be sent from Washington and we would be notified if our names were on it. If not, then maybe we'll be on the list for the flight about October 5.

We'll fly from New York to N. [Natal, Brazil], take a shuttle plane to L. [Liberia], and then on to C. [Cairo]

At least as far as Cairo we can carry 55 pounds of baggage, Pan-Am says. That solves a problem because I thought we could take only 44 pounds. Marie & I weighed my case and typewriter last night and it all totaled 45 pounds. Dan DeLuce came back from the wars today looking fit. The campaign in Burma apparently had left no scars. He said things wouldn't be too bad in India although he didn't expect any excitement in that sector soon. He's probably right but I hope not.

September 27, 1942
New York

No transportation in sight yet. Pan-Am says our names were not on the passenger list for the flight this weekend.

September 28, 1942
New York

Farewells, conferences, a drink with Pappy Kevarick and lunch with Evans for some last bits of advice and instruction. Tickets New York to Karachi $1500. Advance $500 in crisp $10s and $20s—and all set.

Protymans and Riggses over for goodbyes. Marie, Ruth[6] and I taxi to La Guardia airport.

Why is it when you have so much to say the words stick and you're dumb? Marie & Ruth both were wonderful—never a tear—but I guess that came later. God bless them both and look after them.

Our plane took off at 9 P.M.

September 30, 1942
Miami

The trip down was smooth. Met an interesting chap aboard—Capt. Bob Crawford, who wrote the Army Air Force song that is so popular. He was a concert singer until his song clicked and put him in The Long Green, Son of an Alaskan gold miner, Princeton, Greenwich Village, music teacher, amateur pilot—he's in the Pan-Am ferry service, writing songs on the side. Arrived 6:30 A.M. Not much sleep.

Biscayne Bay is bright and colorful through our hotel window. The pigeons wheel and turn in droves—Miami looks and smells so clean after New York's carbonized odors.

A couple of days leisure here would be all right by me but we gotta move on tomorrow morning. The trip is developing faster than we'd thought. Wish Marie could see the view from this window. It's lovely. One of these days so help me we'll do it.

By the time Toby & I began winding up the red tape here we were getting slap-happy and tired. Then my hat blew off and went sailing down the street with me chasing it. That just about finished me for the day.

October 1, 1942
Georgetown, British Guiana

Was it this morning that we left Miami? It seems a long time ago. Time and space lose their values when you're tearing through a cloud-piled sky at 190 mph in a C-54 Douglas transport.

We piled out of bed at 12 midnight, bathed, shaved and got ready for the 2:30 bus to the airport. There we checked with immigration, customs, and navy, had breakfast.

The transport was huge and gray in the night. A squad of troops filed aboard with tommy guns, rifles and full packs. They looked young, tan, tough and capable. There wasn't any horseplay or boisterous talk among them. The trip ahead seemed to have subdued them.

We took off at 4:10 A.M. and the lights of Miami faded. Just blackness outside, deep inky blackness rushing past the windows, and so we tried to sleep.

The sky was beautiful at dawn. Clouds piled up in fantastic splendor that took your breath. There's nothing more beautiful than the never-never land above the clouds.

But still, even the beauty becomes monotonous after a while.

At 8:56 we landed at a field "Somewhere in Puerto Rico," a fine port carved out of the tropic growth by the U.S. Army. A soldier drove us around for a glimpse of the field. The barracks looked cool and comfortable.

"What is there here for amusement," I asked.

"We got movies," the soldier said, "and sometimes we go to the villages nearby or to San Juan.

"There's plenty of rum and women but none of it worth a damn.

"The women are spoiled now. When the soldiers first came down, they could lay the girls for nothing—just take them to the bushes. Then some of the boys began paying the women 25 cents or 50 cents to spend the night.

"And, buddy, it didn't take the girls long to catch on. They're smart about money. Now some of 'em want $1 or $2 for a lay."

After Puerto Rico, we headed for British Guiana. The water below was slate gray and splotched with green and blue patches of ocean. Didn't sight a single ship until we hit the coast of South America where the fishing boats looked like toy sailboats.

The coast was wild jungle with no sign of habitation. Just miles and miles of green foliage broken only by rivers and creeks. Far below the shadow of our plane sailed over the jungle like a wraith. Sometimes the shadow was silhouetted on the clouds—and then it was ringed by a rainbow halo.

Toby organized a World Series pool, the winner to get $4.50 as holder of the lucky inning in which the winning run was scored. The ticket I drew was "Yankees—7th". The Cards won 4–3 in the 8th.

The British Guiana airport looked small in the jungle but the captain set our plane down as gently as a feather floating from a featherbed, with yards to spare on the runway.

We leave at 4 A.M. tomorrow for Natal.

October 2, 1942
Natal [Brazil]

The stars were bright and sharp when we took off at 4:05 A.M. for Natal. Most everyone—acting now like seasoned air voyagers—tried to curl up on the seats for a nap. When I awoke, we were heading into one of the loveliest sun rises I have ever seen. The sun was a red ball of fire over the horizon.

More miles and leagues of savage country below—and you wondered how many pairs of eyes were peering from the foliage at the plane overhead—if the natives had ever heard of a war.

In mid-morning we sailed over the mouth of the Amazon and a short time later landed at an American base in Brazil. Near the equator, the sun beat down hard. Heat waves made everything shimmer in the distance.

Five hours later we were in Natal. Hotel Grande is no Waldorf but it's clean. Even if the bed is six inches too short we'll be comfortable.

Our dinner for five totaled 30.00 milreis or 30 cents each—and I had a very good cocktail, tomato juice, steak, vegetables and dessert.

After dinner to the Wonder Bar, a joint one flight up on a side street. Bing Crosby by transcription sang "The Birth of the Blues" while sailors and soldiers danced with the native girls.

The local talent looked pretty drab but the boys were doing the best they could with the material on hand.

"The local fellows haven't got a chance when there's an American uniform in the joint," a gob said. "After we leave they get seconds."

October 3, 1942
Natal

Did I say the Grande would be comfortable? It was a libel on the good things of this life. Never have I experienced anything like the Grande pillows. Concrete poured into a pillow casing. Stuck my feet through the end of the bed.

We went to the clipper base at 8 A.M. for the flight but something wrong with fuel pump and trip delayed. So back to the Grande in Natal.

Lieut. Morris and Capt. Ash wanted to see the Wonder Bar so even though it was siesta time we took them down. There sat two of our soldiers already drinking with the girls. Boys were busy stringing colored crepe paper from the walls for a big shin-dig.

"These are all amigos, sir," said corporal Jones. He turned to the girls. "Amigos! Comprehend?"

"Si, Si," the girls laughed. We all had a beer to international good will. In the day light the girls looked even sleazier than the night before. The venereal disease rate is very high, Pan-Am officials said.

A few minutes after we sat down a marine MP marched in.

"This place is out of bounds to officers until 9:30, sir," he said "and enlisted men aren't supposed to be in town. I'll have to take them to the guardhouse."

The MP's had rounded up all 13 of our soldiers and put them in the guard house. But later they took them over to the Ideal bar and held them in protective custody.

"I've been thrown out of a lot of whore houses by MP's" one soldier said, "but this is the first time they ever threw me into one."

Lieut. Morris, Toby and I took a sightseeing tour, trying to find a pair of half-top boots of good quality—made in Natal very cheap. We finally bought a pair for $4.50 or 85 milreis. We took off at 5:10 P.M. for the flight to Fisherman's Lake, Liberia. They took us out to the big ship by boat—and it's an amazing craft. There were two main cabins for the passengers and a freight compartment in the rear. Up front were the officers' quarters, kitchenette and toilet. Above them the flight deck.

A crew of 11 was aboard—4 pilots, 2 radio men, 2 navigators, 2 engineers and a steward, in addition to our passenger list of 13 soldiers, 3 officers, a civilian and Wiant and I.

Those 6600 horses in the engines beat a mighty thunder—but as long as they roar there's no cause for uneasiness.

Corporal Jones was poured aboard. Too much beer and wine in Natal. He was stretched out in the rear with the freight—and thus became one of the first if not the first man to fly the Atlantic without knowing it. If Corporal Jones ever brags to the people back home with a description of a trans-Atlantic flight, then Corp. Jones will be lying.

Dinner was a feat of magic which would make an American housewife blush. Our steward produced 30 meals out of that tiny kitchenette with a speed and efficiency that suggested genius.

I've never eaten better steaks—they were as tender as a maiden's dream. The coffee was good. The dessert a bowl of luscious pears.

After dinner six of us resumed a poker game we'd started. I managed to win a buck. At midnight we tried to get some sleep. I put several seat cushions on the floor and stretched out. Several times the ship felt as though it were falling out from under us when it hit the heavy air currents but those motors were a reassuring roar. Once I looked back in the freight room and Corporal Jones was still peacefully unaware that he was partaking of a magnificent drama.

Sometimes German U-Boats surfaced on the Atlantic at night to take a pot-shot at the clippers apparently for the fun of it.

"I wish we could carry an ash can or two," one captain said to me in Natal. "We frequently sight subs but by the time we can code a message and send it, they are far from the spot where we saw them."

In normal times the clippers must be luxurious liners with bunks for all passengers and two stewards to give service. But it's catch as catch can now.

October 4, 1942
Fisherman's Lake, Liberia

The African coast, feathered by white breakers on the beach, was a beautiful sight. Everyone crowded to the windows to gape. Below we could see the thatch-roofed huts of the natives. We landed at 9:55 A.M. G.M.T. and a boat took us to the dock. (13:45 hours for the crossing).

The Pan-Am office was a thatch-roofed native-built shack of ingenious structure. Everywhere there was evidence of a great deal of activity.

We had lunch and were off for the airport.

The dirt road wound through tropic vegetation and many native huts with naked children playing about them.

Ahead of us a Negro woman with a basket on her head trudged down the road. When the bus we were riding was a few feet behind her, she looked around.

Never have I seen such terror in a human face. Her eyes popped open in fear and with a wild jump she scrambled over a ditch to escape the mechanical monster.

This time, for the jump to Accra we piled into a C-53 transport with hard bucket seats. The pilot was a young army lieutenant. He was in a hurry to get to Accra.

We landed at Roberts Field for gas and the pilot must have thought he was handling a pursuit ship. He drove the two-motor C-53 right into the landing strip without even lowering the wing flaps.

It was a few minutes out of Roberts Field that Lieut. Hargrove looked out the window and saw that a gas tank cap was missing on the right wing. He told the pilot and the young chap seemed to be worried. The radio man told the field what had happened but they ordered our pilot to keep flying.

And so for the next 60 minutes or so we were a pretty jittery crew until all the gas had been used from that tank. Meantime the soldiers took me for $4 in a black jack game.

We landed at Accra 5:40 P.M.

This spot, a strategic base for our Air Transport Command, was jammed with soldiers. We had some trouble finding a bunk but finally were settled for the night.

October 6, 1942
Accra

We may get away tomorrow and again we may not. It's getting more difficult to get to Cairo. No civilians are being permitted to go there unless their business demands it—and it's gotta be good.

There's a feeling here that big things are underway. America is on the move in Africa, and it's a great story if it can be told.

There is a vital spot surrounded by Vichy French territory. There are 80,000 well equipped French and native troops across the border of the Ivory Coast. They could raise hell with our supply lines if they moved in or permitted the Germans to do it.

I hear that German subs are basing on Vichy French African coastal points.

"The crews even come ashore and bathe in the surf," an officer said. "We know they're there but we can do nothing about it."

There's talk that the British will be on the move in North Africa this fall. And these boys are nervous about Vichy. They know they're in a hot spot. But if Rommel can be knocked out, the pressure will be off.

Capt. John Henry, P.R.O. [Public Relations Officer], took us on a tour of Accra. It was amazing to watch the Negroes at work on the water front loading and unloading ships by surf boats. With a strange looking three-pronged paddle.

Husky, well-muscled Negroes, running at a dog trot, carried sacks of cocoa beans to the boats, piled them in and then paddled out to the ships. It's primitive but efficient for Africa.

The town itself is a mixture of primitive and modern. The British commercial people and government officials live in big, cool-looking homes with well-kept lawns.

It's a never-ending wonder to see the Negroes carry huge bundles and loads on their heads. Even if it's a beer bottle they carry it on their heads rather than in their hands. It's a remarkable demonstration of balance— like a circus act on a big scale with even the children carrying objects on their kinky heads. Their gait is a peculiar swinging motion that makes their hips appear to be ball bearings. There's many a gawky queen in Hollywood who would give a fortune for such a beautiful carriage as these natives develop by carrying things around on their head!

They call this country "the white man's graveyard." After one year they tell me the inertia and boredom combine to undermine the white man's health. Fevers and dysentery are the dangers plus the innervating [sic] climate. You think you can take it when bang—you're a good prospect for hospitalization.

Boredom and a longing for the companionship of women are the two evils of living in these spots. There is little for recreation and after a few months the men become surly and their nerves cause tempers to flare. Heard a group of men in a normal conversation next door and their voices were loud and rasping. They argued incessantly and seemed to be ready to fight—when actually they were in good humor. Apparently they didn't realize themselves how the country was effecting [sic] them.

Visited General Fitzgerald's residence. A big cool house, well furnished, in which the staff entertains visiting big shots and the local British leaders. The floors were of mahogany as well as most of the furniture. The wood is so cheap and plentiful it's used for every sort of household and office furnishing that requires wood.

Joe Morton heard we were passing through and came down from Liberia to see us, hitch hiking by army bomber. He looked fit and from what he told me, he has the news well covered. If ever I get the chance, I'm going to check on a story Joe said was told to him by a colonel:

Many years ago a tribe living on a small peninsula on the Gulf of Persia found a wrecked British warship on their coast.

They had been more or less secluded from the rest of the world since there were rugged mountains blocking the land entrance of the peninsula. They were great fishermen and became the most skilled mariners in the Persian Gulf. Their chief was the Sultan of Muscat.

After removing the guns and ammunition from the wrecked ship, the Muscat tribesmen mounted them on their own vessels and took to sea as pirates, raiding shipping all through the Gulf.

But one day the Sultan's men seized a ship, and it was American. Among the captives was a red-bearded Irishman of wit and charm who became quite a favorite with the Sultan.

Charmed first by the red hair and beard, the Sultan was even more pleased when the Irishman learned to speak the Muscat language. He became one of the Sultan's most trusted advisors.

"It's all right to raid ships," the Irishman told the Sultan, "but don't ever attack an American ship. America is your friend and we must never have trouble with the government."

By this time the Irishman was a man of high standing with several wives to attend to his needs and provide pleasures. The Mick wasn't averse to a bit of piracy but his sentimental streak toward his native land was built on solid loyalty. Besides, he knew what America might do if the Sultan became a nuisance.

The Sultan took his friend's advice and from that day on the sea roving Muscats never attacked an American ship.

To show his friendship for the U.S.A., the Sultan gave America a base for sea and air transport which is being developed now.

And the red-bearded Irishman did the spade work.

Maybe there will be some red-headed Muscats who can tell the story.[7]

October 7, 1942
Kano, Nigeria

We left Accra at 9:15 A.M. It was raining when we reached Lagos, Nigeria, at 10:55 A.M., and the weather looked bad. I wasn't the only one uneasy about the weather. A sergeant said the storms sometimes were so violent that ships returned with the fuselage twisted. Once, he said, the cargo broke loose in rough weather and knocked the top out of a ship.

However we took off into the gray clouds headed for Kano.

I soon forgot the weather talking to a chubby-faced fat Sergeant, Bob Johnson, from Tuscumbia, Ala.

"Man," he drawled, "this sho' is a long way from home for a country boy. And I'm right hungry for a good mess of hot biscuits and fried chicken. When I get home I'm gonna eat fried chicken every day. And I reckon a batch of biscuits with fried ham and some of that freckle-face gravy would be good, too. And I'll have me four eggs, sunny side up."

Food was troubling Bob. He was thinking of those meals back home and fried chicken had become the emblem that represented the America he was fighting for. Bob knew that if we lose this war he won't get fried chicken like he used to get.

"You know," he said, "some of the northerners don't like fried chicken," Bob shook his head. "I don't see how them folks live without fried chicken now and then."

Well, here's hoping you get back to Tuscumbia, Bob, and that you have great heaping platters of fried chicken every day.

We hadn't been out of Lagos long before we hit rough weather. The ship bucked and bounced as we skirted the edge of several storms. All of us buckled on our safety belts to keep the ship from dropping from under us. Later the pilot said he had to fight to keep the ship's nose down all the way to prevent it being sucked up into the storms. A British Captain was air sick but fortunately for me I didn't get sick. Still, it was a strain to ride a wild ship through the storms. All of us were relieved when we finally landed at Kano at 3:30 P.M. and the pilot decided to spend the night. Poker—lost $10.

October 8, 1942
El Fasher, Anglo-Egyptian Sudan

We took off from Kano at 5:15 A.M. I had expected the country to be similar to Brazil with heavy jungles and dense undergrowth. But the country was flat table land, dreary miles of sandy plains covered with scrub growth. Occasionally I could see small groups of native huts, but there were few signs of habitation.

The ship hit rough sailing and we were an hour late getting to Maiduguri, a small port. There we unloaded some freight and dropped three passengers because the plane was overloaded.

Then we took off for El Fasher which was just a short hop from Maiduguri. Even though the passage was rough, some of us managed to get a nap by sprawling on the floor. We landed at El Fasher at 3:25 P.M., a bleak little airport in the desert country.

We spent the night at the RAF quarters. Again the bed was too short. And for the first time since leaving home we didn't have electric lights and flush toilets!

We may be slow to reach decisions and work the democratic system to the breaking point in getting up steam, but by god Americans can move and move fast once the decision is made. There's no better example of American efficiency methods in the world than in Africa. Wherever you find them they are working harder, faster and more efficiently than the British or any other nationality.

For example the bases we have seen were clean, comfortable and equipped with modern conveniences for the benefit of the soldiers. Sanitation was excellent. In malarial regions, swamps and mosquito breeding spots had been cleaned up. Malaria was a rare illness around the camps. Despite these precautions, free quinine and mosquito nets over the beds were provided.

But here the British have no quinine or at least there is no supply on hand today. There are no mosquito nets. The screening is poor. The prevention of malaria seems to be to stay indoors during the hours of darkness.

Another striking impression one gets traveling across Africa is the vastness of the country. I didn't and couldn't appreciate what the problem of transporting troops and supplies to the African front could mean until I experienced this lesson in geography. It's staggering. Even airplane transportation seems slow despite the fact it moves by the most direct lines possible. When you think of slow moving ships having to sail all the way around the Cape of Good Hope and up the Eastern Coast through the Indian Ocean, you begin to get an idea of the difficulties that lie ahead.

Always before the center of my little universe has been the U.S.A. I visualized the world from that central point. Now I must shift my center to strange places on strange continents. And America seems far removed from the action. It isn't easy to tear up your world and shift it about again as though turning a global map.

Even here I am asked "How long will the war last?" How can anyone tell? The British say they can knock off Rommel in 30 days after starting their campaign. I hope they're right. It would be too bad to step off the plane in Cairo and have a Nazi officer say "Herr Whitehead?"

October 8, 1942
Luxor, Egypt

Tomorrow we reach Cairo. We left El Fasher at 6:05 A.M. Dawn was just breaking. The further we went the more desolate the country. We reached Khartoum at 9:30 A.M. and had lunch—or breakfast—cereal, eggs, jam and bread. At the canteen there were Coca-Colas. The first I'd had since leaving home. With the temperature 105 in the shade, it was the most delicious drink I ever had.

After breakfast we left Khartoum airport for Luxor—a journey of about 4 hours. The trip was rough as the sun rose, and the plane jumped and twisted.

Never have I seen such god-forsaken country as that of the Sahara Desert. It's land scorched by the fires of hell. Just sand, as far as you could see. Hills of sand. Valleys of sand. Black sand. Red sand. Brown sand. It stretched away like a scourge with never a sign of vegetation.

The Nile wound through the bleak expanse like a brown twisting highway and along its banks there were green things growing but we saw little of the Nile on a stretch of 300 miles of desert.

Up at 9000 feet the temperature was 50 but down there it was 130 and up. An RAF pilot made a forced landing in the desert recently. By the time they found the plane he was dead. Whenever I think of hell, I'll think of that land I saw today parched by the blast of a terrible heat.

We landed at Luxor—once the summer home of the Pharaohs—at 3:45 P.M. We stepped into a terrific heat and were brought to the town's deluxe hotel for the night. We got our first real glimpse of Egypt on the way to the hotel.

Out on the desert we'd seen camel caravans from the air, but here the camels, jackasses, oxen and Arabs mingled in a newsreel paradise.

Along the road natives turned ancient wheels and dipped water from the Nile to irrigate their fields. We passed a wailing group of women mourning someone who had died. There were the ruins of an ancient palace with its columns crumbling to dust.

Our room was big and airy with mosquito nets over the beds—and they were the first real beds we'd seen since Miami.

Once more we went through the process of getting the currency exchange straight—22 piastres for $1.00.

After dinner—6 courses including roast beef, potatoes, salad, lemon ice and melon—we went curio hunting. The peddlers swarmed down on us. And there I met the professor—Professor T. Khaled, palmist and numerologist.

"There is something which I will tell you free," he said. "The war will end in April or May, 1943. There will be good news in the first week of January. In July there will be no more war.

"Gandhi will die this year. The King of Italy will die next year.

"By the end of December, the planets Venus, Neptune and Jupiter will be attached. That is the sign of peace."

But I'm inclined to think the professor was a faker. He looked at my palm and found: I'll live to be 84. . . . someone I love dearly, an elderly person, will die in 1947. . . . I will have big success in business. . . . In 1953 I'll go into business for myself. . . . I'll visit England twice. . . . I'll marry twice and the second Mrs. W., said the professor, will be very wealthy. And so my future has been mapped by the professor, the oracle of Luxor.

With Adam, a fezzed Arab, as our guide, we strolled the streets of Luxor past a swarming, seething market of many strange sights and odors. And Adam took us to the Luxor equivalent of a gaiety burlesque.

In a steaming room with no ventilation, two young women danced a while to the rhythm of a mandolin, drum and castanets or its Egyptian equivalent. A dirty-robed Arab served us tea—good tea—while we watched the girls—one with big breasts and the other a broad bottom— give us an interpretation of Luxor night life. They sang in a high wailing sing song that seemed to tear their tonsils. After each dance, the girls passed the cup for the offering—like Papa used to do in the Methodist church back in Harlan. The joint looked like a Coney Island strip tease joint except that the turbaned Arabs filed in to sit quietly and sip their tea while the girls writhed and shook. And that was Luxor.

Two

CAIRO JOURNAL,
OCTOBER–NOVEMBER 1942

October 9, 1942
Cairo

We left Luxor behind at 6:30 A.M. and headed up the Nile for Cairo. With each mile it was easier to understand why the river has played such a lead role in the history of this land of antiquity. In America our rivers are important but not vital arteries of agriculture and commerce. But here—Egypt is the Nile. The desert pushes down to its very shores. It is literally the life blood of a nation.

In the distance we could see the pyramids and then we reached Cairo or rather Heliopolis, a suburb where the airport is located.

There we got our first glimpse of ground defenses, anti-aircraft emplacements, machine-gun nests. We landed at 8:55 A.M.

On the side of the field were piles of plane wings ripped by bullet holes. It didn't seem possible a plane could be shot up so much and still return to base.

We located Ed Kennedy, A.P. Bureau Chief in Cairo, and he arranged room for us at the Metropolitan Hotel. We were lucky for the town is jammed and rooms are precious.

For lunch we had a good steak and Boston baked beans—after we had a drink at the Ermitage bar with a group of American correspondents. Met George Lait of INS [International News Service] and Hank Garrell of UP [United Press] also Frank Martin of AP. Ed wants one or both of us to stay here which would mean we would be accredited to the British 8th Army.

I was dead tired from the trip but felt better after a bath and nap.

Tonight Toby and I went to the Doll's Cabaret for dinner. Steak again. And a very good orchestra and floor show. The place jammed by men in British uniform. Driving through the blacked out streets was an experience. The cab seemed to skim by cars and pedestrians at hair's breadth. The driver didn't even slow down.

In the gaiety and brilliance of the cabaret, it was hard to realize that only eighty miles away the British and German armies face each other. It's a fantastic city but then this is a fantastic war.

October 10, 1942
Cairo

Cairo is quite remarkable, a city living on the edge of a war and trying desperately not to show it. But there is a feeling of tension and a slight hysteria underlying the buzzing voices that beat a steady undertone to the normal noises. Just as in Natal, the natives drive with their horns. The honking, yelping, beeping, blasting symphony of horns never ends. It's a dirty, dusty, throbbing place that's vital and alive with a surface show of business as usual.

The bars are filled. There is no lack of liquor, food, and supplies. But despite its cosmopolitan air, Cairo is pretty much like a Thursday afternoon ladies sewing circle. The gossip runs through the city in an endless chain and the stories are distorted and given new bursts with each telling.

Thirty minutes after Toby and I got here our arrival was a topic of conversation in every bar.

"The chances are," said Kennedy, "that by now they are saying you came to the office, that we had a terrific argument, that I drew a knife and that we fought down the stairs into the street. That's the way everything is magnified."

A few minutes later we met Major Aitchenson of the U.S. Army. He knew our names, our destination and our arrival time before we even saw him.

After lunch, Frank Martin of A.P. took us to the Anglo-American hospital where we were to get cholera shots. We had the serum with us.

A British doctor fumbled with the needle in the vial and then stuck it in my arm. The syringe pulled loose and half the serum squirted out on my bare arm. If I get cholera it will be due to the clumsy fumbling of the doctor.

"A great many British," Frank said, "get all thumbs around an American. They know we're a people who move fast and efficiently. When they try to do the same thing to surprise us they just get all balled up." That probably is an exaggeration of the situation but my clumsy doc was an example that seemed to prove the statement.

Coming back to town we rode in a hack. When we got out Frank offered the driver eight piastres. He wanted ten.

"To hell with you," Frank said. "I won't pay you anything." He walked away. The grumbling driver followed us up the street. He took the eight piastres with a snarl.

"They try to gouge Americans for twice the regular fare," Frank said. "Because you two are in civilian clothes, he thought you were tourists and that you'd pay a big fare without a squawk."

During lunch, the beggars and peddlers crowded to the window for alms and to sell their wares. A baboon performed on the window ledge. A woman begged for coins while a child nursed at her bared breast. A street band played for us. And the cafe manager screamed at the beggars to "Yallah!"—scram.

Wherever they are, Americans are fair game for the natives. The taxi driver, the gharry (hack driver), the porters, the beggars and waiters all expect the American to pay more. Even the servants chisel on meals and services. One American noticed Arabic writing pasted on his back porch. He had it translated. It was a menu with a list of prices for the day's meal. The cook was operating a back door cafeteria on the food he filched from the kitchen.

At Shepheard's we met Frank and a group of Americans for drinks on the verandah overlooking the street. Some wag has said that if Rommel tries to take Cairo, the British will make their stand at Shepheard's bar. And Rommel has said that when he takes Cairo, he will make his headquarters at Shepheard's. The Germans have heard of the hotel and when the British captured a Nazi general, his first request was to be permitted to see the hotel.

We had supper at an Egyptian place—delicious mutton called mufta and kabob and a drink called Kabib. After dinner we saw "The Man Who Came to Dinner."

October 11, 1942
Cairo
Toby and I wrote our first story today on the Americans moving into Africa.[1] We expected it to be a mailer but Kennedy said he would cable it. Had good steak dinner and saw a fair floor show at the Kit Kat Club. Met Zinner and Hart of *Time* and *Life*.

October 12, 1942
Cairo
Ed Kennedy put our story through the censorship—and 90 percent came through intact. He said that was a good batting average. Also he wired

Evans suggesting we stay here unless Grover was in immediate need of relief. So far being a "war correspondent" has meant getting a sore behind from riding on hard transport seats and waiting until someone decides what to do with me. Only one man can be accredited to the British—and an unaccredited correspondent is going to run into trouble getting to the sources of news. Unless I'm accredited I'd rather move on. ChungKing [World War II capital of Nationalist China] might be a good spot.

Frank Martin took us out to see the pyramids. Even with the war on a few tourists still clamber about them—but the visitors probably were all natives.

The great stone piles are impressive and it's hard to believe they were built by human hands without the aid of machinery. Every great block of stone in them was hauled across the Nile and put into place by some tortuous means so that in death the Pharaohs might be glorified.

We walked around the largest of the pyramids to see the Sphinx and found the stone creature had been given a sandbag chin rest as a protection against bombing. Then we visited the temple of the high priest— built of great slabs of granite and alabaster. The stone work was remarkable and each piece fit into the other with a smoothness that showed a high degree of skill and ingenuity. Those old boys weren't bad engineers and craftsmen. A great deal of skill, planning, toil, blood and suffering went into those massive works on the edge of the desert.

Later we walked over to the Mena House near the pyramids and sat on the cool, shady verandah for a glass of lemonade. Once the tourists paid as high as $25 a day to stay at the Mena House. Now the rooms are about $3 a day.

There's a curious sense of unreality to all of this. It doesn't seem possible that life could move so serenely and quietly here while a war is being fought a few score miles across the desert.

There was a young girl at Madras
Who had a most wonderful ass
It was not round and pink
As perhaps you might think
It was gray, and had ears
And ate grass.

October 13, 1942
Cairo

Toby and I wandered through the maze of Cairo's bazaar today—and almost got lost in the winding alleys, streets and courts swarming with Arabs. We started with a guide but it was obvious he only wanted us to stop at the places where he could get a commission on any sales. We dismissed him in a hurry. Back in the native section was like another world. Narrow streets jammed with people. Food, dates and fruits swarming with flies. Dirt, filth and odors of every description but curiously blending into a colorful scene. Cairo is like that. In the midst of squalor we passed mosques in which the courts looked clean, cool and spacious. The Moslems took off their shoes before entering.

After finding our way out, we attended a press conference with Ed Kennedy—and later we wrote a story on our first impressions of Cairo—"Incredible Cairo is living in the valley of the shadow of war trying desperately to be gay and normal and succeeding only in being gay."[2] It is an amazing city. We are only 150 miles from the desert front and yet the war seems remote—something you read about but can't quite grasp as being true. Only last June when it looked as though Cairo was going to fall to Rommel, the city was in a frenzy of terror. "The Flap" they call that desperate period now. But then the British held. The Flap became just a bad memory and life went on as usual. The bars are filled, the cafes crowded, the shops doing a roaring business, the cabarets playing to a free-spending audience.

The favorite pastime is chatter—endless hours of story-telling and gossip, which becomes a bit boring and meaningless after a few days even if it is clever and entertaining. It lacks one essential—and that is the warmth of friendship. Cairo is hard, brittle and glossy but it seems to me it lacks real feeling. The British are afraid of the Americans—afraid they've come to Africa to stay. The Americans are a bit irked with the British stuffiness. Bureaucracy and jealousy feed on each other. That's in Cairo. When the men get together in the battle front and at their bases, I am told, there is none of the pettiness that Cairo breeds. Here the political dry rot is evident. Choice gossip is passed around like a bunch of old women tearing a reputation to shreds. Even the correspondents are caught up in this vice. I may be wrong, but it seems to me too many are forgetting their job is to get the news, and not to sit around the bars being mellow, wise and clever with scotch and sodas as a preventative for gyppy-tummy. Perhaps that's a premature and unfair judgment because I know most of those fellows are capable, experienced men who can hit the ball when they're on a good story. It's just the Cairo influence.

Toby and I were interviewed today by George Pollock, a writer for *Les Images*, a French language publication. He was interested in getting our observations on America at war. Fame already!

October 14, 1942
Cairo

Toby and I had our India visas stamped today. Now we're all set to go onto India if we don't stay here. Also we're measured for a uniform which we'll wear if ever we are accredited by the British. Bye and bye we should reach the status of war correspondents. Right now we're bastard reporters with no real status. Oh, well.

October 15, 1942
Cairo

Met General Maxwell, who is in command of our Mid-East forces.[3] The General has a round, pink face and wide open blue eyes, sandy hair. The first impression is that he's not exactly a ball of fire. He is not a combat soldier but came up the ropes as a supply man. That's all very well while our big problem is supplies, but when the time comes to fight, I'd rather see a combat man directing the show. This is the graveyard of British generals—but I hope it isn't true for us.

We met Major Jones, the General's aide—a young, handsome chap. Others—Major Aitchenson, in the Provost Marshall's staff—West, director of the OWI [Office of War Information] setup in the Mid-East—Nick Parrino, OWI; Jim Lowry, OWI, one-time A.P. man in newsphoto; George [name left blank], OWI, student of Arabic and doing intelligence; Major Bea Stern, former Cleveland newsman.

At the Continental roof, met Lieut. Morris, our clipper friend, and Captain Stratton who invited us to dinner with Colonel Hayne in command of the Services of Supply under Maxwell.

Our table companion was an Egyptian girl who called herself Dinah Lee—a beautiful creature who has become a favorite with the Army. She sings a la Dinah Shore. They say she's one of Cairo's legendary females—but she didn't appear to be digging for gold when I saw her.

Her ambition is to get to the U.S.A. in some way and she doesn't much care how it's done. Says frankly she'll probably marry some old fool and leave him once she's safe in America. Quite a gal and you gotta admire her cold determination even if it isn't exactly a pleasant thing to see. And she might do it, too, 'cause she's got the sex appeal.

October 16, 1942
Cairo

A delightful dinner at Colonel Hayne's residence with Capt. Stratton, Colonel Devenbeck and Major Spicer (he didn't look like the Harlan [Kentucky] Spicers). We had tomato juice, pork tenderloin, sweet potatoes, a strange vegetable I'd never eaten before, chocolate pudding, and figs and dates. Afterward there was Turkish coffee in the living room. Colonel Hayne was military attaché in Moscow for two years and had been in Thailand, the Balkans and in Europe. He's a pleasant, interesting fellow who was very gracious. I'm to see him Monday about a story.

While we were at the Colonels, a sand storm blew up. Soon everything was coated with a film of gritty dust as fine as talcum.

"That's why aeroplane engines only last 150 hours instead of 300 hours," Colonel Devenbeck said. "The dirt works on the parts like emery dust."

Colonel Hayne suggested I should go to Eritrea to see the installations there. I'd like to make the trip to see just what we are doing. At Massua I understand we took over the Italian shops and have hundreds of them working for us.

October 19, 1942
Cairo

We were driving through Cairo's blacked-out streets. A pale half moon cast soft shadows over the dirt and filth and ugliness. The dark buildings were etched against the star-studded sky. Cairo was as soft and beautiful as a woman's body in the twilight of a dim-lit room.

"Cairo is the Paris of the Middle East," the young Captain said. "This is a lovely war."

Yes, Cairo is the Paris and also the Singapore of the Middle-East. It almost makes me afraid to see what is happening here while Rommel's armies are so near. Laugh, drink and be merry—for tomorrow we may retreat!

Cairo is a slut—prostituting everyone who stays here long enough, throwing over them a blanket of inertia that smothers any effort to be independent and aggressive. There's stupidity, bureaucracy and pettiness and a refusal to be realistic that shocks like a cold shower.

I thought we were complaisant at home—but Cairo is worse. There perhaps is some excuse for the Egyptians. They are neutral. Out there is no defense for the British and Americans who are fighting the war from 9 A.M. to 1 P.M. and from 5 P.M. to 7 P.M.—just in time for drinks at Shepheard's and dinner at the ringside of a cabaret.

I called GHQ and asked for Colonel Hayne. The Captain who answered was apologetic: "I'm sorry. Headquarters closes at one o'clock. You see we conform to the British hours."

My God! And the people at home are whiplashed for complacency.

Someone remarked at Ed Kennedy's apartment that the Egyptian stocks had fallen off slightly in the past few days.

"Yes," Ed said dryly. "The news is getting around that the British are going to start a new offensive—and the people figure they're getting ready to make some new blunders. An offensive on this front inspires pessimism instead of optimism."

This is no reflection on the courage and skill of the British soldier. It's just the decay of the old structure and the remains of the deadwood that hasn't yet been cleared away.

The men who have been to the front in the heat and grit and wind and battle deserve their drinks at Shepheard's, their ringside cabaret seats and whatever fun they can find here.

But by god the captains, majors, colonels and generals who quit work at one o'clock should be ashamed to be seen at Cairo's bars and cafes.

Yes, it's a lovely war.

Africa, in early October, 1942, was agog over a great secret.

They were whispering it on the Gold Coast at Accra where the Americans had ripped an airfield out of the jungle on the aerial lifeline from the United States to the Middle East. They talked about it over their warm beer in El Fasher in the Anglo-Egyptian Sudan.

One heard it in Kartoum, where the thermometer stood at 105 degrees in the shade: and in the tea rooms in Luxor, in the Valley of the Kings, where broad-bottomed, big-breasted Egyptian girls sang their weird and doleful chants.

In Cairo the secret was discussed over gin and bitters on Shepheard's Terrace, in cafes, in the smoky, perfumed, sensuous atmosphere of Doll's cabaret as the belly dancers twitched with the nervous excitement of the times, and at the exclusive Gezira Club where the colonels and their ladies gathered to exchange gossip.

Someone remarked one day stocks had fallen on the Egyptian Exchange.

"Yes," said Ed Kennedy of the Associated Press, with sarcasm, "the news is getting around the British are going to start a new desert offensive."

This was the secret being shouted in whispers across Africa.

Everyone wondered how far the British would get this time. And everyone was pretty cynical about another offensive because the memories of defeats were too fresh. Why get excited by another push into the desert which had burned out so many hopes and buried them in the sands?

Early in the war Wavell [Sir Archibald Wavell, Commander of British Forces in the Middle East] *had driven the Italians back to Benghazi and then was forced to retreat before Field Marshall Irwin Rommel's fresh, well-trained, well-equipped Afrika Korps.* [British General Claude] *Auchinlec[k] had pushed almost to Benghazi but his armor had been ambushed and his army driven almost back to the Nile. The British had suffered a heartbreaking record of defeats in the Western Desert with their usual gallantry.*

Now the Desert Rats were going to try again under the command of the virtual unknown—a slender, brusque little refugee from the beaches of Dunkirk, Bernard Law Montgomery.

Cairo buzzed with speculation about Montgomery and his chances against Rommel, whose army was sitting only 80 miles from the port of Alexandria guarding the Suez canal and the open door leading to Palestine, the oil riches of Arabia and Persia and a defenseless India.

The Egyptians were skittish. In fact, everyone knew—although the censors kept it hushed from the public prints—that young King Farouk had been persuaded to name pro-British Nahas Pasha as prime minister only after British tanks had rolled onto the palace ground and trained their guns on the royal domicile. Under the circumstances, Farouk made a hasty pro-British decision.

During this critical period the British in Cairo, a special breed little resembling the home isle product, displayed an amazing and sometimes infuriating show of unconcern which bordered on disregard of the realities. Chin up. No

*necessity, really old man, to change the GHQ office hours of 9 A.M. to 1 P.M.
and 5 P.M. to 7 P.M. The heat y'know.*

The Americans at their new headquarters were taking their cues from the
British. They were a little bewildered and painfully self-conscious in their new
uniforms as the junior partner in the vast and exciting adventure.

Once I called American Headquarters to check a story. Patiently, a captain
explained: "Headquarters always close at one o'clock, old man. You see, we
must conform to the British hours."

Oh, Cairo was a marvelous place. "Cairo is the Paris of the Middle East,"
enthused a fresh-faced young American major. "And this is a lovely war."

Cairo was fabulous, all right, but the price on the tag was high. The
peasants in the fields along the Nile toiled for six piasters (24 cents) a day.
But nobody had time to worry about the peasants. Gold was pouring into
Egypt from all the world. In the shops were silks, broadcloths and exquisite
handiwork from Persia and India, exotic jewels, windows full of watches from
Switzerland, excellent tweeds from Ireland and Scotland, all of the 57 varieties, and good Kentucky bourbon for 125 piasters ($5.00) a fifth.

The bars were jammed day and night. Nightclubs turned away patrons. At
Shepheard's, the Metropolitan and the Continental hotels, reservations were
obtained by knowing a friend of a friend of the manager. The mangy camels
outside the Mena House were busy carrying sightseers around the pyramids
and the bored Sphinx, whose chin rested tiredly on the great pile of sandbags.

Cairo was a strange mixture of cosmopolites and country boys on their first
trip to town. A tall garrulous Red Cross girl who had ventured beyond the
borders of Pennsylvania with expenses paid in search of a husband, was
thrilled with her first chance to ride a real Arabian stallion.

"It's wonderful," she cooed to the cockney in charge of the stables. "All
my life I've dreamed of riding a genu-vine bedou-wine A-rab."

The cynical little cockney cocked an eyebrow: "Man or beast, Madam?"

Troops on leave from the desert crowded the streets and bazaars—
Englishmen, South Africans, Australians, Poles, New Zealanders, Indians,
Americans, Free French and Greeks. They rubbed elbows with beggars and
businessmen, dragomen and drunks, veiled women with the tattoo of caste on
their foreheads, whores, pimps, sheiks and refugees from many lands.

October 20, 1942

It felt good to get out of Cairo to the base where Americans are building
a motor repair center and teaching the British how to handle and service
our new tanks.

Chunky Sgt. Harold O. Frost of Fort Knox, Ky., was just back from the desert where his crew instructed British tankmen on American tanks.

"They've got a lot of confidence in our stuff," Frost said. "And don't let anybody tell you those British boys aren't good fighters. They've got what it takes and I would like to fight right with them."

At least it's good to know the "loveliness" of Cairo doesn't extend to the front.

Frost took me for a ride in a new Sherman tank—our latest model with an all-cast top streamlined to give as difficult a target as possible.

We whipped over the desert with surprising speed and smoothness. We passed an Arab tent camp and a camel peered at the strange clattering monster with indifferent calm.

Propaganda directed at the Arabs creates some peculiar problems— peculiar to the Western mind.

A newsreel was shown in a Cairo theater of German atrocities, bodies hanging from nooses, piles of dead, horrifying brutality.

The Arabs laughed and cheered. They thought it was wonderful.

Simple and primitive, they can only understand force. They admire brutality. They aren't shocked by Axis strong-arm methods. They respect such tactics.

The newsreel was withdrawn quickly.

But movies make good propaganda if handled intelligently.

A great gathering of Arabs in a remote village was drawn for a movie.

First it was announced that the movies were not witchcraft but a new weapon of the Allies, another reason we'll win the war. Then Mickey Mouse flashed on the screen. The announcer had Mickey mouthing curses and obscenities and occasionally poking crude fun at Hitler and Mussolini.

The words had nothing to do with the picture but the Arabs loved it!

Then pictures were shown of American troops, American tanks, guns and factories. Sandwiched into the film was a picture of the local Sheik and his army of 20 men.

"With these great forces as allies, the United Nations can't lose," the announcer said to a wildly enthusiastic crowd.

Such is war in the Middle East.

October 29, 1942

The story is going around that when Churchill visited Stalin in Moscow and they met for the first time, there was no agreement reached on a second front during their first conference. Churchill was tired after the long trip and retired to his room. There he found a beautiful young girl in his bed—nude. He was shocked but what really enraged him was that the maiden was only 12 years old. Winston called Uncle Joe. "I'm enraged and insulted," he stormed. "What do you mean putting a nude 12 year old girl in my bed."

"Well," said Uncle Joe, "if you're as slow with the girl as you are opening a second front, she'll be old enough by the time you get down to business."[4]

Beer, belligerence and benefits just don't mix—not at $5 each for the benefit.

It happened this way. Nick Parrino of OWI and I were in his room having a drink when a young lieutenant called and asked us to go with him and his date to a Royal Egyptian Benefit.

We drove to the benefit and Nick and I started in, thinking the Lieutenant had complimentary tickets for us. We found he didn't and went out to ask the price.

"It's not worth a fin to me," I said. Nick agreed.

"But let's tell the lieutenant good night," Nick said. We went to the gate and asked an Egyptian in tuxedo to call our friend over.

Instead he started shoving us away. "No tickets, get out!" he said.

We shoved him back. "Listen, chum," said Nick, "We are Americans and we're not going to be shoved around."

The Gyppies [Egyptians] swarmed around but we said we wouldn't budge until somebody called the lieutenant over. We were going to say goodnight or know the reason why.

Finally the place was in an uproar. Half the crowd was for us—half against us.

Then a couple of Australian MP's came up to see what the trouble was.

"All we want," we said, "is to tell our friend goodnight. And we don't like to be shoved around."

"I don't blame you, buddy," the Aussie growled. "I don't like to be shoved around either."

P.S. We said goodnight to the lieutenant.

Henry was a Maori [indigenous inhabitant of New Zealand]—and a tougher looking soldier I've never seen in my life. He was all muscle. He swaggered when he walked like a sailor at sea. The brown eyes in his coffee-colored face were never still.

Henry was a little dubious when Nick and I asked him to sit down and have a steak with us.

He looked at me and shook his head. "Your face I have seen somewhere, no?"

I told him I'd just arrived in Cairo.

"But your face, I swear I've seen it somewhere."

It finally took my passport and War Correspondent card to convince Henry that I wasn't pulling a fast one. And he looked at Parrino.

"Your name sounds Italian," he said accusingly.

"Sure, but I'm American," Nick said, producing his identification. "You see, Henry, in America you can be Italian, German, English or African and still be an American. That's what we call Democracy. If you should come to the United States and get your papers, you would become an American, too."

Henry's face was a study in thought. Then a smile broke over his stony features.

"I think I understand now," he said. "Forgive me if I have hurt your feelings. I am sorry. I will leave now."

"Sit down and forget it," Nick said. "Here come the steaks."

Henry ate his steak slowly.

"I've met Americans," he said. "By God they were real men. The American Volunteer Ambulance Corps. They come right to the front looking for wounded. They seem disappointed when they don't find any. But they're always there on the job."

Henry beamed. "The war's over. When America come in, the war's over."

He stared at me long and hard.

"I'll swear I've seen your face . . ."

At 10 P.M. on October 23—a clear Friday night when the moon bathed the desert in soft light—Britain's Eighth Army opened its third offensive against the Axis on the western desert.

We knew it was coming but we didn't know when.

E.K. [Edward Kennedy] called me into the office to tell me he had decided to have me accredited to the British and that Wiant was to cover American activities. That suited me fine. It meant I could get into the desert or travel to any military area in this section.

"Personally I'm sick of the bureaucracy in Cairo and I want to get away," Ed said. "I'd rather be out on the desert myself because out there the fellows are fine. There's none of this cheapness and pettiness you find in Cairo which is the hell-hole of the Middle East."

And so did I. I was fed up with Cairo. I wanted to see some of the unvarnished, untinseled side of this war.

But next day Ed took off to the desert with the RAF.

"You're in charge of the news in Cairo while I'm gone," he said.

The next day the offensive began—and I was sitting on a powder keg.

My first assignment an offensive—tossed into my lap as a beginner, before I'd had time to make my contacts or know my way around. I didn't even know the routine.

But there it was and there was nothing that could be done about it except dig in.

It wasn't as difficult as I thought it would be to get back into the swing of spot news. The difficulty was to have the censors cut obvious stuff from the stories. In one case they even censored their own handout.

Such incredible things happen in censorship. We couldn't say it was an offensive—only an attack. We couldn't say from what sector of the front the heavy attack began although I presume Rommel had a pretty good idea. We couldn't say this and we couldn't say that. All "off the record."

For two days the army advanced sending infantry ahead of tanks to clear paths thru the German minefields. Then there were light clashes of armor—but we were in a fog as to how the battle was progressing. There was a feeling that everything wasn't going as well as hoped but that was largely due to the sudden stop of news from the front.

Still, I think we managed to get the big story out—that this is the big show—the drive to shove Rommel from North Africa.

Ed is back from the desert trying to rush my accrediting so that I can get to the desert to relieve Martin.

The spectacular drive across the Western Desert was a contest to determine which could run the faster—Montgomery's Eighth Army or Rommel's Afrika Korps. Rommel had a head start in the race and all Monty could do was give chase with the knowledge that sooner or later his enemy would have to stop and fight. The only question was—where?

During the start of the chase, I was fighting the battle of communiqués at the Cairo press headquarters in the Immobilia building, learning the art of writing what are known to the trade as "colorful" and "gripping" battle stories for maps, briefings and handouts.

The routine rarely varied. Each morning at 9 o'clock (4 A.M. in New York) the correspondents gathered in the press room for a briefing by a colonel from public relations, who had been no nearer the front than a tall rum drink on Shepheard's Terrace. The colonel would explain the action that had taken place in the past few hours and give us such names, places and other information as were considered within the bounds of security.

Officers from the American Air Force headquarters and the RAF would hand out prepared releases on the air activity, the number of sorties flown, the objectives and the damage done, and the number of planes shot down. The phrase "All our planes returned safely" failed to mention those limping back as full of holes as a sieve and with crewmen dead or wounded.

Occasionally we were given tid-bits such as an interview with a pilot hero and his crew just back from a desert mission. Then we would sit at our typewriters dashing off bulletins and adds at a furious clatter for an hour or so. The dispatches went from the censor's office to the cable office for transmission to London and from London they were cabled to New York for distribution to Associated Press member newspapers. Supplementing these headquarters' stories were the reports from the men in the desert with the army.

No war book would be complete without at least a passing remark about censorship, the army's often arbitrary and confusing interpretation of what constituted security which was a cross borne by all correspondents, a hair shirt of irritation and an absolute necessity.

The mental gymnastics of censors were strange and wonderful to behold at times. More than once they became confused and censored their own censored handouts. But as time goes by my feelings toward the censors become a little more tolerant because they were continually being hammered by the correspondents while caught in the vise of military restrictions.

The poor censor was in a much worse position than Lo, the poor Indian. If a story brought unfavorable reaction from a General, the censor who passed the story caught hell. If there was a "poor" public reaction, from the army point of view, the culprit was the censor. He was bedeviled, be-damned, berated from all sides. And each story he handled was potential dynamite to his army career and the goodwill of his superiors.

The basic difficulty was in the correspondents' interpretation of security and the military interpretation. Too frequently the military went beyond the bounds of security to impose censorship as a cover-up—as in the Patton slapping incident, the shooting down of our own planes over Sicily, and the tragic time in Italy when American infantrymen mutinied. Lieut. Gen. Mark W. Clark killed the mutiny story on the grounds that it would not only create an uproar at home but would give aid and comfort to the enemy.[5]

As a matter of fact, in suppressing the story, General Clark lost a chance to show the people at home how undermanned his army was for the job it had to do, how badly he needed fresh divisions to relieve his worn out troops who had fought to mental and physical exhaustion. But more later about the tragic Italian campaign which was an adventure into futility.

There were courageous censors and public relations officers who stuck out their necks and placed them squarely into the noose because they fought to get news released and permitted commonsense reporting and interpretation of events at the risk of a reprimand, banishment into the Siberia of the combat infantry, or loss of promotion.

There were men like Capt. Robert Myers, a South Carolinian who honestly believed it was his job to help the correspondents clear the hurdles of censorship and who had the courage to fight for his convictions. Unfortunately, men like Myers were in the minority and too often public relations was used by the army as a convenient catch-all for incompetents who had neither the desire nor the intelligence to be realistic.

Once outside Saint-Lô in Normandy I took shelter in a ditch with the troops during an enemy bombardment of the road leading into the town. A young lieutenant slumped down beside me with a piece of shrapnel embedded in his back. With each breath the blood oozed from the wound in crimson bubbles as we carried him in a jeep to a dressing station, from where he was rushed to a hospital for an emergency operation.

That evening I wrote the story of the American entry into Saint-Lô and described the wounded youth. I told of the blood bubbling from his body with each tortured breath. I tried to give the people at home a glimpse into the horror of war and of how men suffered as life slipped out of them in crimson bubbles.

Later I checked and found that all references to the blood "bubbling" from the wound had been blue-penciled from the story. I asked the censor why this had been done.

"Every mother who has a son on this beachhead would think it was her son," he said. (The names of seriously wounded could not be used in a story.) "Besides, the description was too gruesome."

"But war is gruesome!" I argued. "And the blood did bubble from the wound!"

"Yes, but your story shows this was a lung wound . . ."

It was useless to argue against such reasoning. The only hope was to raise hell and hope for a better break next time or a more liberal censor.

But to return to the Cairo headquarters scene: After the cleanup of the morning briefing, we usually retired to Churchill's bar or Shepheard's Terrace for a drink before lunch, which was the custom of the land and one which few violated. The briefing routine was repeated at 5 P.M.

A few correspondents enjoyed the ordered routine of headquarters life, the creature comforts, and the vicarious thrill of reporting battles without the inconvenience of the desert life, poor food, fleas, no hot-water baths, and, incidentally, being shot at.

The headquarters job was a necessary and vital part of war reporting and somebody had to handle the communiqués, handouts and conferences. But most of us were fed up with the bureaucracy and the feeling of frustration that seems to cling to headquarters. We envied the men with the field assignments.

I had been accredited as a war correspondent to the American armed forces but I did not have a license from the British and consequently could not go into the desert inasmuch as the British controlled the movements of correspondents in the Middle East. But finally the War Office in London approved my accreditation and my boss, Ed Kennedy, then Middle East Chief of Bureau for The Associated Press, told me I was to report to an advance RAF fighter group which was supporting Monty's advance.

Here was the opportunity I had been seeking, the chance to become a combat correspondent. Those of us in the trade developed a snobbish pride in drawing a distinction between a "war" correspondent and a "combat" correspondent. WE righteously considered our combat status a step higher in the correspondents' caste system and, consequently, we had the same clannish feeling that bound combat troops against the rear echelons who had never heard a shot fired in the war.

November 7, 1942
Cairo

But for a review of events leading up to this point.

On Sunday, Nov. 1, I drove to Tewfik on the Red Sea to do a story on the arrival of the *Aquitania* with 7000 troops and nurses. The great old luxury liner was drab in her black battle dress. Fat barrage balloons sailed over the port and the super-structure of a sunken freighter jutted from the water—victim of a Jerry raid. Bob Landry of *Life*, Harry Zinder of *Time*, Kaye of UP, Tom Treanor of San Francisco and I were on the party. A launch took us out to the *Aquitania* and we were shown over the ship by a conducting officer. Not a man was lost on the trip and 11 major operations were performed. There was a lot of bitching by the officers about the lack of fresh water for bathing and crowded conditions but apparently there wasn't a great deal of room for complaint—and no pun intended. The nurses aboard seemed to take the inconveniences in stride. The troops had only one complaint—that the food served by the British was monotonous and no matter how you cook mutton it's still mutton after 42 days at sea. After looking over the ship we visited the temporary camp where the soldiers were resting before going on to their stations. Then we came back to Cairo.

Then the merry-go-round started. Toby Wiant who was at an American air force base took an operational flight with Kennedy and other correspondents. Major Jones of Maxwell's headquarters raised all manner of hell—threatened to have him brought back under arrest and refused to pass his story of the flight. Toby had taken the trip at the invitation of Colonel Backus of the 12th Bombardment Group and with the authorization of General Strickland,[6] Brereton's chief of staff. Nevertheless Jones sent a report to the War Department and a few days later A.P. cabled that Wiant's credentials had been withdrawn. Toby was heartbroken, of course, and brooded over the thing until I was worried about him. I went to Jones and he professed ignorance of the war department's actions. Personally I'll always think Jones sent an unsympathetic report without recommendation when as a matter of fairness the report should never have gone out of his office. It was drastic, unthoughtful and an example of a military upstart trying to be officious. Toby gets worse as the days go by, waiting to hear if New York will be able to do anything.

On the news side—the British are chasing Rommel after breaking through the El Alamein mine fields and defenses with reversed blitz tactics. Instead of tanks leading the way and getting knocked off by the German 88's, the British sent the infantry in at night with bayonet charges which cleared out the advance gun positions. Then there was a heavy concentration of artillery fire—1000 guns laying a shell over every seven yards of German-held soil—or sand. There has been no report of casualties, but I hear they were heavy—particularly among the Aussies and New Zealanders who led the bayonet charges. Paul Lee Barber and I alternated on the conference stories.

I met Air Vice Marshall Tedder at an RAF press conference.[7] He said the air assault was the most concentrated pattern of bombs ever laid on German troops. While Allies didn't hold air superiority at the start of the campaign, he said, we gained it after first terrific air blows which knocked out dozens of Rommel's planes on the ground and in the air. (Later I heard we had superiority in numbers of planes at the start of the drive—so I suspect Tedder was hedging on a point of technicality as to the definition of air superiority.) However the air forces did a magnificent job and the Americans are going great guns. They've taken a page from Chenault's AVG Tigers who evolved their own method of fighting the Zeros with their greater altitude. Since our planes can't get the altitude of the ME109 [Messerschmitt] because of heavier armor and equipment the boys make the Germans fight at their best level—from 12000 to 16000 feet. If the ME's stay too high, the Americans let them stay there because they can't do any harm. But when they come down the fight is on. So far our score is about 10 to 1. And Lieutenant Lyman Middleditch is our first hero of the Middle East. The kid shot down four ME109's—three in one scrap. He was outnumbered 4–1 in last fight but he got a triple, and won the DSC [Distinguished Service Cross]. However he was on a mission at the time of the presentation and didn't get to Cairo to get the award pinned on his blouse.

General Frank Andrews has replaced Maxwell as commander in chief of the ME command, glory be! Unctuous bland Maxwell takes a back seat. If this had happened earlier then perhaps Toby wouldn't have gotten into difficulty. Cairo becomes more nerve-racking as the days go by. This place gets on your nerves, in your hair and rasps like a file. It's the politics, the gossip and the petty problems which only hamper any effort to get a job done. I'm still waiting for the British to come through with my credentials.

Tuesday November 10, 1942
Cairo

At last London has cabled the British PR that my credentials have been approved. I'm to leave Thursday for an advanced RAF landing ground. Meantime my credentials are being stamped and signed. Frank Martin is back from the front with a Nazi Swastika, two machine guns, a pistol and a couple of rifles he picked up at the front. I went out today to sign all the necessary papers for my cards of identification. I'll get them tomorrow.

Wednesday November 11, 1942

I'm pooped out tonight. I'll get to bed about 2 A.M. and then get up at 6:30 to report to the RAF. I finally got the necessary papers from the British and American Headquarters—the British at 9 Sharia Nabatat and the Americans at 5 Sharia Walda. It's the hardest thing in the world to do anything in a hurry here. I spent the entire day getting food and equipment for the desert and picking up my credentials. Three bottles of whiskey and a little pile of canned food and chocolate came to more than $30. Paul Lee is taking over Room 213 at the Metropolitan.

Thursday November 12, 1942
Bug Bug [Buq Buq, Egypt]

Bob Landry, *Life* photographer, Walter Graebner of *Time* and I met at RAF public relations at 8:30. Farnsworth Fowle of INS was to join us later. There was one place open in a plane going to an advance aerodrome so we matched for it and I won. When Fowle arrived I offered to let him have the plane sent so I could be with Landry and Graebner on the auto trip. I figured I could see more by automobile than by air. But Fowle thought the same thing. He chose the auto trip. I left them and drove to the airport at Heliopolis, outside Cairo, and there was a Blenheim waiting. The only other passenger was a British major going up on an observation flight. I sat in the glass nose of the ship. The pilot was a 20-year-old yellow-haired kid named Peter Bartlett, of Nottingham England. He'd been flying with the RAF for almost three years. We left Cairo at 10:10 and headed Northwest. Below was the green valley of the Nile checkerboarded with its farms. Up ahead I could see the brown desert. The sand was patterned by auto and tank tracks in a crazy jumble. None of them seemed to be headed anywhere in particular. We were flying at about 500 feet when Bartlett suddenly turned the nose of the plane down. I thought something was wrong when it looked as though we were going to plow into the sand. I looked back at Pete and he grinned. Then we leveled off just above the sand. We couldn't have been more than three feet off the ground, roaring along at almost 200 miles an hour. Somehow though I wasn't nervous. The kid made you feel perfectly safe. Ahead I saw the littered wreckage scattered over the El Alamein line. The desert was spotted with burned and wrecked tanks and vehicles. And the German defenses were thick. It must have taken a tremendous lot of power to break through those defenses. We flew over the graveyard of Rommel's tanks.[8] The plane was so low Peter had to hedgehop them. Then we zoomed over the Daba landing ground where there were dozens of wrecked Nazi planes scattered about the ground. Most of them destroyed before they could get into the air. Tanks, trucks, guns, vehicles of all kinds—twisted into grotesque shapes, blackened by fire. There were thousands killed down there. Hundreds of bodies were still unburied as we flew over. Along the coast road moved the British convoys going forward. A long brown river of men and machines flowing westward as far as you could see. It was a wonderful and terrible sight. I'd never seen an army on the move before. Now I know what the German army must have looked like pouring across Poland, Belgium, France and the Balkans. It was shortly after noon when we reached the Bug Bug airfield which the Germans had held a few days before. There were wrecked planes lying about and bombs abandoned by Jerry. A desert landing ground means just a flat place in the desert. The heat was intense. I caught a ride in an army truck to advance air headquarters. We drove for 90 minutes in the convoy and turned off to the white sand dunes by the Mediterranean. The RAF conducting officer whom I was to contact already had gone further forward. So I went over to the American Hqts. I was going to put up my cot nearby when General Strickland said "Don't sleep out here, son. Come on over to our tent." So I moved into headquarters. [Major General Louis] Brereton was quartered in a camouflaged trailer nearby. It was getting dark so I opened a bottle of Canadian Club and asked one of the officers to have a drink. I hadn't heard his name when we were introduced. We were sitting on a cot in the semi-darkness and I poured him a slug into his canteen cup. The talk turned to horses. I began giving him pointers on racing and sharing my knowledge of the turf.

"I own a little farm in the Kentucky Bluegrass on the Paris Pike," he said. "I breed a few horses." One of those small-time operators, I said to myself, and asked what his best horse was.

"I haven't got any good horses right now," he said. "The last good one I had was Equipoise [famous mid-thirties race horse]."

My blushes could have illuminated the tent. He was Lieut. Col. C. V. "Sonny" Whitney, a helluva swell guy. Later we went to Brereton's trailer and had hot chili warmed over a gas burner. The trailer was furnished only with a bunk, table, chair, radio and washstand. Then we listened to the radio news about our army's progress in the West. It was cold and damp my first night in the desert. I was glad I was sleeping under a tent.

———————

Three weeks after the Battle of El Alamein opened, I checked out of the Metropolitan hotel and Hassan, my favorite porter, put my bedding roll in a taxi. Sadly he gave me the international farewell salute—an arm extended with upturned palm.

The scoundrel had been filching my small change for weeks but I never had the heart to dampen his sunny spirits or question his loyalty with an accusation or reprimand. Hassan was a thief and I knew he knew I knew he was a thief. But his melancholy countenance quickly changed to a toothy smile when I placed a pound note in his hand and bid him goodbye.

At the Heliopolis Airport on the outskirts of Cairo a Blenheim was being warmed up. The pilot was a yellow-haired young man named Peter Bartlett of Nottingham. He was only twenty but he had been flying with the RAF for three years and was a veteran of the Battle of Britain. His youthfulness startled me, but then I never got over the surprise of seeing modern warriors with little more than a heavy fuzz on their cheeks.

"If you are ready," Peter said, "we'll be off." He suggested I sit in the glass nose of the plane for a better view of the desert.

The old Blenheim, almost flapping its wings to get into the air, rose over Cairo and headed toward the Mediterranean. Below was the lovely green valley of the Nile checker boarded with farms. The pyramids and the Sphinx squatted ageless and mysterious where the brown of the desert rolled in to meet the green of the valley. I thought it would be appropriate to jot down some wise observations on the inscrutable Sphinx at this stage of civilization's progress, but nothing brilliant occurred to me and I devoted my time to watching the desert rolling monotonously below.

We had been flying about an hour when the plane suddenly nosed toward the desert. The earth came rushing up and when I thought we were going to plow into the sand, the ship leveled off and we roared along no more than ten feet above the dunes.

I looked back and Peter grinned and pointed up ahead. There in front of us was the graveyard of Rommel's hopes to capture Egypt—the fire-blackened skeletons of tanks, trucks and guns, abandoned gun positions and trenches already filling with drifting sand. It was the desert prominence known to the Arabs as "The Hill of Evil Men," where Rommmel's tanks made their first stand to halt the rush of Montgomery's forces through the broken El Alamein defenses.

The tell-tale wreckage led toward the West, and marked the path of Rommel's retreat. But the retreat was not a riot. Rommel had saved most of his Afrika Korps and his armor by abandoning Italians. Leaving them without transportation, food or water under the pitiless sun.

Our plane skimmed the desert alongside the brown, dusty horde pursuing the Desert Fox. To our right was the blue Mediterranean and the coast road over which streamed endless columns of traffic writhing across the desert floor like a great brown snake enveloped in a fog of dust.

Hurtling over dunes and dipping into depressions, we roared over pens of German and Italian prisoners. Some instinctively broke and ran for cover when they saw the low-flying plane. Others stood and stared stupidly, too dazed or too tired even to move, looking at us with drawn, sun-blackened faces.

Once the Blenheim climbed to five hundred feet above the coast road and then a couple of Hurricane fighters moved in to look us over. They dived in like lean hawks on a fat goose but when they saw the RAF markings they veered off to keep their vigil over the lifeline of the army.

Shortly after noon we landed on a desert air strip at Bug Bug which was pitted with bomb craters and cluttered with the wreckage of German and Italian planes. No one knew where I could find the RAF unit which I was to join—except somewhere vaguely forward. It was moving close behind Rommel's rearguard.

I learned that Major Gen. Louis Brereton's desert air force headquarters was nearby on the shore of the Mediterranean, so I hitched a ride in an air force truck, reaching the camp site just before dusk.

I was preparing to spread my bedding roll on the sand when lean, leathery Brig. Gen. Auby Strickland, commanding the American fighter command called to me.

"Hell, son! Don't you go trying to sleep out there in the open. There is an extra cot in this tent."

I accepted the invitation gratefully, for the chill of night was settling over the desert. No one else was in the tent at the time, but as I was taking a drink from a bottle of Canadian Club, an American Lieutenant colonel entered.

"Have a drink?" I asked.

"I'd love one! I haven't had a drink in days."

We sat in the semi-darkness sipping the whiskey and enjoying the pleasant warmth it gave. We began to talk and I mentioned I was from Kentucky.

"I suppose you like horses," the colonel said.

I was feeling nostalgic. I told the colonel of the beauties of Kentucky and the loveliness of the Bluegrass when the sun slants over the rolling, purple-hazed meadows. I told him of the magnificent farms where the great thorough-breds are foaled and trained, of the races I had seen, and which horses were Kentucky's pride—and why. I gave the colonel quite a lecture on Kentucky, mint juleps and the finer points of thoroughbred breeding.

"Kentucky is a beautiful state," he said finally. "I own a little place myself on the Paris pike."

I said: "Do you have any horses?"

"Not many."

Ummm, I thought, a small-time farmer. "Have you ever bred any racing stock?"

"Yes, but I don't have any good horses now."

I persisted. "What was your best horse? Maybe I lost a bet on the hayburner."

"The last good horse I had," said the colonel, "was named Equipoise."

Even in the darkness, Lieut. Col. C. V. "Sonny" Whitney probably could see the blush that suffused my burning face. But he was a gentleman. He didn't laugh.

Friday November 13, 1942
Bug Bug

Brereton said I could ride with the U.S. convoy to Gambut tomorrow. I haven't heard what progress Landry, Graebner and Fowle have made. After lunch Whitney and I walked to the beach for a swim in the Mediterranean. The beach was beautiful. The water was clear and blue-green but cold. I took a cake of soap along for a bath but it was useless. The soap wouldn't lather in salt water. Nevertheless the swim made me feel cleaner. We went to the British mess tent for supper. Whitney and Finch were there. I had just finished eating when we heard the planes coming over. Jerry planes, probably from Crete. Then suddenly there was a terrific explosion. Everyone jumped to get on the ground and turn out the lights. We lay in the darkness, and listened to the planes. They went on toward the highway and there we heard more bombs dropped. All this time a group of British soldiers were singing. They never missed a beat even when the bombs dropped. I finished my dessert and went up on the dunes. I sat with Finch, Whitney and Lieut. Keith Siegfried under the stars while the German planes circled overhead.

"Dammit, I'd like a cigaret," Finch said.

"Sure, so would I," Whitney laughed. "But this is no time for smoking."

"And look at that full moon," Whitney added. "This is why I don't like full moons anymore."

"My girl back home can't understand why I don't like a full moon anymore," Keith said. "She thinks I'm not as romantic as I used to be."

We went to bed a little later when the planes left. But when I was in bed I heard them coming over again. I counted at least twelve. Over by the road I could hear dull explosions. Jerry was hitting at the convoys. But the British boys never stopped singing.

Next morning, after a dip in the sea, a group of officers and I went to a nearby British mess for supper. We had finished the meal when we heard the enemy planes, probably over from Crete to hit at the British columns rumbling along the coast road through the night.

Suddenly there was the eerie whine of falling bombs. We dived for the ground. I fell across Whitney and someone doused the lights as the earth shuddered under the explosions. We lay there listening to the planes overhead and to a group of Tommies singing in a nearby mess hall.

"Bless 'em all, bless 'em all,

"The long and the short and the tall . . ."

They sang defiantly and did not miss a beat as the bombs fell. And then the crash of bombs came from the directions of the highway and the drone of motors faded. We picked ourselves off the ground and went up to the dunes while another flight of planes circled overhead. Colonel George Finch of Atlanta and Lieutenant Keith Siegfried of New York were with us.

"Damn! I'd like a cigaret!" Finch growled.

"So would I," chuckled Whitney, "But this is no time to light a cigaret. I'll bet those Jerries can see us sitting down here."

Keith said: "My girl back home can't understand why I don't like moonlight nights anymore. She thinks I'm not romantic like I used to be. It would be a hell of a note to have my romance busted up by a big, round, beautiful moon!"

When we were in bed the Jerries came back again, bombing the highway. But the British boys didn't stop their singing.

"There'll be no promotion this side of the ocean,

"So cheer up, me lads, bless 'em all!"

Three

IN PURSUIT OF ROMMEL (LIBYA),
NOVEMBER 1942–FEBRUARY 1943

Saturday November 14, 1942
Gambut [Libya]

Again I've just missed the RAF advance party. It's hard to get anywhere traveling in convoy. We broke camp at 6:30 this morning after a cup of hot coffee for breakfast. I rode with Keith Siegfried who shepherded the convoy. We reached Halfaya Pass at 10 A.M. and never have I seen such a traffic jam. Almost as far as I could see the plain between the escarpment and the sea was filled with trucks, tanks, cars and everything on wheels, waiting to get up the winding steep Halfaya Pass road or over the Solum Pass some five miles further west. The First Armored division was creeping up Halfaya in clouds of dust and exhaust fumes. They seemed to creep along at a snail's pace. It didn't look like we could get through for hours. The army had priority and so we had to sit. Keith and I lunched on a can of vegetable stew (cold) and a hunk of cheese. After two hours in the hot sun Keith said "to hell with it." He lined up his trucks and broke into the convoy line. We went crawling up Solum Pass. It had been bombed or dynamited at one place but repaired. At the top of the escarpment we stopped to look back at the plain below us. For miles and miles we could see the convoys packed by the roadside. And others were coming up. The plain was littered with abandoned German equipment, destroyed vehicles, clothing, hats and shoes. I don't believe I ever saw such a bleak, desolate land except for the Sahara. Little white crosses marking German and Italian dead dotted the sand.

"God, what a place to have to die in," Keith said. He was right.

We made better time on top of the escarpment—and we heard later the Germans came over after we'd passed Halfaya and bombed the concentration of vehicles.

We rolled into the dusty advance headquarters site at 5 P.M. This time I dug a slit trench but I didn't have to use it. Jerry didn't pay a night call. Still, it was the same story over again. The RAF unit was up ahead. I got a good little yarn from Strickland. Lyman Middleditch's DSC caught up with him. Brereton, Strickland and Cunningham went to the advance American base to present the award. Middleditch had gone off in a jeep to look over a damaged German plane. He came walking up for the ceremony in his flying clothes with toilet paper streaming from one pocket. After the medal was pinned on his jacket, he took off on an operational flight. Late this evening the *Yank* photographer, "Slim" Aarons, came in with General Andrews. He (Slim) and I—not the General—will go up together tomorrow.

We broke camp at 6:30 next morning, November 14, and after a hurried breakfast of coffee and chocolate bars, our convoy headed for Gambut, the site of the next advance air force headquarters. We reached the plain below Halfaya (Hell Fire) pass at 10 A.M. and our convoy was halted by a bad traffic jam. The plain between the escarpment and the sea literally was one huge parking lot jammed with vehicles of all descriptions waiting to get up the winding road through Halfaya Pass or through the Solum Pass a few miles westward.

The British First Armored Division was creeping through Halfaya in clouds of dust and exhaust fumes. The armor had right-of-way and no other vehicles were permitted on the roads until it had passed.

Beyond Solum Pass, we drove across the flat, dreary plains into Libya and at dusk arrived at Gambut where I found my old friend, Sergeant George (Slim) Aarons, photographer for Yank *magazine, who was on his way to join the same outfit I was chasing.*

Sunday November 15, 1942
Tobruk [Libya]

Slim and I found a RAF film unit going to Gazala so we hitched a ride. The headquarters outfit is moving too slow for us. It was blowing up a blinding dust storm when we left. The dust coated our faces, gritted on our teeth, filled our hair and rasped our eye balls. We drove to the landing ground first and the fighters were taking off. The base was being moved forward again. We found a NAAFI [Navy, Army, and Air Force Institutes] and bought some canned goods, fruit drops and cigarets. Then we headed for Gazala. Two or three times we almost ran off the road passing trucks. The dust changed to rain. The desert became a sea of mud. This Libyan desert is scruff growth and sand-clay. When it's hot it's dusty—then the dust changes to mud. And the winds were cold. We reached Tobruk late in the afternoon. The city was a shambles—an eery place of horrors with its sunken ships in the harbor and its buildings reduced to stunning, battered rubble. Slim and I wandered about the ruins. Soldiers camped in groups in the streets and in the few houses where there was a roof.

It was almost dusk when the bells of Tobruk began to toll. In the center of town was a Catholic church. The steeple somehow had escaped the bombs, and the bells were tolling. The soldiers paused in the streets to listen. It probably reminded them the bells were ringing in England, too. When the soldiers entered the roofless church, they instinctively removed their hats. They talked in whispers and walked on tiptoe. The floor was littered with debris. There were no pews, probably they had been broken up for firewood. Near the center was the figure of a Madonna, looking peaceful and serene in all the wreckage. On the pedestal were written many names. But the one I remember was Guiseppe [*sic*] Scire of Fredonara who wrote "Madonna Mia, look over and protect me and my family." We found a house next to the church for our cots—an air conditioned room on the second floor with shell holes through the walls. Our dinner was hot tea, hardtack and peaches. I was standing at the front window when three German planes came over flying low. Wham! a bomb dropped in the harbor area one block away. I could feel the shock. They dropped four others. Tracer bullets swarmed upward in orange colors like a fourth of July celebration fireworks display. But Jerry veered away into the low clouds. We could hear the motors in the clouds for several minutes then they died out. Slim and I went down the dark streets to the regimental headquarters of the Queens Regiment. We neared the gate and two sentries threw up their bayoneted rifles and shouted "Halt!" It was like a scene in a Hollywood super-duper special. We said "Friends" and advanced to be recognized. A minute later we were chatting with the guards like old friends. The headquarters was in a building formerly used by Rommel. The windows were blacked out. Oil lights spluttered dimly in the corners of the corridors. We found Colonel Sellers and his staff at mess. We had a cup of Chianti and a very pleasant evening. Then Slim and I returned to our quarters. The streets were dark and silent. The sentries were ghostly shadows pacing their beats. The jagged walls of ruined buildings were etched in tortured forms against the sky. Tobruk was just a ruined shell of war—a name in history—with its wreckage the monuments of a graveyard for thousands of dead. There was the feeling of death and creepy horror about that stillness in Tobruk.

During the mosquito-filled night a cold wind blew in from the sea. Doors swung on rusted hinges and broken shutters clattered on the windows. Slim slept with his clothes on just in case Jerry paid a return visit.

I don't believe I ever felt as lonely and far from home as I do tonight. It's a peculiar sensation that leaves an emptiness so great it almost hurts. I suppose it will stay with me to a certain degree as long as I'm abroad.

We decided to hitch our way forward next morning with a RAF film unit. A cold wind was shipping up a dust storm when we left Gambut and headed across the sandy-clay desert for Gazala where we hoped to find our outfit.

Dust sifted through the doors of the truck, coated our faces, gritted between our teeth and powdered our hair. Each blink of the eyelids rasped sand grains across our eyeballs and I began to understand why desert fighters always had a blood-shot tinge to their eyes. Goggles helped a little, but even goggles could not keep out the talcum-fine sand.

In midmorning the dust cleared under a steady, chill rain. The desert became a sea of brown mud which was good luck for Rommel. Our fighters could not take off in weather like this to harass the enemy's fleeing columns.

We drove mile after mile through the custard-like mud. Our driver, a youth from London's wrong side of the tracks, stared glumly ahead.

"Cheer up," I said. "It isn't too bad. At last we're on the right road toward home."

He shook his head. "I was thinking of my girl back home," he said. "She wrote she'd love me 'til the sands of the desert grow cold.'" He looked out across the dreary, muddy scene and shrugged. "The sands are bloody cold today!"

We rolled into Tobruk in the late afternoon and decided to spend the night in its ruins rather than the open desert. We found a building with part of the roof intact and made camp.

Slim went exploring and yelled back from the basement: "Look what I've found!"

I went down and Slim waved to dozens of cases of Mussolini's best mineral water, a liquid treasure. We stripped and poured bubbling quarts of aqua minerale naturale over each other to wash away the dust and mud of the day's travel. "I'll bet," Slim grinned, "this is the first time any American ever has taken a bath at 6 o'clock on a Sunday in Tobruk with specially bottled Italian mineral water imported from Milan!"

We dressed and went out to look over the battered town where the British had made their gallant stand in 1941 after being cut off by Rommel's drive toward Egypt.

Small groups of soldiers were camped in the streets or in the buildings which had roofs. War had rolled over Tobruk in waves, each wave leaving a little more destruction, a little more desolation and the smell of death and decay.

Dusk was settling when Slim stopped suddenly and whispered "Listen!"

It was the bell of Tobruk. Its silvery tone rang out across the sand caricature of a town with the sweetness of a benediction, clear and startling, the only clean thing left in all this shambles of war.

Soldiers paused to listen and then slowly walked in the direction from which the sound came. There in the center of the town was a little Catholic church. Its roof was torn off by shells and shrapnel had left gaping holes in its sides. But somehow the steeple remained upright and someone was tolling the bell.

As the soldiers entered the church they instinctively removed their helmets. They spoke in whispers and walked on tiptoe as though they might disturb the ghosts which people dead cities. There were no pews. Probably they had been used by the troops as firewood during the Siege of Tobruk.

The troops tiptoed through the debris littering the floor of the church and some of them knelt and bowed their heads at the shattered altar. Near the altar place was a figure of the Madonna, looking peaceful and serene in all the wreckage. On the pedestal on which the figure stood were many names— British, Australian, New Zealand, South African, Italian and German.

But the one I remember was that of Giuseppe Scire of Fredonara who asked in a penciled scrawl: "Madonna mia, look over and protect me and my family." Little boys who scrawled on sidewalks and fences had grown up to be soldiers who scrawled their names and prayers on a pedestal below a Madonna.

Slowly the light faded and the shadows moved silently out of the church and into the night.

Slim and I returned to camp and with our driver prepared a supper of stew, hardtack, and canned peaches. Afterwards we walked through the dark streets to pay our respects to the commanding officer of the Queen's Regiment stationed near the waterfront where masts and hulks of sunken ships jutted from the water.

A sentry challenged us and then we were led into the blacked-out building where the regimental staff officers were finishing their meal. They were using the building which Rommel had occupied a few days earlier.

"Have a cup of tea with us," urged the commanding officer, a colonel.

A batman brought two steaming mugs of tea and then I saw a look of utter horror in the eyes of the colonel. I looked around and saw Slim calmly spooning jam into his tea.

"But . . . I say, old man!" the colonel exclaimed. *"You are putting jam into your tea!"*

"Oh sure," said Slim. *"I always put jam in my tea. My grandmother taught me that when I was a kid in New England. It's good, too."*

"But I never . . ."

"You'd better try some, colonel," Sergeant Slim said. He reached for the jam but the colonel grabbed his cup.

"Oh, no, please!" the colonel sputtered. *"If you don't mind, I'll just drink the tea with a bit of cream and sugar. I've grown to prefer it this way."*

He looked sharply at Slim. "Jam in tea! Most unusual! Most unusual!"

Slim drank his tea and spooned the jam from the bottom of the mug. "I like tea just as much as any Englishman," Slim said. *"But jam gives an added flavor that makes it different. I prefer strawberry jam myself, but blackberry and red raspberry are all right, too."*

It was near midnight when the party broke up and the colonel acted as our guide through the dark, silent streets.

I suppose the colonel, after that night, always had his doubts about the Americans as an ally. A people who put jam in their tea!

Monday November 16, 1942
Martuba [Libya]

We left Tobruk about 8:30 A.M. and then it began to rain. The desert was a wasteland of scrub growth and mud. Occasionally we passed Arab caravans and wogs [pejorative for Arab natives] peeking through the ruins of a truck or tank looking for loot. Out in the most God-forsaken places, the wogs were standing by the roadside holding up eggs for sale. They didn't want money, but sugar or tea. Near noon we drove into a muddy field and found Gherity Marsh, the RAF conducting officer for whom I had been looking. He was an actor in England before the war. Slim and I walked through the mud transferring our rolls to Marsh's car. We set out for Martuba where the advance landing grounds were located. Out in the Cyrenean desert the storm had made small rivers which sometimes inundated the road. We had to drive carefully because there were many unexploded mines the sappers hadn't recovered. Just ahead of us a jeep was blown up. Dozens of cars and trucks had passed the spot before but the jeep happened to hit the mine in the right spot. Three men were killed. When we reached Martuba we pitched our tent on a flat table land, rocky and wet, between our trucks and cars. They helped shelter us from the cold wind. But we found a bottle of Chianti had broken and soaked the canvas, giving it a dark purple tinge and the alcoholic odor of a wine cellar. Our bedding was damp to make matters worse—but even so we managed to be fairly comfortable. The other correspondents in the party were Peter Duffield, an Australian, and a veteran of the desert, Richard Caple of the *London Daily Telegram*. Caple is reputed to be the only man in the desert who can take one cup of water, drink half of it, and still have enough left for a shave and a bath. He's an interesting old codger. Bach and Beethoven are his first loves and he publishes a music quarterly of critical articles. Once a member of a party began singing "Frankie and Johnny," Caple got out of the car, furious. "It's blasphemy," he said, "Bastardizing the classics."

The rain started falling again next morning as we left Tobruk. Occasionally we passed Arab caravans and natives picking through the wreckage of trucks and tanks looking for loot. Some stood by the roadside in their rain-sodden robes holding eggs in their hands and crying "Eggus! Eggus!" They were willing to swap eggs for tea or sugar.

The storm sweeping the desert created little rivers which sometimes inundated the road and progress was slow. Our driver was careful about running off the main road for the Germans had sprinkled the shoulders liberally with mines. A jeep ahead of us swung out of the main line of traffic and touched off a mine. They were lifting three torn, lifeless bodies from the wreckage as we passed.

At noon we reached the RAF airfield at Martuba, a brown stretch of mud which had been captured from the Germans the day before. But it was too muddy for fighters to land on the airfield. Advance ground crews of the 211th RAF Group and the American 57th Fighter Group were preparing ground installations to receive the fighters when the field dried.

Slim and I located Flight Officer Gherity Marsh who was in charge of our public relations unit.

"You are just in time to help us get up the tents," Marsh said.

We pitched the tent between a car and a truck to get some shelter from the wind. But our new home smelled like the inside of a lost weekend. A jerry can full of red wine, discovered at Tobruk, had spilled out and soaked the canvas.

Our tentmates included Peter Duffield, an Australian correspondent, and a British correspondent, Richard Caple. They made us welcome and shared with us the wine they had left.

Caple was one of those brilliant eccentrics sometimes found in the desert. He had been in the desert with the RAF for months and legends had begun to grow up about him. He made a fetish of conserving water because he had seen men suffer from thirst and he alone among us knew what it meant to be in the desert with an empty canteen.

I watched him carefully pour one cup of water in the morning, drink part of it, and then wash his teeth, bathe, and shave from the single cup. I chuckled when I saw this performance for the first time, but later I was to find myself doing the same thing.

The others in our group were comparatively callow youths compared to Caple. He was a scholarly man in his late fifties, tanned and dried out by the desert sun. He rarely left the desert and when others returned to Cairo for relaxation in the flesh pots, Caple remained to edit a music quarterly published in London. He was as meticulous about reporting a battle as he was about criticizing the modern school of music.

Once when two correspondents, riding in the same vehicle with Caple began singing a modern ditty, he shouted for the driver to stop.

"It's blasphemy!" he cried angrily. "I refuse to ride further until you stop bastardizing the classics!" The bastardizing stopped.

One of the more hilarious Caple stories concerned the trip of a female correspondent who came into the desert as a guest of the RAF unbeknownst to Caple.

Women correspondents were taboo with the Eighth Army. Montgomery had refused to have women traveling with his troops because he regarded them as an unnecessary nuisance. But the RAF was more liberal than The Master and this time slipped the woman into the desert to give her a quick look at the front.

This gallantry required additional conveniences for the sole benefit of the female correspondent—specifically, a Chic Sale affair surrounded by a wall of canvas and placed at a discreet distance from the camp. As for the men, they had only to pick up a shovel and walk over behind the nearest sandhill.

Caple arose one morning and looking across the horizon saw the inviting and unusual structure. Unaware of the arrival of the young woman, he decided to avail himself of the privacy offered. He no sooner had settled himself comfortably within the canvas walls and opened a book of verse than the woman *correspondent came across the sands. She entered her private little convenience, and was shocked to see a man sitting there.*

"Why . . . why . . . you horrid old man!" she spluttered angrily. "What are you doing here!"

With all the dignity which the occasion would permit, Caple retorted: "My dear young woman, even a person of your limited intelligence should know what I'm doing here!"

The female visitor left for Cairo a short time later.

With such characters as companions, I saw I was going to enjoy life in the desert.

Tuesday November 17, 1942
Martuba

We changed our camping place today to be nearer the 211th RAF group. It took quite a bit of wandering around the countryside to locate the outfit but we finally succeeded. They are near the Americans. The landing grounds are so muddy the fighters haven't been able to land yet. I wished for them this morning when a Jerry plane came over leisurely and bombed the road near our camp. Slim and I passed the evening playing poker dice with two RAF boys. I broke even. Earlier I had finished the story of my trip to Martuba and sent it back to Cairo by dispatch rider and plane. I hear Ed Kennedy is hereabouts but I haven't seen him.

Wednesday November 18, 1942
Martuba

I went over to see the Americans today. A big red bearded lad from Nitta Yuma, Miss., Corporal Johnson, was the cook and he dished out a lunch of stew, beets, jam, hardtack and coffee. "I'd sure like some pancakes for breakfast," he said, "but we ain't got no baking powder and pancakes are purely flat without baking powder." The boys were living on British rations and weren't liking it at all. The British just don't feed their troops as well as we feed our men. Nor do they pay them or clothe them as well either. It's a sore point with the British troops. George Oldfield of Tonawanda, N.Y., a technical sergeant, was working on a captured German ME109. "I'll have it in the air in a day or two," he said. The Black Scorpion squadron has claimed the plane as its own. They're anxious to get the ship flying and see what it's like to be in the enemy's aircraft. A British armored car patrol had surprised several German fliers on the field a couple of days ago. This plane belonged to the commandant of the field, a German who had been educated in the U.S.A. "Okay, boys," he said in American slang when the armor came up. "You've got us." We'd slashed one tire on the 109 and broken the radio. Otherwise the ship was in good condition. Late in the afternoon Ed K. walked up. He'd come back from Giovanni Berta [Libya] for supplies with George Lait of INS and Harry Zinder of *Time*. He asked me to take over with the army. When I mentioned I had a couple of bottles of liquor, Ed was delighted. He hadn't had a drink in days. So Ed, Harry, Capt. Krosnick of the U.S. airforce and I retired to my tent to pass the bottle around. Later I took my bedding to the American field and we slept in a large tent.

Thursday November 19, 1942
Giovanni Berta [Libya]

We were up at dawn and drove to Giovanni Berta, a little Italian colony which was one of Mussolini's prize colonization projects. The Germans had moved on two days ago. The village was a beautiful little place built on the side of a small hill. The village square was dominated by a Catholic church. The padre was the only Italian left in G.B. [Giovanni Berta], a dark skinned gray bearded little man. The church was beautifully kept and looked quite rich for such a small village. The houses were built of stucco and gleamed white against the dark hills. All the Italians had been evacuated by plane. In the British drive last year many Italian colonists chose to stay with their farms—and the Arabs massacred many of them in retaliation for the Italian massacre of the Senussi [Sanusi][1] tribesmen by Graziani[2] during the Itie [Italian] conquest of Libya. The natives swarmed about in their dirty but picturesque costumes. Many wore Itie clothing or an Itie coat above Arab dress to give them the incongruous look of scarecrows. They brought eggs, fresh vegetables and chickens to trade for tea and sugar. Our camp was in one of the abandoned villas overlooking the village. The kitchen chimney was blocked and when a fire was built the smoke filled the rooms. But it was cold and so we huddled in the kitchen for warmth even tho our eyes watered from smoke. Enroute to G.B. our truck had stalled in a detour of a dynamited bridge. So we had to send a tow car back for it. Wes Haynes, A.P. fotog [photographer], came by with a party of British naval officers enroute to

Bengasi [Benghazi] and took a flock of pictures of me around the town— for A.P. promotion.

Friday November 20, 1942
Giovanni Berta

Tomorrow we go on to Bengasi. The British are moving in on the city. It's cold and raining.

Saturday November 21, 1942
Bengasi [Benghazi, Libya]

We broke camp and left G.B. [Giovanni Berta] early this morning. The roads were being swept by the sappers looking for mines and so we stuck to the paved road as much as possible. Before coming to Barce [Pass] we drove through the Jebel, where the Arabs live in caves and tend their flocks of sheep and goats. The Barce pass had been dynamited but we detoured on a narrow winding pass into a beautifully cultivated plain. The farms were plowed and farm implements stood in the fields. But the country was deserted. We stopped in the town briefly and the natives swarmed about our car. We went into the hotel that once had been a very attractive place. The register was still on the desk. The last entry was Nov. 7. We signed the register before going on—giving our destination as "Berlin via Rome." Several miles out of Barce we went down the blasted Tocra pass to the coast road and then drove toward Bengasi. We could see the city in the distance across the flat coastal plain. Columns of smoke hung over the skyline. We drove through an arched gateway to the city at midafternoon. The smoke was from burning rubber dumps and an Italian tanker in the harbor which had been hit by American bombers in a raid two weeks earlier. Bengasi was torn and battered by bombs and shells. The civilian population had evacuated. The only Europeans were British prisoners of war in a hospital. They had been captured at Tobruk last summer. Bengasi was a filthy, stinking city of death. Tobruk was battered worse, but Bengasi was more depressing. At one time it was a modern, progressive seaport. There was a park near the harbor which must have been a beautiful spot. Now it was gouged by trenches and shelters and the trees and shrubs were torn and dead. In the business district the shops were shambles. Twisted steel girders and masonry were piled in the gaunt walls of buildings hit by bombs. On the waterfront

were miles of barbed wire entanglements. They must have been afraid of
Commando raids. The wires were strung with tin cans so that if anyone
touched the wires pebbles rattled in the cans. The twin-domed cathedral
wasn't badly damaged. Its ugly exterior was pocked by shrapnel and
some small shells had penetrated one of the domes. But the Italian marble
walls were almost untouched. The figures of the saints were damaged but
the place still had a majestic look—though it wasn't as warm and friendly
looking as the little church at Giovanni Berta. I had expected the entrance
to Bengasi to be a thrill. But it wasn't. It was depressing to see so much
destruction, waste and filth. Lait and Warrener located an apartment
building and we moved into a flat after sweeping out the trash and filth.
However we had a maple dining room table, easy chairs, china closet,
sideboards, book cases and odd tables at no extra cost, left by a tenant
who was in a big rush to get out. Ince's Court was the name of our abode
and before nightfall most of the correspondents had moved in as our
neighbors. It was quite a cozy and comfortable place.

Sunday November 22, 1942
Bengasi

We toured the ruins of Bengasi today, poking about in dark, silent buildings littered with trash and discarded clothing and household odds and
ends. In the Jewish quarter the rabbi said the Germans had hung four
Jews as a warning not to be friendly to the English. The word "Jew"
was printed on the doors of their homes and the little stalls in which they
had their shops. In the harbor the navy is getting ready to sweep for
mines and to get supplies into the port. Once this harbor is working it
will ease the strain on the lengthening British supply lines. I'm still chasing the war but there's not much chance to see any action until the front
becomes static.

Monday November 23, 1942
Bengasi

Met Haynes again today—more pix and another tour of wrecked buildings. Wes had some chocolate and it was delicious. You get to crave
sweets out here and you're like a child when someone gives you a chocolate bar. I never cared particularly for canned fruit—but when we open
a can of pears or peaches we exclaim over them as though they were

nectar. But we had bad news. The army wants our quarters. We gotta find another place to live. Luckily we have a supply of the mineral water we found near the Cathedral. The water in Bengasi is contaminated and dangerous. It's not very satisfying but it's pure—and a laxative.

Tuesday November 24, 1942
Bengasi

We moved into new quarters today, a little villa on the edge of Bengasi which had been headquarters for a German signal unit. It was filthy as everything else but we cleaned it up with the help of Arabs and moved in. The place has two large bedrooms, a small bedroom, dining room, kitchen and basement shelter. Morrison and Zinder left us today to return to Cairo, not before they dropped 14 L.E. [lire] in a poker game by candlelight last night. Lait won about 10 quid and I won the rest. Our new place is comfortable. There are shutters on the window for blackouts and we have our broken candelabra for the candlelight meals at night. Between the dining room and kitchen is a small opening in the wall through which we pass the food. We hung nets over the door and window to keep out the flies with another net over the opening to the kitchen. I was commissioned then to bring Bessie of Bengasi into our household. I drew the figure of a robust Amazon—nude—on the wall and the net made a skirt to hide what would have been Bessie's middle. Each time the plates were shoved from the kitchen it looked as though they were coming between Bessie's legs. Anything for a gag to break the boredom of waiting for the next move. The army is moving up but it's slow over such distances. And it looks as though Rommel will make a stand in the El Agheila line which appears to be stronger than the El Alamein position. The 8th army is keeping contact with armored patrols but no big push can be staged until the heavy stuff gets forward.

Thanksgiving
Thursday November 26, 1942
Bengasi

We had a Thanksgiving dinner today of Bully beef, hardtack and tea. The b.b. was cooked in a hash but it still was bully beef. Lordy, what a good turkey dinner would taste like with hot rolls and then a chunk of lemon or banana pie for dessert.

Saturday November 27 [28], 1942
Bengasi

DeWitt Mackenzie [venerable AP foreign news analyst] barged in today. He's on a tour of the Middle East and came up for a look around the front. I took him on a sight seeing tour of Bengasi—and he brought along a quart of Bourbon from Kennedy plus some cigarettes. Mac said he would call Marie when he gets back to New York. He's a bit impatient because he can't get in touch with the generals by picking up a phone. He can't quite understand the name Mackenzie doesn't mean a damned thing out here. Still Mac's a good guy even if he does take himself too seriously.

Sunday November 28 [29], 1942

Frank Martin arrived in Bengasi today. He's supposed to join the RAF and American fliers but came up on a sight seeing tour. Said Turner and Farnsworth had arrived and Wiant had gone on to India after getting his credentials straightened out.

Thursday December 3, 1942
Bengasi

Lait, Warrener, Mackenzie and I are going back to Cairo tomorrow. We are told that unless we go back now and get equipment and supplies, there will be no chance later. When we get to Tripoli it may be there will be an expeditionary force found for an invasion attempt. For no reason we acted like children at the prospects of good food, a hot bath, and a soft bed.

Field Marshal Irwin Rommel staged the big bluff of his African retreat at El Agheila, south of Bengasi, where he skillfully made the pretense of digging in for a stand or perhaps lashing back at his pursuers with a counter-offensive. The position was ideal for defense. To the south was a vast marshland impassable for tanks, and to the north was the Mediterranean. At the entrance to the corridor between the sea and the marshes Rommel sowed the heaviest minefield ever laid in the desert.

This display of fight was enough to halt Montgomery. Methodically and with his usual thoroughness, The Master sent out armored patrols to keep contact with the enemy while drawing up his forces for another massive assault. He wasn't keen about advancing further until Bengasi harbor was opened to receive supplies from the sea. The long overland haul from Alexandria was beginning to put a heavy strain on his lifeline. An open port at Bengasi was needed to keep the advance rolling into Cyrenaica and on toward Tripoli.

Wavell had reached this point and been driven back. Auchinlec[k] had suffered the same disappointment. Monty was taking no chances.

I had left the RAF at Martuba to take over an assignment with the ground forces. My traveling companions were George Lait of INS, Harry Zinder of Time magazine and Chester Morrison, then of the Chicago Sun. Our conducting officer was Captain William Warrener of the Green Howard Regiment—companion, nursemaid, advisor, desert authority, and a credulous audience for Lait's lurid stories of life in the United States.

Waiting for Monty's next move, we settled down in a little house on the outskirts of Bengasi along with our drivers, Private Bertram Baker and Private Harold Crocker.

Correspondents are inclined to glamorize their rugged lives, remembering only the exciting, dangerous or amusing things that happened to them. In reality, life with the army in the desert was for the most part an endless fight against flies, fleas, mosquitoes, boredom, loneliness, and the monotony of Private Bertram Baker's cooking.

The British appetite, I discovered, is a strange and wondrous thing. I don't know whether the English housewife's cooking has destroyed the nation's taste buds, or whether the Englishman's indifference to food, with the exception of roast beef, has stifled the culinary arts on the little isle. Whatever the reason, the average Englishman will thrive, without complaint, on unvarying monotony in his diet. If American troops had been forced to subsist on British rations for three years, as the Eighth Army, they never would have finished the war. There would have been revolution which would have made the post-war demobilization uproar resemble the fretful prattle of little children.

American troops in combat had K and C rations which caused loud complaints because of the lack of variety. But troops behind the lines had 10-in-1 rations offering such delights as roast beef, meatballs and spaghetti, chicken, peas, beans, tomatoes, carrots, peanut butter, tinned cheese, jam and other substantial food.

The British gave their troops practically the same rations the army had been eating since the Boer war and bastard brands of cigarettes even worse than the cigarettes in the American K ration. The basic British desert ration was bullybeef and hardtack, supplemented by tasteless M and V (meat and vegetable stew), potatoes, flour, treacle, and tea. When supplies were plentiful there were issues of bread, orange marmalade, and bacon.

Private Baker, it developed, was a sharp trader even if his cooking left a great deal to the imagination. Each day he carefully hoarded the limp tea leaves collected from the teapot. He spread them in the sun to dry and then placed them in a can, sprinkling over the top a layer of fresh tea. Apparently his conscience did not bother him when he traded the lot to the Arabs for fresh eggs, and so far as I know he was never caught.

Warrener and our drivers were happy if they had a daily dinner of meat and vegetable stew, boiled potatoes, and tea. But occasionally our American bloc would revolt and then we would get a Spanish omelet or meat and vegetables disguised by a few sauces.

One day Baker came proudly into the dining room carrying a dish filled with a steaming, sticky, corpse-gray substance covered with black spots looking suspiciously like a cloud of trapped flies.

"What in hell is that?" Lait demanded.

Private Baker beamed. "This, sir, is Yorkshire f————g pudding!"

"I never saw Yorkshire pudding in this condition."

"Well," Baker admitted, "It's not exactly like me old mother used to make. I just mixed up some f————g water and f————g flour and put in a few f————g raisins. I think it will be all f————g right with treacle, sir."

Strangely enough the doughy mass did taste very good when smothered in syrup, but I would not recommend the f————g recipe to anyone with ulcers.

Occasionally an Arab would appear at our door and draw a chicken from the folds of his robe, and then we would have chicken stew. On one memorable occasion, we managed to get two chickens with Baker's disguised tea leaves. They were sad, scrawny fowl but the American bloc voted to have fried chicken, Southern style. Since I had been born South of the Mason-Dixon line, I was elected chef. I wrung the necks of the two victims, plucked the feathers, and cleaned them while beating off swarms of flies. I dipped each piece of chicken in egg, rolled it in crushed hardtack crumbs in lieu of flour, and dropped it into a skillet of hot bacon grease.

The aroma was delicate and altogether pleasing! But the evening breeze must have wafted the tantalizing odor into the street, for a British brigadier and a colonel who had been passing stopped in for a visit and there was no choice but to invite them to help consume the daily dish.

For weeks I had been dreaming of fried chicken, great platters of crisp brown fried chicken. And now these two were muscling in on our meal. I never cared much for British brigadiers and colonels after that.

Friday December 4, 1942
Cairo

What a day! Bombed before dawn in Bengasi and now I've had a good hot bath and am ready for bed in Cairo. I found seven letters from Marie waiting for me at the office. It was wonderful to hear even though hearing has made me blue. The sound of planes awoke me this morning at 5:30. Then the bombs began to fall—and the anti-aircraft opened up on the planes. I rushed out to watch. The sky was lit with flares making it bright as day. The Jerries were after a convoy in the harbor. The heavy ack-ack guns whammed away. Machine guns rattled and the Bofors [Swedish 40mm anti-aircraft gun manufactured on license by Britain, Canada, and the U.S.] spat shells into the sky—120 a minute each. The tracer shells and bullets streamed into the heavens in balls of red white and green. It was a weird fantastic picture. The bombs shook the ground and rattled the window shutters. The concussions rocked me backward. Spotlights fanned across the skies. Suddenly one picked out a parachute drifting slowly to earth. Two planes had collided and a crew member had jumped. The din continued for 45 minutes. Then the sound of the motors faded. The guns stopped roaring. The sun began to rise. We drove to the Benina airport and I got on a ship with Mac. We were in Cairo four hours later—and after getting my mail I dived into a tub to soak for an hour.

Sunday December 6, 1942
Cairo

This has been a day of labor for me. Friday the American Liberators raided Naples and we had no one aboard. Martin was supposed to go but he was in Bengasi and the message didn't get to him. Kennedy was furious but the damage had been done. I suggested we could only get hold of someone who had made the trip and get a byline story. So I spent the day getting a story from Lieut. Col. Kane who led the raid. I got it through censorship along with the U.P. story of the raid so we got an even break. Now I understand Martin is going to India and Tucker will take over his credentials with the British.

Wednesday December 9, 1942
Cairo

I've spent five days in Cairo and now I'm ready to leave again. The place gets on your nerves after a few days. You feel better in the desert, too. I've spent my time collecting gear and knocking around with Tucker and Farnsworth and Mackenzie. Paul Lee came out of the hospital from a round with infected sinus and I turned over my room at the Metropolitan to him and moved in with Farnsworth at Shepheard's. Then Tucker came in from Alex and had no room so we took him in. Funny how grown men can act like kids at times. Tucker didn't check in. We tied the twin beds together and slept three in a bed. We ordered our breakfast sent to the room—so when the waiter came in, Tucker crawled under the bed to hide while he was in the room. Tomorrow I leave again for Bengasi. We'll go up on an American plane.

Thursday December 10, 1942
El Adem [Libya]

Lait, Ed Stevens and I left Cairo this morning—Lait with a terrific hangover. Chet Morrison was to come with us but the night before had been too much for him. We were to get aboard an early plane but at the last minute a bulldozer was loaded aboard and the pilot said he couldn't afford to carry anymore. We managed to get aboard a DC3 carrying a jeep. I slept on a pile of bedrolls until we reached El Adem where we were to catch another ship to Bengasi. But we missed the plane by about 30 seconds. The Americans invited us to spend the night in one of their vacant tents. I had a bedroll and rubber mattress and a Capt. Bowman supplied blankets. This outfit has been doing a great job transporting supplies to the front. They left the U.S. with 52 planes last month and got all of them safely to Egypt. They went into active service in the desert almost immediately.

Friday December 11, 1942
South of Bengasi

We rode from El Adem to Benina airport near Bengasi. They put us in separate planes because the ships were carrying drums of gasoline. The colonel explained the risk involved if anything happened, but we were anxious to get away. We flew very low over the desert, startling wild dog, herds of gazelles and camels. The ships all made perfect landings. I hitchhiked to Bengasi to get our truck to pick up our gear. Then we set out for a new encampment, leaving Bessie behind together with Akedia, a little Arab boy who had been our house boy. Akedia was in tears when we left.

Saturday December 12, 1942
Agedabia [Libya]

Last night was miserable. We had no sooner got into bed in the open than it started to rain. We all jumped out of our cots—in the nude—and put up the utility tent—but when we were settled again the tent began to leak. I pulled my bedroll up over my head and said to hell with it and went to sleep. Bill Warrener spent the night in the car. Now we've made camp again and hear that Rommel may be retreating from El Agheila.

Sunday December 13, 1942
Mersa Brega [Libya]

Rommel is in retreat! There will be no battle of Agheila. Just as the British were ready to strike, Rommel pulled out and ran. We were the only correspondents on the ground—most of them being in Cairo—so I think Lait and I have a good beat. If we don't beat the communiqué we'll at least have the first descriptive stories.

Monday December 14, 1942
Mersa Brega

It will be interesting to know why Mr. R. left the Agheila line, and where he will make a stand. This line is a maze of thousands of mines and booby traps, and it's hard to see why he pulled out of such a strong position. There are marshes through which tanks and trucks simply bog down. Infantry would be mowed down trying to cross the flat marshes and barbed wire entanglements without tank support. *I'm beginning to believe R. may not be going to make a stand before Tripoli.* He's left probably his stoutest position on the coast—and mines and traps are thick, slowing up the British advance. However we hear the New Zealanders have swung south and are moving fast.

Wednesday December 16, 1942
Mersa Brega

The bodies of Scotsmen lie in the minefields where they were caught by exploding traps, growing black in the sun. Mines are everywhere. I saw a desert burial of a young Scot beside the road, while the bagpipes played in the distance. The padre said a few words and the soldiers stood silent with their heads bared. On the road a few yards away rolled the tanks, guns and trucks. Planes roared overhead—but the group at the grave seemed oblivious to all the noise and uproar. Now the Scotties are furious at the Germans. "I'll never take another prisoner," one Scotsman said grimly. "Not after what I've seen."

When the Eighth Army, rested and reinforced, was ready to attack, Rommel suddenly began retreating on December 13. He had stalled for time and gained it. Monty had sent his New Zealanders on a left hook around the marshland and planned to drive forward with his Highlanders spearheading the advance. But the sudden withdrawal gave The Master a victory without battle.

The British began working their way through the maze of minefields and booby-traps. A flame of anger ran through the troops because the Germans had begun to mine and booby-trap everything, including the bodies of their own dead. This devilish practice was to become a common thing later in the war as the enemy grew more desperate but at this time it seemed a particularly vicious and unsportsmanlike act. But we hadn't heard much about Dachau and Buchenwald.

The bodies of Highlanders lay in the minefields growing black under the sun. Sappers were busy clearing the roads for the advance and could not take the time to recover the bodies. The stench of death lay heavily over the desert.

Once we stopped and watched the burial of a young Scot beside the road. Across the sands rolled the high, reedy wailing of the bagpipes, a thin and mournful dirge in the roar of planes overhead and the rumbling of tanks and trucks along the road. Soldiers stood with heads bared while the chaplain intoned a prayer. The body was lowered into a shallow grave and covered with sand. The white cross looked lonely and incongruous marking the mound already being rippled by the wind.

The advance beyond El Agheila stirred a new hope in the hearts of the troops—the capture of Mussolini's last North African stronghold, Tripoli!

Men who had fought so long in the desert, for a cause that at times appeared hopeless, saw the first ray of victory, and the dazzling light brought cheer to their tired spirits.

"Good old Monty! He knows how to do a f———g proper job!"

It was here the troops began to believe in Montgomery, to realize that victory was ahead. They had crossed the black abyss of defeat and they saw a long fair road ahead of them. They accepted Monty as their hero, and this feeling among the troops was transmitted to the people at home. Blood, sweat, toil, tears, were beginning to pay off.

The supply line lengthened until it stretched more than one thousand miles from Alexandria. And although supplies were flowing into Bengasi by sea it was necessary to conserve food, gasoline and water. Each of our little group was rationed to six mugs of water daily—five for tea and the sixth for our toilet. I learned the tricks of brushing my teeth, shaving and bathing in a single cup of water. The secret of the bath was to wash only under the arms, between the legs, and between the toes. The rest of the body didn't matter and besides once you got sufficiently encrusted with dirt, the fleas weren't such a nuisance. At the end of the first week without a full bath, you begin to smell your companions. At the end of the second week, you start to smell yourself. And at the end of three weeks, there is no known odor that is particularly offensive.

Teatime was at 10 A.M. and 4 P.M. Trucks, guns, tanks—the entire desert war—came to an abrupt halt twice daily while the army enjoyed its cup of tea, a strong scalding brew that lifted one's spirits by the nape of the neck and shook them vigorously.

Tea is both a stimulant and a sort of mystic rite with the British. There is a communion of spirits over the cups, a strengthening of the ties that bind Empire, and a rejuvenation of the soul. I actually have seen them brewing their tea while fighting a tank attack. My dad was an Englishman and I learned to like tea at an early age. But the vapid, listless stuff I knew as a youth had no relation to the desert brew. It was like comparing a mild, sweet blackberry wine to aged authoritative Kentucky bourbon.

I am convinced that the best way to defeat a British army is to cut off its tea supply. British troops can do without proper weapons, food or clothing. They will hang on with their bulldog tenacity when everything seems lost. But I believe they would disintegrate, division by division, without the stimulus of the little leaves marketed by Sir Thomas Lipton.

Saturday December 19, 1942
Marble Arch [Libya]

Yesterday we jumped from Mersa Brega to Marble Arch—more than 100 miles. The New Zealanders swept through from the South to take the airdrome and cut off some of Mr. R's rear guard. We're only about 385 miles from Tripoli now. This place gets its name from a massive arch across the road built by Italo Balbo.[3] It looks gaunt and absurdly bare standing out in the desert with nothing but barren land for miles. The Ities like to build arches, monuments and statues at every camel track. This is an excellent camping ground near the sea. We went swimming today—the water was cold but it felt wonderful—and we got some of the grime off. It isn't as cold here as it was at Mersa Brega. Last night was beautiful with a soft moon almost full. There's nothing much to do except wait for developments so we can move forward. The mines are bad ahead and we must be careful of our transport.

Sunday December 20, 1942
Marble Arch

Fourteen years ago Marie and I were married—our fourteenth anniversary and I'm sitting in a tent in the desert 10,000 miles from home. It's windy today and the dust is blowing across the flat country like a brown mist. We tried to find a NAAFI to get some chocolate but when we arrived we couldn't get it—the supplies were for the sappers. We pouted like a bunch of disappointed school boys, for chocolate suddenly became the most desirable thing in our lives. But finally we could laugh at ourselves. It was funny, four grown men beefing about not getting a little bar of candy—angry as though it were a vital thing affecting the outcome of the war. We tried to find water, too, but no luck. Our supply is low and this is one of the most arid parts of the desert. After being in the desert a few weeks you need very little water to drink. One little tin can half full is enough for me to shave and wash in. Warrener, Stevens and I walked about mile tonight to a little tent on a desert hillside to listen to the radio. An armored car had a German tank radio. The armored car boys in their leather jackets were lying about on the ground. They looked big and tough, but they laughed like kids at the corny jokes. It's cold tonight.

Monday December 21, 1942
Marble Arch

After days of close association the characters and little facets of personality begin to show in those you live with and you find yourself adjusting to your opinions of your companions. And you learn of the quirks and foibles of men whose names back home are big in journalism. They aren't the supermen you'd thought them to be. Sometimes they seem simple and childish—but there's one characteristic of the top-notch men. Most of them are gregarious, they love company, and like to spin tall stories hour after hour. That's only a superficial observation on the human side. Ed Stevens of the *Christian Science Monitor*—educated abroad, speaks several languages, has covered wars in Finland, Russia, the Balkans, and the Middle East. Married a Russian girl, is only 32. Ed is a peculiar mixture of cosmopolite and naive youth. He's well read and has traveled many lands, but he still hasn't grown up. He's a fidgety, restless fellow who's never satisfied to be where he is—he always wants to be somewhere else. And his voice has a little boy whine of petulance. He's perpetually beefing about something.

George Lait of INS is one of those likeable, bawdy, friendly guys who manages to stay in good spirits all the time. He's a good desert man and one of the most unselfish men I've seen. It shows up in many little ways—giving his American cigarets away, helping those on the party, sharing whatever he has. George is full of George's own importance as a war correspondent but it isn't objectionable. He never runs out of stories, most of them ribald and dirty. Three drinks and he's drunk—and next day he's bragging about how much liquor he can drink. He's paying alimony to four wives—or so he says—and pokes fun at his own foibles in love. But when he's tight, George likes to talk of his last wife. He's still in love with her. George's stories of his war experiences grow day by day. He embroiders on each of them a little bit, polishing them up with each telling. He's been a war correspondent for 20 years and knows his way around. He gets a laugh with his stories of how the French insist on calling him "Mr. Milk." While in France he got special permission to spell his name Laité to avoid embarrassment and annoyance. Whenever he'd register at a hotel, the clerk would always giggle and say "Monsieur Lait—Meester Milk! How fonny!" George likes to give the impression that he's hard, cynical, and independent. Actually he's a sentimental, kind hearted, tolerant man with a need for company and a great enjoyment of his job.

Bill Warrener has the typical English reserve that gradually dissolves as you know him. He rarely talks of his war experiences but one night he began reminiscing. He was in France with his Green Howard Regiment. His company had to fight a rearguard action at Dunkirk. All but three of the company were killed. Bill and two others lay in the fields as though dead, while tanks and troops passed by them. When night fell, the three began trying to reach the beach at Dunkirk. The Germans saw them and began shooting. Flares went up. But Bill got out. At Dunkirk he waded into the water and was heaved aboard a boat. He's a great guy to have as a conducting officer.

Bill came back from the ration dump with a haul of 26 oranges, jam, raisins, fresh bread, and cans of hard rations. With several dozen lemons we picked up from an old German ration dump, we have enough fresh fruit for several days.

Tuesday December 22, 1942
Marble Arch

This has been a lazy day in camp. Tomorrow we move up again closer to the front. It's hard to figure out what's going to happen. Rommel still has an army of some 50,000 or 60,000 men. But no one seems to know whether or not he'll fight before reaching Tripoli. I'm going out on a limb to predict he won't make a stand. The Christmas holiday season came to the desert tonight. I opened a bottle of Old Taylor before supper—and another after. Lait got out his Very pistol and we shot flares over the tents of the British correspondents near us. Our auto driver got drunk and he was yarping all night. Poor kid probably had never been drunk before.

Wednesday December 23, 1942
Nufilia [Libya]

We broke camp in a dust storm this morning. Stevens and I rode behind the truck cab and the dust was blinding. We stopped at a German ration dump and picked up a case of rice and meat stew. They had left dozens of cases of canned food about. I found an American Tommy gun in the sand. It's rusty but a little work will put it in good condition. It was midafternoon when we got to Nufilia, a little Italian village in the desert—600 kilometers from Tripoli. The village is a cluster of white stucco buildings, the principal section forming a square about a fountain—waterless of course. On one side is a beautiful little Mosque looking like a toy house with its white dome and minaret. However we moved into a fort atop a hill overlooking the village. It might be part of a scene from a Hollywood thriller with Beau Geste dashing from the Iron gates on a white steed to lead a charge against the Arabs. The fort gates were barred, but we entered cautiously, looking for booby traps, and found the place deserted. On one side of the square were two large connected rooms, very clean, with a smaller one between. We moved in where the Caribinieri Reali [Italian Royal Military Police] had once been quartered. In the center of the courtyard is a round lookout tower. The walls and rooms of the fort have guns slits and ramps leading to the top of the walls where riflemen could stand. It's an absurd place, however, for one small cannon could batter the place to bits. The soldiers once quartered here probably lived well. There was running water in some of the rooms once but before leaving the Ities damaged the well and punctured the water tanks. Still it's good to have a roof over our heads again.

Christmas Eve

We left the fort tonight to visit the boys in the village. The correspondents and drivers gathered in the little mosque to sing. An English driver was playing the harmonica beautifully. He once had been a concert player in England and could make the harmonica do tricks with Rhapsody in Blue, Star Dust and Moonglow. We sang everything from carols to Mademoiselle from Armentieres, and listened to the kid play. The acoustics in the mosque were fine. When we came in a driver whispered "Here are the American correspondents. Play the Star Spangled Banner." "I don't know it," the kid said. He compromised with Stars & Stripes Forever. Back at the fort Lait and I filled stockings for our drivers with bully beef, handkerchiefs, oranges, lemons, chocolate and some money.

Christmas
Nufilia

It's been a nice day even if it is so far from home—a box from E.K. [Ed Kennedy] and a packet of letters from Marie, the first I'd had in more

than two weeks. The correspondents played the drivers in a soccer game
in the morning. We lost 3–1. During the ceremony Major Guy Mostyn-
Owen arrived with Brigadier Gehu of the British Indian P.R. to present
Bill Warrener with the Military Cross for bravery in action on the Alamein front where Bill saved an officer's life under fire. Had lunch with
the Brigadier & Major as our guests. Tonight we went to the New
Zealand mess for Christmas dinner—soup—turkey and pork, potatoes,
carrots, peas, pudding, fruit cake, coffee and fruit salad. Quite a spread
for the desert, and a very pleasant time with ale and whiskey to add a
bit of cheer. The Brigadier—Kippenberger—extremely pessimistic about
getting to Tripoli—thinks February 15 will be normal if Rommel makes
a stand and he expects a counterattack by the Germans. We drove back
in darkness with Warrener on the running board to keep us from running
off the road or through a road block! It was only 12 miles but it took us
two hours to make the trip.

Saturday December 26, 1942
Near Sirte [Libya]

We moved up today to 7th Division Hqts. We chased Baker for miles
across the desert when equipment and luggage began dropping off the
truck. Just as we would almost catch up we'd have to stop to pick up a
chair or a shovel or a bag. Luckily we stopped him without losing anything. The nights are getting very cold. It's a chore to get out of bed
each morning.

Sunday December 27, 1942
Near Sirte

We left our camp this morning for Sirte, which was abandoned by the
Germans in the morning mists Christmas day. We wanted to be the first
in the town. Enroute we came upon a picturesque fort in the desert—
Gabr El Hadi [Gabr Abd el-Hadi, Libya]. There had been a furious battle
there a couple of days before when the British came upon a German
garrison there. The walls were spattered with bullets. The gates had been
torn off. On the battlements were splashes of blood. The strings from
hand grenades lay about. There had been stables inside the walls for
horses and camels. Handmade camel saddles and handwoven straps were
still lying about. We had a lunch of bully beef, cheese and sardines and

went on to Sirte. The town sits on a slight hill at the edge of the sea. It's another ghost town—silent, depressing, lifeless except for one fat cat which slinks about the vacant buildings. The Germans had taken everything of value even to the furniture. The place had been evacuated both by Italians and Arabs. Many buildings were wrecked, some by the RAF and others by German demolition. Booby traps filled the place. The sappers had been in but they had barely touched the traps which were attached to doors, chairs, toilet pull chains, hidden under steps and along paths. We walked gingerly. The jetty at the little bay had been dynamited. On the walls were caricatures of Churchill, Stalin and Roosevelt. "We'll see you again at Alamein," and "We'll be back" the signs said, or "He laughs best who laughs last, Englishman!" Again there was the smell of a dead city. The airport below the town had been plowed up. We got the first story of Sirte.[4]

Monday December 28, 1942
Near Sirte

The gods of good fortune must be with us. How we ever got out of Sirte without being blown to hell I'll never know. God must be kind to fools. We walked all over the town and into many buildings to see as much as we could. A few hours later three officers were killed and ten men wounded by booby traps. One officer stopped his car on the main street and walked around behind it. A trap under a cobblestone exploded and killed him.

"You've been over more mines than you'll ever know," Driver Baker said. "Remember coming into Bengasi when I swerved and almost ran into a ditch? I just missed a mine." It was the first time the kid had said anything about it. He didn't want me to worry about any danger.

Tuesday [December 29, 1942] with 4th L.A. Brigade

Lait ill today so Stevens and I went forward with the Fourth Light Armored Brigade. I was in a truck with Driver Bill Poor. The convoy moved over the desert as far as you could see. Late in the afternoon we came to the Wadi Chebis, a great depression like an old valley gouged out of the sand by a river long dried up. The trucks and armor moved across it in a stream, a magnificent sight. The Germans had been there this morning but withdrawn. God knows why. The place was a natural defensive position. Even machine guns on the escarpment would have caused a lot of trouble. Late in the day, at dusk, we lingered 15 miles from the Germans. It was cold and sharp when I got into my bedroll beside the truck.

Wednesday December 30, 1942

I'm bone tired and wearier than I can remember tonight. It took no urging to get me into bed. First, there was little sleep last night. I'd been asleep only a short time when I was awakened by an uproar. Earlier a patrol had captured a German hunting gazelle in a staff car. He'd been a professor of languages at Heidelberg. A smart chap, he refused to talk very much. A corporal was left to guard him. About midnight the German rolled suddenly out of his bed and dashed around a truck near me. There was an uproar of shouting. Dark figures leaped over my bedroll. The corporal ran the prisoner down without shooting at him. We were up before dawn. An officer in a jeep ran about the camp yelling "Wakey, wakey! Breaky Breaky! GET THE HELL OUT OF BED!!" Doughty little General Harding[5] called his officers in for a conference. He was getting ready to go on a patrol with two American-made honey tanks with the turrets cut off. He said Stevens and I could go along, so we piled our bedrolls on the tank. I left my typewriter as I thought we were coming back to the brigade headquarters. We hung on to the top of the tank as it bucked across the desert into "no man's land." Our tank went first. The general's followed. The cocky little general does his own patrols. The tanks lumbered across ditches, sand hills and wadis [dry river-beds]. On the horizon we sighted MT [Military Transport] which disappeared over the ridges as we approached. Once we came up over a hill and there was an armored car. The tankmen eyed each other through binoculars. It was an electric minute—but then the tank commander said, "It's one of ours." We pulled over to it for a powwow and then went on. When a few miles from Buerat—we could see the town in the distance, we turned in a wide sweep for home, plunging over rough trackless country. It was late afternoon when I climbed wearily from the tank back at Division Hqts. The ACV [Aide-de-Camp to the Viceroy] sent a message to the Brigade to send back my typewriter. I was all in—but the General seemed as chipper as ever. "Sorry I couldn't show you more excitement," he said. "It isn't always this dull."

Thursday December 31, 1942
Near Sirte

This is the most beautiful camp site we've had. It's in a palm grove near the sea. The scent of night-blooming stock fills the air. The beach is white. Near us is a well. I had my first bath in three weeks today. Went on a flea hunt as I'm being badly bitten again during the night. Celebrated New Years Eve with the fig pudding, listened to the radio in the fitter's truck nearby and then to bed about 9:30.

Friday January 1, 1943
Near Sirte [Libya]

A lazy day with breakfast in bed. Near camp found a cache of stolen Arab stuff buried in the sand—shoes, sweaters, buckets and clothing—most of it Italian. Got a quart of Canadian Club from S.K., cigarets from Tucker who's with the RAF. Had a flea hunt.

Saturday January 2, 1943

A miserable night and it's cold and damp today. The wind never stops blowing, chilling you through. The tent leaked during the night and Bill scrambled into the car. I just pulled up my mackinaw over my head. Ed Stevens left today for Cairo. Looks like a lull ahead as Rommel seems to be dug in at Wadi Zigzaou [Tunisia]. Our heavy stuff is coming up. Tonight we all climbed into the back of the truck to eat supper. Opened the bottle of C.C. [Canadian Club] which eased our cold pains.

Monday January 4, 1943

Rain and more rain—cold, steady and monotonous. The truck has become our home—the only dry spot in camp. Our bedding is soggy and a dripping dampness saturates everything. We're all browned off with close confinement. Days like this are a strain on tempers. Fortunately this crowd gets along well together or we would have been cutting each others throats by now. I tried to write letters in my tent but the drips of water splotched the paper no matter where I sat. Finally gave up in disgust—wandered about in the rain—soaked.

Tuesday January 5, 1943

The sun came out today. It's marvelous what physical and spiritual effect it can have. We all felt better and hung our sodden bedding to dry. The flies came out in swarms but we didn't mind them so much. We'll probably move in a couple of days to the Wadi Tamat about Sirte. Things may pick up in another ten days and again we'll be on the move. I'd like to get to Tripoli but Ed K. may take over before that time comes and I'd have to miss the show.

Thursday January 7, 1943

I had a bath in hot water today—news in any desert. Found a large oil drum which had been cut in half, so I heated a tub of water. It felt wonderful. We bought five eggs from an Arab so there will be a fried egg each for breakfast to break the monotony of fried bacon and fried bread. The flea situation is a little better although my legs and waist look as though I had measles, the bites are so thick.

Friday January 8, 1943
West of Sirte

We broke camp and moved about 15 miles west of Sirte near Wadi Tamat. Our camp site is in the dunes, near the sea again, where we can hear the surf. It's cool tonight but not as cold as it has been for the past week. Warrener's birthday—he's 28. The Germans had a large camp in this area. Slit trenches and dugouts are thick so they must have had a healthy fear of our air force. They celebrated Christmas, too. We found a Christmas tree made from twigs of desert bush tied to cross pieces set in a box. Ornaments were made from tinfoil wrappings from wine bottles and cigarets, and strips of colored paper. There was candle wax on the branches. Apparently each man received a small box as a gift—probably with candy, razors, and small trifles as gifts.

Saturday January 9, 1943

Lait and I hitched a ride forward trying to find Tucker. At the Tamat airdrome there were hundreds of tellermines [German pressure detonated device] and S mines [German antipersonnel device] stacked beside the fence. I don't know whether they were left by the Germans or dug out of the road and field by British sappers. Got a ride back with Captain Oliver, Harry Zinder, Norman Clark and Lloyd Williams. We've got no cigarets left but Warrener left this morning to find rations.

Sunday January 10, 1943

The little angel looking over us at Sirte is still working overtime. We've been going in and out of our camp site with no thought of mines as the engineers had apparently cleared our track. Today a S mine exploded at the entrance to our track, killing one man and wounding three others seriously. I walked down to see what had happened. "For Christ's sake, you're standing on a mine!" an RAF officer shouted, "Step in the road." I was standing by a tin can which had been used to mark the mine. Later the engineers took three more mines from the back. Bill Warrener had to spend the night in the desert when the gas line became clogged with sand. But he came back today with rations.

Monday January 11, 1943

The Stuckas [Stukas] and Macchis [Italian fighters] raided the airdrome near army. We could see the planes diving, the whump of bombs and the puffs of anti-aircraft shells. A Spitfire drove a Macchi out to sea. The faster Spitfire kept forcing the Macchi lower and lower until it crashed in the sea. The Spit didn't fire a shot.

Wednesday January 13, 1943

We moved to army hqts for the night. We're losing Bill Warrener as our conducting officer. He goes in as DADPR [Desert Army Director of Public Relations] succeeding Major Mostyn-Owen who has been the victim of political intrigue. The old man is broken up about it. He came over for supper last night. It's tough to lose Bill. I went back to 7th AD for my pistol and typewriter—saw dozen tanks, transports streaming over desert moving up for the next show. Chet Morrison re-joined the party, flying up from Cairo. The other reporters poured in, too, having heard the show is to start in a short time. Actually it's to get underway the 15th. E.K. sent up chocolates, mail, cigarets.

Chet, George and I left army to join the 7th Armored for the big show. We're ready to move and it looks like we'll reach Tripoli in 10 days. The Germans appear to be ready to put up only a rearguard action and not a real stand. Our troops will move south and west of Misurata to reach Tripoli and then may move on toward Tamis. Our air force is hitting at the Jerries hard today. It was wonderful to see the bombers going over. I can hear the thump of bombs in the distance. We'll stay here until the armor begins moving and then join the drive. Tomorrow the commander's message will be read to the troops. It says: "Personal message from the army commander to be read to all troops.

"1. Leading units of the 8th army are now only about 200 miles from Tripoli. The enemy is between us and that point, hoping to hold us off.

"2. The 8th Army is going to Tripoli.

"3. Tripoli is the only town in the Italian Empire overseas still remaining in their possession. Therefore we will take it from them. They will then have no overseas empire.

"4. The enemy will try to stop us. But if each one of us, whether frontline soldier or officer or man whose duty is performed in some other sphere, puts his heart and soul into this next contest—then nothing can stop us. Nothing has stopped us since the battle of Egypt began on Oct. 23, 1942. Nothing will stop us now. Some must stay back to begin with, but we will all be in the hunt eventually.

"5. On to Tripoli

Our families and friends in the home country will be thrilled when they hear we have captured that place.

B. L. Montgomery."

All through the latter part of December and the early days of January, 1943, the Eighth Army moved up behind Rommel through Cyrenaica into Tripolitania brewing their tea. The enemy maintained a rearguard action and then appeared ready to make a stand southwest of Buerat at the Wadi Umm er Raml, a dry stream bed which nature had made into a formidable anti-tank ditch.

Once again Montgomery carefully drew up his forces, this time for a push on Tripoli. The plan was for the Highlanders to spearhead a drive along the coast while the veteran Seventh Armored Division, the original Desert Rats, drove across the inland desert country. On the left of the Highlanders were the Fourth Light Armored Brigade. Then the Eighth Light Armored Brigade, the New Zealanders and finally the Seventh Armored.

Word came from Montgomery's headquarters the attack would open before dawn on January 15. Our correspondents' group voted to join the Seventh Armored in its desert push.

At dusk on the day before the attack, officers gathered their men in little groups and read them Monty's personal message.

Silently the men listened to the message. Then they went back to their tanks and vehicles to wait for the zero hour. Overhead our bombers thundered across to pound the enemy's positions. A pale half moon rose above the horizon and a cold wind stirred.

Thursday January 14, 1943
With 7th AD

The attack begins in the morning. On the coast are the Highlanders, then the 4th LAB 8th LAB [Light Armored Brigade] and New Zealanders, spread over a 40-mile front. Seventh Div. moved soon after breakfast this morning. We moved to the eastern edge of Wadi Umm Er Raml and there leaguered [set up for the night] for the early hours of darkness. "We move at midnight" we were told. It was cold, a bitter cold that made your clothes seem thin. Earlier the soldiers gathered in little groups to hear the commander's On To Tripoli message. They didn't cheer. They listened quietly and then went back to their vehicles to discuss what lay ahead. They must have known earlier the big push was coming. When we leaguered there was a pale half moon. The stars were bright. Lait, Morrison and I sat in our car with the drivers for warmth. And then at midnight a whistle blew. The motors turned and we headed West, plowing through sand and over rocks. The columns looked ghostly— shadows moving in the moonlight. Each shadow followed the shadow ahead—and a jeep bounced ahead of the lot. We drove until the moonlight faded at 2:30 A.M. and then the columns halted.

Friday January 15, 1943
With 7th AD

The attack opened this morning all along the line. Before dawn the tanks roared by us over a ridge with the thunder of a freight train. It took them an hour to pass. We tried to get some sleep in the car though the crash of artillery on the coast was loud and flashes lit the horizon. I crawled in the back of the utility with tommy guns, boxes and typewriters for a bed! The cold was bitter, penetrating, and numbed you through. I dozed occasionally. Chet slept on the seat, George in front of the car. We were up before dawn. The tanks ahead of us faced the enemy across Wadi Umm er Raml southwest of Buerat. The Germans and Italians had a tank screen of guns with some tanks across the wadi. There was a five-hour skirmish and then the Germans retreated again. We followed them closely across the flat country gashed by depressions of soft sand. During the afternoon we reached Wadi Umm er Raml and camped for the night, again closing into leaguer at night fall. This time we slept in our bedrolls.

Saturday January 16, 1943
With 7th AD

There is no greater mental torture than climbing out of a warm bed before dawn into the freezing cold. You lie in dread of the first move and then take the plunge like a swimmer diving into cold water. But unlike swimming, the first shock isn't the worst. Our columns dispersed at daylight and fires dotted the desert as tea was brewed. Then we moved again in chase of the enemy. The movement of tanks, trucks and armored vehicles was an awesome and spectacular drama on a grand scale. Not even the vastness of the country could dwarf it. As far as you could see they rolled. In the sands was the story of the first fighting—burned out tanks and blasted enemy gun positions. During an afternoon stop the Messerschmitts came. They dived, six of them, on our encampment with machine guns rattling. The antiaircraft guns roared. Some soldiers even shot at them with rifles and machine guns. The Jerries were daring and it was a magnificent display of fine courage and good flying. Once finished with strafing, the six raced along the ridge a few yards from us, dipping within a few feet of the ground. The bofors and machine guns threw a hail of lead after them but I believe they got away. Later I heard the ackack boys got two of them. Two killed—a vehicle burned in the raid was our loss. But we didn't have the desert entirely to ourselves. Once a frightened rabbit dashed through the tanks and trucks trying desperately to get out of the bedlam.

Sunday January 17, 1943
With 7th AD

We covered a lot of ground today and tomorrow may see a battle. We're near Kir el Dufan and the road to Misurata, with the chance of cutting off some of the enemy on the coast. We had another Stuka parade. The planes wailing like banshees in their dives. We're getting out of range of our own fighter protection and the Stuka raids will be more frequent. We're just a little more than 100 miles from Tripoli. About 20 miles ahead the enemy has a strong position with some armament. There may be a scrap. Even the Arab farmers have their troubles. One of them had a little patch of barley planted in a moist spot God knows how many miles from anywhere. But the army went plowing across his fields. Another crop plowed under. We passed two burning vehicles which the Stukas hit. A young officer drove up. "Can you tell us where we can find a padre?" So some of the men didn't escape.

Monday January 18, 1943
100 miles southeast of Tripoli

It has been a hellish day—miles of the roughest rockiest country I've ever seen. But still we've moved ahead. And the Germans continue their retreat so the expected battle didn't develop. We've driven through vast fields of rocks, fields that looked as though rocks were being cultivated. The constant bouncing and shaking made your neck feel as if it had been jammed into your skull. From level country we began to get into the hills. They were naked and bald, the same harsh cold brown. We're dirty, tired and unshaven. We haven't much water and washing is too much of a luxury. It was cold last night. It will be cold again tonight. We talk of many things but food is the main topic—reconstructing our favorite meals. Instead of philosophy, politics or world affairs, the conversation is about beefsteaks, pies, cakes, delicacies, and drink. Food, drink, and the luxuries of a bath, clean linens, and clean clothing become important. There have been no more Stuka raids. The advance is going well. The stars and moon are hard, sharp and bright in the cold blue of the sky. The trucks, tanks and guns are shadowy blobs around us. You hear occasional laughter, sometimes see the flare of a match. But the troops get to bed early. To our left the artillery is booming. Probably a pocket of rearguard resistance. The flashes light the horizon. The earth trembles with the shock. Our bedding is damp and clammy. There has been no chance for five days to air it. Overhead I can hear the planes pass occasionally. You wonder if they can see your convoy in the bright moonlight. Probably not or else they have another and more important objective. And you lie and listen to the throb of the motors, try to see the plane in the sky. You find your muscles tense when the plane approaches and when the motors' roar begins to fade you relax involuntarily. Now the wind is cold, biting. A young Tommy said: "If my girl ever says she'll have me 'til the sands of the desert grow cold' I'll say 'nuts!' because they're cold at 7 o'clock." We passed several German gun positions today and several captured Germans and Italians. The British were crowded about the Germans. The Italians were ignored. They were weary of war, or so they said. But a few hours before they were fighting. One gunner who kept firing from an anti-tank position had his head blown off. The others surrendered. The gun pit was littered with guns, ammunition, clothing, and personal effects of the men. In an overcoat pocket was a half loaf of stale bread. An Italian postcard showed a gallant Italian soldier atop a disabled tank labeled "Made in USA." The Ities like their propaganda bold and embroidered with the theme that the Italian soldier is a lion in battle. It's amusing and pathetic.

Before dawn the tanks roared by with the thunder of a passing freight train, plunging across a ridge and into the wadi. Guns began to flash all along the line with the rippling light of summer lightning. They dueled for five hours and then the armor burst through the enemy's wadi defenses and we began to move toward Tripoli.

Occasionally Messerschmitts dived from the sky and we dived for cover. Once I saw a frightened rabbit break from hiding and run through the columns frenziedly trying to escape from the bedlam. The columns moved swiftly across an incredible stretch of sand and stone.

One evening we watched a camel caravan in the distance, slowly negotiating the barren country.

"Camels will be blown up for years to come by the mines left by the Germans," Captain Warrener remarked.

"Oh, no," said a colonel. "The camel is a truly a remarkable animal. He distributes his weight so evenly while walking there is never enough pressure on any one foot to touch off a teller mine."

Thursday January 19, 1943
near Tarhuna [Libya]

We may be in Tripoli tomorrow. It's a race now to see who gets there first. The Highlanders on the coast smashed through at Buerat in the first attack and have followed the coast road to Misurata and then West toward Tripoli. Apparently the Jerries didn't have time for much mine laying. Our armored stuff has come all the way by desert, a hard spectacular drive that has been magnificent in its execution. We traveled along the high rocky plateau today at break of day. The sun touching the tops of bare brown hills was a beautiful sight. The columns filed down a steep escarpment into a valley. The Arabs had cultivated the place quite extensively and for the first time since leaving Cairo I saw grass, patches growing along irrigation ditches now dry. Clouds of dust swirled in and about the car. Then we stopped shortly after noon. Ahead the guns began again but were soon silent. My guess about Jerry not defending Tripoli was right. There's been only a rearguard action and none of that very strong. There was a bit of a scrap ahead of us today. Jerry was holding a ridge with 88's. One shell burst exploded near a tank on which General Harding was standing. His arm was badly hurt and he may lose it. Shrapnel hit him in the side and thigh. I hated to see the little guy hurt. I'd admired him very much since making the patrol with him. Got a Luger from a Jerry prisoner.

Wednesday January 20, 1943
Tarhuna [Libya]

We were too optimistic about getting into Tripoli today. The Germans are holding a narrow defile near here on the road to Tripoli. I'm worn out, this has been one of the damndest days in the desert. We started for Tarhuna early, going for the paved road. We cut across country and mired in the sand, sand as fine as talcum. The more we tried to get out the deeper we mired, only 50 feet from the road. A truck hit a mine near us and was wrecked. That was the beginning. A few minutes later a jeep hit a mine. The shrapnel whistled over our heads. One piece hit Lait in the chest but didn't hurt him. We were sitting in the middle of a mine field. Then a group of Arabs came up with two camels to look over the truck. A camel stepped on a mine and was blown into a chunk of raw meat. One of the Arabs had a mangled foot. We gave him first aid and sent him to a Red Cross station for attention. When it looked as though we couldn't get out of the sand, Morrison walked over to a tank and asked their help. They drove over to pull us out but the tank got stuck, too. However, the British boys worked for an hour and finally got us on hard ground. Tarhuna looked clean and quite civilized from the top of a ridge above the town. We drove through rows of Eucalyptus trees to the main square, and then toured the place. A few civilians had been left. We located a house and moved in. Late in the day the civil population was called to the city hall. The brigadier of the occupying troops told the people they had nothing to fear from the British, that they would be protected and every effort made to provide for them but if anything happened to remember they had only their own government to blame. Women holding children in their arms, men and boys listened in silence. They had been frightened. After being abandoned by their own troops they could hope for little from the English. When the brigadier finished his talk they began to laugh and shout.

I recalled the colonel's remarks next day as we neared the town of Tarhuna south of Tripoli. We cut across the desert to reach a paved road leading to the town but our vehicles bogged into the talcum-fine sand. Neither would budge and perhaps it was lucky they didn't. A truck passed us and was blown up by a mine. The badly injured driver was carried to the road and rushed to a first aid station. And then a jeep went up on a mine.

Several Arabs had seen the explosion and one of them—leading a camel by a rope—came over to see what he could find in the smoking truck. Suddenly there was another loud explosion, and the frightened Arab turned to find his camel was only a big hunk of raw, mangled meat.

Never believe a British colonel if he tells you a camel will not explode a land mine! Brother, I know!

A tank driver rescued us from our dilemma by hauling our vehicles onto the road.

Thursday January 21, 1943
Tarhuna

The Germans were still holding the pass today so we stayed in our house. Lait and I got the hot water heater working and had our first hot bath since Sirte. Late in the day a young American pilot came to see us. We'd seen a plane fall in flames the day before in the desert and watched a parachute falling from the sky. It was this kid, 23-year-old Richard Kimball of Minneapolis, a second lieutenant with the U.S. Fighting Cock squadron. Kim had been on a mission to dive-bomb a road south of

Tripoli. Coming back his ship was hit by ground fire. It caught fire and he baled [*sic*] out. Now he's going on into Tripoli with us.

Friday January 22, 1943
Castel Benito

We left Tarhuna this morning. The road was clogged with traffic. After some 15 miles we passed through the defile which the Germans had held and came out on flat plains. Near C.B. [Castel Benito] we stopped for a while by the roadside and I met George Tucker. Then we pushed on. At one point the column stopped. Gunners ran out to mount guns. There was the crack of rifle fire. Three Germans were captured in a field near us. We drove on through olive and almond groves and blooming apple trees. It was a peaceful looking countryside. The farms seemed prosperous and were well kept, each with its white stuccoed buildings. On either side of us the tanks moved through the trees in battle formation. Suddenly our column halted. Officers ran out to confer over a map. They ran back. The trucks wheeled and dispersed into the fields. We sat all alone on the highway, wondering what was around the bend in the road. We pulled over behind an embankment and waited—eating jam and crackers. Then the 25-pounders came up and were put in position behind us. We learned the Germans were holding a strong point just ahead. So we drove down a side road to an abandoned farmhouse and set up camp for the night. I walked through the plowed fields to the guns with T. E. A. Healy of the *London Daily Mirror*. We watched the crews prepare to open up on the German position. The guns were concealed under the trees but soon they were whamming away. The shock and noise of the guns was more than I'd expected. The shells had an eerie whistle. When the noise quieted I heard one of the gunners whistling "Dark Town Strutters Ball."

Saturday January 23, 1943
Tripoli

And so we entered Tripoli today![6] The long haul is over. And what a mixed day it has been. We raced into town early this morning. The Arabs waved and shouted greetings. The Italians looked on stolidly. Most of them seemed dazed as though they couldn't realize what had happened. A few laughed and waved. The armored cars and trucks and tanks rumbled through the streets crowded with civilians. The soldiers were happy. It was the end of a long road for them. Their mates were chasing Rommel west of Tripoli but no one in Tripoli was worrying about that. The fall of Tripoli was the thing. The Buffs [nickname for the Royal East Kent Regiment] came into town before dawn. Then came the armor. Unofficially the race to Tripoli was won by the desert division. But it was close enough to be a dead heat. We pulled into Piazza Italia. There was a meeting of the correspondents, shaking each other's hands. Then we rushed to write our stories and get them back to Cairo. We got rooms at the Grand Hotel facing the harbor—which was cluttered with the wreckage of ships. The harbor was badly battered but the rest of the city wasn't damaged much by the American and RAF bombing. The stores were closed. Civil life was at a standstill until the British got things organized. The lights & water were on, but there isn't much food in the city at present. In the afternoon Tucker, Zinder, Lloyd Williams of Reuters and I went down to the Ghetto. Never have I had such an experience—it was embarrassing and shocking. As soon as the Jews learned we were American and English, they mobbed us. Men threw their arms around us and kissed our faces. Women patted us. Children clung to our legs and kissed our shoes. Everyone wanted to shake hands. A husky fellow grabbed us by the arms and pulled us through the crowds down a dark stairway into a room where a patriarch in a white robe sat at a bare table. Dozens crowded into the room. The doors were barred. They gave us wine, nuts, candy. We were given a royal welcome as though we personally had liberated them. They told us the Italians had treated them worse than the Germans. The night before our troops entered the city Arab policemen massacred many Jewish merchants. They knew nothing about the British victories until our tanks rolled into town. We finally managed to get away—all of us tipsy from the wine.

We drove into Tripoli on the morning of January 23.

Arabs and Jews waved and shouted greetings. The Italians looked on dazed and dejected, unable to comprehend the disaster that had befallen their empire, fearful of what the conquerors would do to them. Piazza d'Italia was a madhouse of happy troops celebrating the victory. And above the shouts rose the clatter of typewriters as correspondents sat on curbstones and vehicles to write their dispatches.

After finishing our stories, George Tucker of the Associated Press and I decided to look over Tripoli's ghetto in the old section of the city where 16,000 Jews were crowded. We followed Harry Zinder, who could speak Yiddish.

We walked through an arched gate guarded by military police. When the people recognized us as Americans, the emotional outburst was riotous. Bearded men threw their arms about us and kissed us. Women kissed our hands and children clung to our legs and kissed our dusty shoes. A husky young man suddenly grabbed us by the arms and shoved us through the crowds into a courtyard and down a flight of dark steps into a cellar room where sat a white-robed patriarch with a long white beard.

The torrent of people flowed after us until the room was jammed and no others could squeeze their way inside. Women brought us wine and bread and cheese. Everyone who could reached out to touch us or to grasp our hands as though we were Messiahs and a touch would heal the wounds they had suffered in body and spirit.

They were laughing and crying and shouting. We were the symbols of liberation to these people. We represented the hope that had burned in their hearts for so long. We were freedom come at last.

And suddenly I felt humble and ashamed . . . ashamed that any human being could suffer the indignities these people had suffered. Ashamed that they should have reason for such gratitude.

I felt like weeping. And I did.

Sunday January 24, 1943
Tripoli

We had a sidewalk breakfast today. We slept too late to get anything in the dining room so Tucker, Morrison, Lait and I started on a tour of the city. We drove around the hotel and there on the sidewalk a British Tommy was cooking eggs and bacon and fried bread for Slim Aarons of *Yank.* Slim invited us over, and we had a fine meal with hot tea. The eggs came from a Senussia Arab who stood by to watch. There was quite a gathering around by the time we finished. We walked through the picturesque old fort of Tripoli and the maze of narrow streets in the native Suc [Souk, Arab market]. Again we ran into our friends of the day before and they said they could get me a camera. We were taken around back alleys and into old buildings with heavily barred doors. Finally we went into a dark room and from an old chest, one of the men brought out several cameras. He said the Germans had forced him to give them

180,000 lire worth of cameras and equipment before they left. I bought a German-made Kodak for 16 L.E. and three hours later was offered 25 L.E. So I got a good buy.

Monday January 25, 1943
Marble Arch

Tomorrow I'll be back in Cairo. Three months almost from Cairo to Tripoli. Two days to return. Slim Aarons and Burgess Scott of *Yank* and I went to the Castel Benito airport together this morning. I was in a financial daze. My hotel bill for the Tripoli stay was 59 lira—about 50 cents. We waited only a short time at the airdrome which was cluttered with wrecked and captured enemy planes. Several DC3s landed and we went over. Major Williams Denner of Carmel, Cal., was the CO. We piled on his plane and a few hours later arrived here. We had a good supper of cole slaw, stew and peas, cake & coffee. I went over to say hello to Col. Jerome B. McCauley of Denton, Texas, and Major C. C. Bowman of Kew Gardens, N.Y. Had a long confab [confabulation, casual talk] and got material for a story on the "Flying Commandos." Went over to Denner's tent and he produced sardines, baked beans, chocolate. When I started back to the tent I got lost, wandered about the camp for an hour before a sentry put me on the right road.

Tuesday January 26, 1943
Cairo

The ecstasy of a hot bath with the steam vapors rising from the water! The pure luxury of relaxing between clean cool sheets! The delicious food! And mail from home. What a day. We left Marble Arch at daybreak. Enroute we landed at Gambut where I met Col. Morsalis. He took me to his tent for a drink. Promised to get me a hand-woven bed spread from the Arabs. Nice guy. We arrived in Cairo in midafternoon and I came to Shepheard's after picking up my mail at the office. Later I met E.K. for a drink and for dinner.

Wednesday January 27, 1943
Cairo

A busy day and yet I've accomplished nothing. That is typical of Cairo. Went out to airforce HQ and met Keith Seigfried my friend with Brereton. Also saw Sonny Whitney again. Had dinner with Nick Parrino of

OWI, E.K. seems pleased with the job Tucker and I did in the desert. He cabled NY we deserved special credit. Also Ed has written Evans saying my work has been very good and that I've "made a place" for myself in the Middle East. He said he thought I was good prospect for bureau chief. It was a swell boast.

Thursday January 28, 1943

Four months ago tonight I left La Guardia field for Miami and the beginning of my assignment abroad. A great deal has happened since then and I've been lucky to see as much action in such a short time. Some of the other boys haven't been as fortunate. Had dinner again with Parrino, looked at room in same apartment house. I'll move in tomorrow. Tucker got back from the desert. We had dinner together in the hotel room at Shepheard's. Tucker excited as a kid about his mail.

Friday January 29, 1943

My new address is Midou Ismailia, Bahhara Building. The new room looks good. It's large and has a balcony from which I can see the Nile and the pyramids. The tops of Cairo's buildings are like ships at sea with the radio aerials as masts. The weather is cold, a damp cold that chills you through. I never knew sunny Egypt could be this cold. Slim Aarons and Burgess Scott of *Yank* and I got a jeep from HQ and went out to Kilo 13 to the quartermaster's depot. I got two heavy undershirts to combat the cold, gloves, and an American uniform. The young lieutenant in charge didn't want to let me have it at first but he finally agreed. Then we went over to see General Strickland who is in the hospital with a case of jaundice. The general was eating a whopping meal when we went in with a box of candy as a gift. "Here, taste this sweet milk," he said, "just see how good it is." We all took a sip of milk and it was delicious, the first real cow's milk I'd tasted since leaving home. All they serve in Cairo is buffalo milk which is thin and tasteless. We sat down and talked for almost an hour about our desert trip and the entry into Tripoli. The general was astounded when I told him how the Jews of Tripoli were overjoyed by our entrance and the reception they gave us. A major, captain and lieutenant came in and stood around the wall while we talked—making quite a room full. Slim never stands on military formality. It wasn't "Goodbye sir," when we left, but "So long, General."

Saturday January 30, 1943

There's a good story about a mixup of copy in the censor's office. Seems that Lumby of the London *Times* was a quiet, intellectual chap who appreciated the beauties of nature and often indulged in picturesque descriptive matter when in the desert. MacMillan of WP [World Press] is a chap who milks everything from a story, and he likes the hardier more colorful school of journalism. A page of Mac's copy was inserted by error in one of Lumby's yarns during the campaign last summer. Lumby's story went something like this: "It's quiet and peaceful today in the desert with the soft browns of the sand peculiarly restful. There's a gentle breeze carrying the soft fragrance of night blooming stock." Then the next page (MacMillan's): "The guns are thundering as I watch the Australians charge into battle with the sands running blood. There's blood dripping from the bayonets. Dead men are all around me."

Another page: "Somehow I am reminded of England by the fragrance and peacefulness which soothes the senses and drugs the mind . . ."

Played poker and shot craps at the apartment, losing 4 pounds.

Sunday January 31, 1943

I saw Winston Churchill for the first time tonight. The correspondents were told to be at PR headquarters at 6 P.M. There we were told Churchill would see us in the British Embassy ballroom. We went over, more than 50 correspondents. The ballroom was a huge place. Red plush upholstery. On the walls were coats of arms, and medallions covered with old guns, swords and knives. Churchill came in a side door with a cigar in his hand. He looked younger and more baby-faced than I expected. Except when he stuck out his lower lip in a typical tough expression, he didn't have the well-publicized bulldog look. Just back from Turkey, he discussed the war's progress and the understanding that had been reached with Turkey. He was in good spirits and his travels from Casablanca, where he met FDR, to Turkey and then to Cairo apparently had not overtaxed him. He warned against "audacious speculation" about the British-Turkish agreement, saying it would be better to let the story unfold chapter by chapter as the author preferred. Before going to the conference I became involved in a crap game with the OWI boys. Won $600.

Tuesday February 2, 1943

Went window shopping with Tucker today and purchased canapé sticks to send home. Tonight a stag party at the Metropolitan in honor of Guy Mostyn-Owen. Fair.

Wednesday February 3, 1943

You live in a never-never land of unreality in a foreign assignment. The big job is going to be to keep my perspective and not go haywire. If I can just make myself look at this job as an interlude—then I can't go wrong. But it's not a normal existence. Everything is exaggerated. It's easy to lose your sense of values. Most of these men out here aren't going to be able to go back home to a sane life. Money has no meaning and is spent like water running over a mill. Drink and conversation are the two major activities. You feel restless, unsettled and never quite satisfied with your life—because I suppose there is always the longing for home and those you love.

Thursday February 4, 1943

Ed K. went to Tripoli today and left me in charge of the office—a job I'm not very keen about. I'd like to stay in Cairo a few more days and then get out myself.

Friday February 5, 1943

"Admiralty advises Crockett fatally wounded Mediterranean buried at sea." The message from London confirmed the rumors we had heard, and brought us up with a jolt. The death of Harry Crockett brought the dangers of this business close to us. Harry's the first A.P. man to die in World War II.[7] He came to Cairo last May and two weeks later was in the desert when Rommel began his attack. From that time he saw plenty of action. George Lait knew Harry well. He said Harry was scared when the shells and bombs fell—he jumped everytime he heard one. But he wouldn't let his fear get out of control. "If you're so scared why in the hell don't you get out of the desert?" Lait said. "I'm scared but I'm going to stay and do my job," Crockett replied. I suppose Harry was really a brave man. We don't know yet how he died. He messaged the office 31/

1 that he was returning to Cairo to have a foot ailment treated. The last time he was here was Christmas Eve. Then he went to Malta. Apparently he was aboard a ship which was torpedoed or else in a plane that was shot down. An RAF chap told Chet Morrison Crockett was in the water between a raft and a destroyer. He was dragged onto the destroyer and given artificial respiration. Then he was buried at sea. Tucker went to Alexandria at noon to gather up his personal effects and to try to find out what really happened. You can't help but wonder at times if the same thing will happen to you. So far I don't believe I've really been scared—actually frightened that I might be in danger. I've been nervous and jumpy when bombs have fallen nearby and mines gone up around us. But I've never had the feeling any of it was meant for me. For some reason I feel I'm going to get through the war safely. I've had it ever since I left home and even at the front I never felt I was in much danger personally, even when I saw the dead. Probably the nearest I came to fright was flying from Lagos to Kano. Our ship tossed and twisted in the storms like a blowing leaf. We were overloaded and knew it. The sensation of falling in the down drafts left you tense and gulping for breath. Still I didn't doubt we'd make it safely. The bombing at Tobruk was like watching a scene on a screen. The bombing at Bengasi was a thrilling, magnificent spectacle of lights, flares, and bursting color. But again it was like looking on a stage setting. Perhaps you don't feel fear until death is near you, for I know I'd be scared if I thought danger was near me. I just haven't felt that way yet. And even though you know you run risks, there's the feeling nothing can happen to you. I suppose all of us have it. Harry probably felt the same. Sometimes I think Ed has a premonition he won't get through the war. He's a strange man of moods. Tucker and I wrote a story on Crockett and sent a message of sympathy to his family, on behalf of Ed, who's still in Tripoli. I had the RAF message Ed about Crockett. He's going to be broken up about the news.

Saturday February 6, 1943

Tucker went to Alex [Alexandria] today to collect Crockett's personal effects and to find out just what happened. In the afternoon Barber, Slim Aarons and I went to the Ghezira racetrack, the first time I'd attended one of the Egyptian races. The atmosphere was reminiscent of all race tracks with the program boys and touts [vendors of information on race horses and their prospects] rushing to sell you their booklets. The Arabian horses looked very small and I was surprised by the number of grays. The track was very pretty. The strangest thing of all was the shock of seeing the horses running clockwise around the track. The infield was part of a golf course and between races the golfers and their caddies would stroll across the track and continue their game. I lost three bets, one by a head. Slim hit a 9–1 shot in the sixth race. Tonight I went out to Kilo 13 to a dinner at the quartermasters, riding in an open jeep. The boys put on a wonderful dinner, all GI food. There were about 12 courses, ending with peach pie and custard. Others present were Bruce Manning, Colonel Stanley, Nick Parrino, Slim and Scotty, George Corley. Slim had taken a date, the only girl present, and she posed for cheesecake after the meal.

Sunday February 7, 1943

Tucker came back tonight from Alex[andria] and this is the story of Crockett's death which he got from Commander Roe: Harry embarked at Malta on a destroyer bound for Alexandria. On Monday night, Jan. 31, the ship was torpedoed. Harry was in the wardroom having a drink when the torpedo hit. Roe said he was drunk and that when he went into the sea he swallowed a lot of seawater which resulted in shock and congestion of the lungs. Roe claimed Harry had been drunk for days. "My God," he told Tucker, "why do men make damn fools of themselves like that? He might have had a chance if he'd been sober—but as it was he didn't have a chance." Crockett apparently left his personal belongings in Malta, or else it went to the bottom of the Mediterranean. He had only 16 L.E. on him and a few odds and ends such as identification cards. In our office here are two unopened Christmas packages for Harry—and a letter from his wife dated January 13.

Monday February 8, 1943

Roped in on a luncheon with Renee Ventura by slow thinking. A black-haired, dark-eyed French youngster who is our office boy. We took the tram to Maadi. The natives shove and crowd until you can't see how another soul could get aboard. Then they hang on the steps like scarecrows with their night gown dress flapping in the breeze. The luncheon was really very nice. The flat was on the third floor of an apartment

building. A balcony overlooked a well kept lawn and garden. An Arab
was asleep under a tree. After lunch Renee took me to see the Maadi
Country Club—not a bad place for play. Then home again on the
crowded train. After the conference I came back to the apartment.
George Carley, OWI artist, showed us some of his water colors painted
in the Congo region—violent blues, greens, reds, purples, yellows and
blacks. I liked his portraits and gave him a Tommy gun with the promise
he would do a portrait of me.

Tuesday February 9, 1943

This is the story of Harry Crockett's death as told to Tucker by Flight
Lieutenant Normal Shirley Jenks of Dorset, England:

"It happened about 7 o'clock at night on Monday, Jan. 31. We had
embarked earlier in the afternoon. We were in the wardroom having a
cup of tea and talking about our families and it was then I learned Harry
and I were the same age. We were both 31. We talked about our homes
and he told me he had been married since he was 20. He described his
wife to me, and his children . . . he was just telling me about his children
when the first torpedo hit us. Then we were hit again and for a moment
I thought the walls were going to come in. We got on deck as fast as we
could. Luckily the lights didn't go out. I saw Harry later and he had his
life belt on. He was grinning. We all had our lifebelts on. We laughed
about it. We didn't believe the ship would sink. Two destroyers were
only four hours away and steaming toward us. We thought we'd be
picked up and towed to port. Then suddenly, about an hour later, she
lurched over. I slid down her side—a dangerous thing to do because
you're apt to injure yourself badly if the ship has barnacles. But I was
lucky. I hit the water and began to swim away from the ship as fast as I
could. When I had covered about 40 yards there were a number of explosions. These were our cargo of depth bombs. It was these, not the torpe-
does, that caused such heavy loss of life. I was in the water about six
hours, from 8 o'clock that night until two in the morning. I could see
men everywhere swimming in their life jackets. There were a few badly
overloaded life rafts. From time to time I would rest on one of these
floats—holding on while my feet and body hung in the water. Then I
saw Harry. He was having a pretty hard time of it. He had swallowed a
lot of water and when you swallow too much sea water, you are in
trouble. He was in the water but two men on one of the rafts had him by

the shoulders. They were holding his head above water and trying to keep him from drifting away. His feet were troubling him and he couldn't swim properly. I called out to him but he couldn't hear me above the noise. The men were all singing. You never knew such pluck. They sang songs and cracked jokes. One man yelled out that he would never curse the desert again. He said he'd take the sand and heat to the sea any day. They sang Roll Out The Barrel, and Hallelujah, and Swanee River and John Brown's Body. The rafts and the men were dark blurs on the water. There was no moon. It rained now and then. I remember thinking I'd never known rain to be so wet. It turned bitterly cold. Along about 1:30 in the morning the destroyers arrived. I could see Harry still being supported by two men on the raft. Then the raft swung in toward the nearest destroyer. For a moment—certainly not more than fifteen seconds— Harry's head was under water. I could see him between the raft and the side of the destroyer. The men got hold of him again and heaved him on deck. Men were going up the sides from bow to stern. When I got on deck I saw two men working over Harry. They worked over him for more than two hours but I think Harry was gone before they got him on deck. You must remember all of us were suffering from exposure and shock. We were numb. And Harry's feet were in bad condition. He couldn't swim properly. Later they told me Harry and two British seamen had died. At ten o'clock next morning the entire ship's company and all others able to leave their quarters assembled on the quarter deck. We were running through a turquoise sea. The *Belvoir*'s flag flew at half mast. That was the ship that picked us up. The sister ship accompanying us had her flag at half-mast, too. There were three canvassed figures lying on deck. One of these, I knew, was Harry. We stood with bared heads in the warm sunshine. The captain stepped forward. He looked at the flags and at the blue sea and at the three figures lying so quietly on deck. Then he began to read the service of burial for those who die at sea.

This is the service:
   "I am the resurrection and the life, saith the Lord: He that believeth in me, though he were dead, yet shall he live; and whosoever liveth and believeth in me shall never die. . . . We therefore commit his body to the deep, to be turned into corruption, looking for the resurrection of the body, (when the sea shall give up her dead), and when the life of the world to come, through Our Lord Jesus Christ; and who at His coming

shall change our vile body, that it may be like his glorious body, according to the mighty working, whereby He is able to subdue all things to Himself."

A message from Kent Cooper today, not to assign anyone else to the fleet. It's been a bad luck job for A.P. men—except that Allen[8] got the Pulitzer prize for the work he did.

Wednesday February 10, 1943

We're almost out of a job in the Cairo bureau. General Alexander[9] exploded a bombshell when he gave correspondents an interview this morning. The little conference room at "Gray Pillars," British JHQ [Joint Headquarters], was crowded. We all stood when Alexander walked in, a fine looking man of medium height, black hair, strong jaw. He began by lauding the Eighth Army for its achievements—Rommel is now driven out of Tripolitania. He praised the war correspondents for the job they did in telling the story. Then he announced he is going to Tunisia to take over the ground forces under Eisenhower. Tedder already is there in charge of the air forces. Soon there will be a unified command over all the North African Operations—under Eisenhower. The announcement will come in about 15 days. The principal communiqués will be issued through Eisenhower's headquarters. Cairo will be chiefly a supply base. This means the news center shifts to North Africa. Cairo becomes a secondary news source—because as Alexander put it, "The Eighth Army has fought its way into Eisenhower's battle." So there will be a great exodus of newsmen from Cairo. After writing my story I had Barber send a signal to Kennedy that he should return at once. This afternoon Tucker, Lait and I went to Kilo 13 by jeep. I got gloves, underwear, handkerchiefs and insignia. Lait says he turned down an offer to join the A.P. I wonder. Morrison says he has an offer from N.B.C. I'm well stocked with cigarets again. Marie sent three cartons of Camels, a shirt, sox, soap, and candy. Reminded me of Christmas. Then a package from Pop with two cartons.

Thursday February 11, 1943

Ed Kennedy returned from Tripoli today. He had been to the front. I gave him the news of developments, and filled him in on details of Crockett's death. After going over all the files, he seemed to be satisfied with the way the job was handled. Says we will open a bureau in Tripoli. George Turner and I were at U.S. Headquarters when DeWitt Mackenzie came in. Mac has been to China, India, Iran and Iraq. He was held up at Basra three days but managed to get aboard a plane after wrangling for priority. He leaves for home tomorrow.

Friday February 12, 1943

Harry Zinder is back from Jerusalem, enroute to the states. Says he will take my Luger home with him. It's one of my prize souvenirs. I took it from a German colonel on Jan. 19 near Tarhuna, the day General Harding was hit. We were with the armored cars and tanks when we topped a ridge. There was a German staff car racing over the sand toward a road leading to Tarhuna. They probably hadn't expected the British to move so fast. One of the guns on a Sherman whammed away. There was a burst in front of the car, and it plunged into a ditch. A few minutes later we drove over. The driver was badly wounded, with a chunk of metal in his side. A colonel who had been in the car was standing under guard—a grinning Scotsman who obviously was proud of the catch. "I'd certainly like to have a Luger," I said to the Scottie. "Well, there's no better chance than right now," he said. "Take that one off this bloke." So I marched up to the colonel and unhooked his belt. He didn't protest and appeared not to care. Had dinner tonight with Bob Gilmore and Mike Mason of *Parade*—ate white bread and then for dessert had two pieces toasted with butter.

Saturday February 13, 1943

Henry Cassidy came in yesterday from Moscow enroute to New York. He's a small, quiet, likeable fellow with thinning hair, been in Russia three years and glad to get out for a change. Says food situation is bad and civilian sacrifice for army. Militarily Russia is strong, he says, but economically weak. The government is ruthless in seeing that the army gets what it needs even at the expense of civilians. Says there is no mail service between Russia and the U.S., consequently none of the boys there can receive or send letters. Cassidy doesn't think Farnsworth is the man for Russia—too moody and sensitive. But Clyde can't get in unless Cassidy gives up his credentials as no news agency can have more than two men accredited. Kennedy doesn't like Farnsworth either. Clyde's a strange fellow. He looks impassive and easy going—almost phlegmatic. Actually he's a bundle of nerves, sensitive, and keyed up inside. He must be suffering tortures on this assignment. Ed, George, Henry and I had lunch together at the apartment. Tonight I had a "going away" drink with Zinder who is returning home for a visit.

Sunday February 14, 1943

Beer with Cassidy and Tucker, then George and I went to Shepheard's. I took George, Lait, Morrison, Monroe and Twitchell to lunch. Tuck and I went window shopping, met Kennedy and went to the office for a bull session. Kennedy is about as fantastic a person as I ever encountered. Now he has a plan to kidnap Mary Brock in Teheran and bring her to Cairo to be his secretary. I don't know whether Ed is in love with the girl or not. She's the wife of Ray Brock of the *N.Y. Times*. He talked about her for two hours—what a marvelous girl she was, how intelligent and kind. But he said she was entirely irresponsible and unable to handle her own affairs. She came out of Greece with Ed. Now she's in Teheran doing odd jobs and, Ed says, going to pieces. He wants to have her arrested and brought to Cairo. This may sound strange—but it isn't strange for this part of the world. You seem to develop into a harmless, mellow sort of screwball if you stay with the job long enough. It's a shame Ed has stayed abroad as long as he has. He's slowly going to pieces from too much liquor and this dream world he moves in. One minute he's laughing and in top spirits. A few minutes later he may be moody and snappish. Tucker and I seem to be his favorites but you can never be sure where you stand with Ed. We talked for hours. Ed is a fascinating story teller and has a good mind. It's too bad he's letting himself crack up this way.

Monday February 15, 1943

Went out to headquarters to see Lieutenant Campbell about the change in the PR setup. He doesn't seem to know what the score is. Also went over to see Major Randall about a story on our air transport. Later in the afternoon I dropped by the office and found George and Ed Cassidy came in with a quart of Scotch to add to a case of beer which George and I had bought. We had dinner together at the Ermitage.

Tuesday February 16, 1943

Dropped by the office tonight and Ed said I should return to Tripoli as soon as possible. That suits me fine. I'm fed up with Cairo and want to get back to work on something besides conferences. I'm to see Lt. Col. Bob Parham tomorrow about transportation. I went with George to dinner and then to his hotel room. We had a long talk about the local situation. Ed's moodiness and unpredictable temperament, and our position. George is bored and restless with inactivity. We agreed to stick together and help each other as much as possible. I like George. He's one of the most sincere, likeable fellows I've met in a long time. There's nothing phony about him and he's someone worth knowing. As a writer he's one of the best. I helped him outline ideas for several stories, including a request to King Farouk for an interview.

Wednesday February 17, 1943

I'm to leave for Tripoli next Tuesday. I got my travel orders from Parham after signing the usual releases absolving Uncle Sam of any liability just in case. Now I must get my kit ready for the trip. I won't take so much this time but will travel as light as possible.

Thursday February 18, 1943

Have a rotten head cold and don't feel so well. There seems to be an epidemic of colds in town. Stayed in the apartment most of the day.

Friday February 19, 1943

My cold isn't much better—but it's no worse. Gave myself the milk of magnesia cure. I've given my tommy gun to Tuck. He's going to try to get it home by breaking it up into parts and sending each of them home in separate bundles.

Saturday February 20, 1943

The cold seems better. This afternoon Nick Parrino, J. O. Williamson and I made a tour of Cairo's "Streets of Sin." We went into a small narrow street. The harlots lounged in the doorways in kimonos calling to passersby. Some grabbed our arms and tried to pull us into their houses. They were a tough, drab looking collection. They wiggled their hips and shouted suggestive phrases. Outside the doors of most of the houses was tacked an arm with the five fingers extended—the price tag—five piasters an assignation. We went in one of the houses to look it over. Three girls and a woman lounged in the hallway in scanty wraps. The madam's two daughters worked in the joint. We climbed two winding flights of well-worn stairs to a little hallway in which there was a divan. Four unpainted doors opened off the hall. One of them opened and an Egyptian girl came out pulling up her blue panties under her slip. She welcomed us with a grin revealing a gold tooth. Behind her came a man buttoning up his trousers and buckling his belt. He waved a friendly greeting and went down the steps. The man of the house came in and I ordered a beer. The girl wanted me to go to her room but I convinced her I wasn't "feeling well". She said she received 50 piasters for each visitor, half of it going to the house. That was the price to Americans—Egyptians paid much less. But business is so good there are eight new houses to be opened just for American trade. Another caller came in with a girl and stopped to chat. "I like it here," he said. "It's nice and it's clean. You don't have to worry about nothin'." He went into the room and shut the door. Business seemed to be good. After a few minutes we left and walked through the other red light streets, all patrolled by MPs to keep the men in uniform out of them. These places are "out of bounds" to Allied troops, so we wore civilian clothes for our tour. I wouldn't want to walk those streets at night. Not only would you be liable to be raped—but you might have your throat slit if you carried more than a pound note.

Sunday February 21, 1943

Stayed in bed most of the morning because of my cold. Went to the conference and found Tucker mad as a wet hen. He'd gone in the office and found Kennedy alone. "I said 'Hello, Ed,' and he glared at me a moment and then walked out without speaking," Tuck said. "I'm damned tired of this attitude of his. You never know where you stand with him. One minute he's laughing and joking, everything is hysterically funny. The next he's sullen and moody. I don't have to take that kind of treatment from anyone and I'm not going to." George is sore, too, that Ed hasn't kept his promise to let him go with the army. I don't blame him.

Ed is unpredictable and is going to pieces. I had lunch with Bob Gilmore and Zola of *Parade*, and spent the afternoon in the apartment.

Monday February 22, 1943

Picked up my movement orders from British PR. Warrener has been promoted to Major and I'll take his crowns up. At U.S. Hq. met a Major Lester from Danville, Ky. We discovered we had played football against each other in high school. Gave Col. George Finch a letter to take home for me. In the afternoon I packed for the desert trip. Cleaned up my room tonight and stored my bags with J. O. Williamson.

Tuesday February 23, 1943

I was up at 5:45 this morning. The wind was howling. Rain beat down. The weather was more like New York than Egypt except there was no snow. I took my kit down and my saffragi [officiant, waiter], Ibrahim, dashed into the rain to get a cab. It was a two-cylinder car of God knows what vintage—probably pre-Ford. We started for the airport. The streets were running water. Egypt seldom gets a rain as heavy as this. There is no drainage system to carry off the rivers flowing in the streets. Halfway to the airport the car wheezed and stopped. The driver tried to crank the engine. His helper lifted the hood to look helplessly at the motor. I was screaming at them to get me another cab. Finally one came by. We transferred my luggage and drove on to the field. I arrived just as all trips to Tripoli were cancelled. So I headed back for Cairo. My driver was a Sudanese. He was an intelligent negro. Said he earned $6 a day hacking and was making more money than he'd ever made in his life. Before the war he made about $12 a month. Now he's making almost $200. That's what the war boom has done for Egypt. "I have a wife and two sons in Cairo," he said, "and I take care of my mother and father and my wife's parents, too. They live in the Sudan. About every four months I go back for a visit and take lots of tea and sugar and clothing as gifts. I am a big man in my village. There always is big celebration when I return. They have plenty to eat but no tea or sugar." His name was Mohammed. I went to Shepheard's and had my stuff taken to George's room. Tuck was still in bed, of course. We ordered breakfast sent to the room. I stayed in the room writing letters home until late in the afternoon when George and I went to the office. Had dinner with Kennedy who was in high spirits. George has broken down the Tommy gun into 14 parts and is going to send them home piece by piece. He's getting a great kick out of it.

Wednesday February 24, 1943
Tripoli

It took me almost three months to reach Tripoli the first time. Today it took nine hours. George Lait, Ned Russell of UP and Jack Belden[10] of *Time* and I left Shepheard's together at 6:30. The weather had cleared. We put our gear aboard a DC3. The walls of the plane had been plastered with pictures of nude women—an art display leaning more to nudity than art. A YWCA woman came aboard, enroute to Tripoli to lay the spadework for a social center for ATS [Army Transport Service] girls, WAAFS [Women's Auxiliary Air Force Service], and other women in the services. She was one of the first women to come to Tripoli by air. She was a broadfaced, middle aged woman from New Zealand. Her name was Jean Begg. She steadfastly ignored the nude pictures. Shortly after noon we landed at Benina airport near Bengasi and had lunch from American rations. I was ravenous. We landed at Castel Benito at 6 pm. Bud Warrener met us and we put our gear into a truck and were driven to PR quarters in Tripoli. It was dark so we didn't see much of the city. The quarters are very comfortable.

Claire Hollingsworth, an English woman correspondent, managed to get accredited and finagled the Americans into bringing her to Tripoli. As soon as Montgomery heard about it, he was furious. "I'll have no women correspondents with my army," he said. "Don't let her into Tripoli. Get rid of her. I don't care if the Americans did bring her up, she can't stay." So Claire did a quick return trip. He's a cocksure little guy. "We'll knock them off the continent," he told his officers. "I was at Dunkirk. I was on the beach at Dunkirk. We'll give them a Dunkirk of their own at Tunis. We'll smash them."

Before Alamein, Monty told his men: "Our job is to kill Germans. That's every man's job—to slaughter Germans. You're soldiers. That's your job. If you ask a soldier what his job is and he says his job is to repair vehicles, tell him he's wrong. His job is to kill Germans and then to repair the vehicles. That's his job—to kill Germans." Monty looked at a padre who was present. "And you padres. Your job is to kill one German each weekday—and two on Sunday."

Monty said: "Fighting a war is easy. It's the easiest job in the world as long as you keep it simple. Keep it simple, that's the way to do it. It's when you try to make war complicated that you have difficulty. Keep it simple. I never make a move until I get what I want. I won't move until I do get it. I get everything I need. Then I double it and I'm ready. That's the way to fight a war."

But among all these restless thousands there were few who knew anything of Montgomery. Even the British correspondents had only a skimpy knowledge of his background.

Monty had been an unexpected choice to lead the battered but desert-wise Eighth army. He had taken over his command on August 18 after Lieut. Gen. Henry E. Gott, originally selected for the command, was killed in an airplane crash.

Montgomery brought something new to the desert—a cocky, supreme confidence in the army and in himself. His cock-sureness sprang from something his men did not know: the knowledge he was to be given more guns, men planes, tanks, truck, supplies and material than any British commander in the Middle East had ever been given.

Wavell had operated literally on a shoestring with outmoded tanks, an airforce composed of a ridiculous assortment of fighting planes, and an ill-equipped, poorly-supplied, half-pint army. His supply line was held together with baling wire like an old model T. His troops whipped the Italians in one of the great desert campaigns but were no match for Rommel's Afrika Korps.

Auchinlec[k] was a little better prepared than Wavell but not much more— and he could count on no such promise of aid as Montgomery had received from the Allied high command.

Always before the reinforcements and supplies had been "too little and too late." But Monty knew his army was on high priority. American Sherman tanks were arriving in a steady flow, with crews to teach the British how to use them. American airmen, in American-made bombers and fighters, were learning the art of desert warfare under the tutelage of the South African Air Force and the RAF. Supplies with the Made-in-America stamp were piling up in desert dumps.

Montgomery was in a favored position and he was well aware of this fact as he planned his offensive against Rommel. He cut the deadwood from his headquarters and avoided as much as possible the inertia of Cairo GHQ which was a notorious dumping ground for those who had failed in other theaters. He surrounded himself with bright, eager, loyal young officers who soon were calling him The Master. He began to overhaul the discipline, the operations, and even the thinking of his army.

To understand Montgomery's campaigns it is necessary to understand something about the man himself and his theories of fighting a war. Monty had supreme self-confidence and was credited with great ambition.

One of his favorite stories concerning Montgomery was that King George slipped into No. 10 Downing Street one evening for a chat with Winston Churchill.

"Winston," said the King, "I'm disturbed by the talk about this fellow Montgomery."

"Don't worry, your Highness," Churchill chuckled. "I've heard those same stories. I'm not afraid of him getting my job."

"Your job," exclaimed George. "The blighter is after my job."

There is no doubt Montgomery regarded himself as a man of destiny in British history. He had a canny sense of showmanship to keep the public informed at all times that Montgomery was commanding the Eighth Army. Even that fine soldier, General Harold Alexander who commanded the Middle Eastern theater, was overshadowed by Montgomery.

Monty lived simply and severely. He neither smoked nor drank and had few if any of the common vices. Everything he did was precise and ordered, according to plan. He was dedicated to being a soldier.

Being something of a fanatic about his pet theories and enormously self-sufficient, Monty frequently snubbed his superiors, trod on unguarded Allied toes, ruffled the feelings of others, and maintained his charted course with little regard for the opinions or the feelings of others.

And yet, Montgomery was precisely the personality the Eighth Army needed after being kicked about in the desert until the troops had acquired a complex of resignation to the inevitability of defeats and retreats. The army needed an egotist who talked of victory, not in a dim future but now. Monty restored their confidence in themselves and in the future.

A member of Montgomery's staff gave me an insight into the Master's theory of war with this story:

After Monty had driven Rommel beyond Tripoli, he was discussing one day the proper method of directing an army in combat.

"Fighting a war is easy," Monty said. *"It is the easiest job in the world as long as you keep it simple. Keep it simple: that is the way to do it. It is when you make war complicated that you have difficulty. I never make a move until I get what I want. I will not move until I do get it. I get everything I need. Then I double it and I am ready. That's the way to fight a war."*

And that was the way Monty prepared to attack Rommel at the El Alamein line. He waited until he had superiority in everything and was certain Rommel could not match his strength. He kept it simple. And while he built up the army's striking power, he built up the fighting spirit of the men.

"Our job is to kill Germans," he said to his commanders with his peculiar habit of repeating himself for emphasis. *"That is every man's job—to slaughter Germans. You are soldiers and that is your job."*

"If you ask one of your troops what his job is, and he says his job is to repair vehicles, you tell him he is wrong. His job is to kill Germans, and after that he can repair his vehicles."

And then Monty turned to the chaplains.

"You padres," he said. *"It is your job to kill one German on weekdays and two on Sunday."*

The Master also had a sense of humor.

Montgomery had been in command less than a month when he had a chance to slaughter Germans and to show his troops this fellow Montgomery had not come to the desert to lose battles.

His intelligence informed him Rommel was preparing for an attack, a final desperate push to drive to the Nile and then seize the Suez Canal. He prepared his defenses accordingly, setting an ambush for Rommel's tanks as Rommel had set an ambush for Auchinlec[k] a few weeks earlier near Bengasi.

Before dawn on August 31, 1942, Rommel attacked with his tanks on the southern flank of the El Alamein line, north of the Qattara depression, while his famous Ninetieth Light Infantry division attacked on the northern end of the line.

The fighting quickly spread across the entire thirty-mile front. The battle for Egypt was underway. All day the Nazi Fifteenth and Twenty-first Armored Divisions plunged into the British defenses. At dawn the following day the armor had penetrated the British lines to a depth of fifteen miles.

Monty had anticipated precisely the direction of the armored thrust. When the shock of the first attack had spent itself, the British gunners opened up on the tanks with concealed 25-pounders. They poured a murderous fire into the iron columns.

The battle raged for three days and then, on September 3, Rommel began extricating his battered divisions, pulling them back behind his El Alamein defenses.

And while he withdrew, the Nazis in Germany were making another mistake. They were attacking Stalingrad.

Here was the turning of the Nazi tide. Here was the beginning of the long, bloody march that would lead to Nuremberg, a vial of poison for Hermann Goering and a hangman's noose for other criminals who plotted with Hitler to bring slavery to millions of people.

But no one knew it then. The crystal balls still were too hazy. Few realized in fact the Eighth Army had won a major victory in the desert—a victory that had doomed Rommel's Afrika Korps.

Montgomery knew Egypt was saved. He knew Rommel's armored strength had been drained. He knew his Eighth Army was a master of the situation and all he had to do was to keep the battle simple and he would be the victor.

Monty wanted England and the Allies to know he had won an important victory, He knew the tired, war-weary people of his homeland needed the tonic of a victory. But he did not want to make an official announcement. Himself.

As it happened, Wendell Willkie was passing through Cairo on a trip to Moscow. Montgomery invited Willkie to visit him at his desert headquarters, and there he told Willkie of the victory and what it meant. He asked him to make the announcement.

Willkie's statement at a Cairo conference that Egypt was saved hit the headlines with a resounding bang. The defeated presidential candidate was promptly and soundly chided in editorial columns for making such a rash pronouncement, setting himself up as a military expert on the basis of a few hours in the desert. Some thought that Willkie merely was making political hay, edging himself into the limelight.

So far as I know, the public never knew Willkie was doing a favor for Montgomery.

Having disposed of Rommel's final offensive threat to Egypt, Monty went about the task of preparing for his counter-offensive which was to be coordinated with the Allied assault in North Africa to squeeze the Axis out of Africa and open the Mediterranean.

With the greatest secrecy possible, he massed his tanks, guns and troops before Rommel's El Alamein defenses. At 10 P.M. on Friday Oct. 23, Monty sent his Eighth Army crashing forward behind a barrage of more than 800 guns.

Unable to withstand this overpowering assault, Rommel began to retreat. Ruthlessly, he abandoned Italian divisions and took their transport to save his Afrika Korps. His retreat across the Western Desert was tactically magnificent. And Monty took up the chase.

Thursday February 25, 1943
Tripoli

Jerry was over last night and all hell broke loose. The harbor is ringed with antiaircraft guns and guns are in the orange groves at the edge of the city. Tracers poured into the sky. A big gun outside my window roared. The shutters shook as though kicked by a mule. The building trembled with the concussion and my cot did a jitterbug—not from my trembling but from the concussion. The raid began at 11 P.M. under bright starlight. The guns were silent after 30 minutes and I could go back to sleep. I'm to be in Captain Gordon's party with Ronald Legge of the *London Daily Telegraph* and Eric Bigio of the *London Daily Sketch*. Lait, Russell, Belden and I took a drive around Tripoli with Bill Warrener. There isn't much change except the civilians have come out of hiding and are going about their normal pursuits again. A month ago the shops were closed. Crowds stand on the sidewalks looking sullen, incredulous and afraid. The only traffic was tanks, guns and trucks. The city's economic life had come to an abrupt halt, paralyzed by the sudden entrance of British troops. Today civilians strolled the sunwashed streets and harbor promenade. Gharries [horse-drawn cabs] rolled through the streets and bicycles were a common sight. Near the Grand Hotel was a huge bomb crater. A German bomb had torn out the railing and sidewalk along the harbor front. I wanted to go back to the ghetto to see how my Jewish friends were—but at the entrance was a typhus warning. It was not surprising that disease should have broken out in the crowded quarters where the Jews had been herded. The shops were open, selling cheap souvenirs and fruit. The food situation is acute because there are no more imports to supplement the food grown in Tripolitania. After the tour we came back to PR quarters. They are villas in an orange grove. A young Italian youth showed us the place. Oranges were ripening on the trees. In the barnyard—clean and neat—were four cows and two horses. Small rabbits hopped about. In another pen were chickens, turkeys, a gazelle, rabbits and a goat. This family lived well. We asked the youth if he liked the British better than the Germans—but he would not commit himself. "I love the land," he said, "all I want is to be free to tend the land. I like anyone who is kind to me." I suppose that's the way millions of people in occupied countries feel. All they want is to be left alone—free to seek happiness without the aid of anyone.

Friday February 26, 1943
Tripoli

The Jerries paid a return visit last night—or rather before dawn today. And the guns opened up again with a terrific barrage which lasted for almost an hour. You could hear the planes diving out of the star filled sky—hitting at shipping in the harbor. The ackack guns brought two down and the night fighters two more. But I saw no damage in or around the harbor today.

Saturday February 27, 1943
Zuara [Libya]

Bigio, Legge, Captain Gordon and I left Tripoli this morning. We stopped at the American fighter base and I met Major Archie Knight of Fountain City, Ind. I explained I wanted to stay with the group a few days to do a story about them. He invited me to stay with him and Lt. Col. Arthur Salisbury, commanding officer of the 57th group. I walked into the mess tent of the Black Scorpion Squadron and there were pans of fluffy, golden, beautiful hot biscuits—the first I'd seen since leaving home. I made a meal on biscuits and butter. Then I took my kit over to the tent and put up my cot. Knight, group operations officer, took me over to meet Salisbury, and Hugh Allensworth, intelligence officer from Texas. In the operations trailer were maps of the front showing the bomb line and the objectives. Then I noticed on the wall the roster of American pilots. I looked for the name of Dick Kimball, the black haired kid we saw shot down at Tarhuna and who went with us into Tripoli. I found his name—and beside it was the word "missing". The kid finally got it. He'd been on a strafing mission this morning over Gabes [Tunisia]. The ackack was heavy and our fliers were jumped by the Messerschmitt 109s. The pilots heard one of their mates shout into the radio "Kimball's got it! Kimball's got it!" A captain Sneed was shot down, too. Salisbury came into our tent later in the day and threw himself on his cot. He's very young but he has the look of a man as old as I am. And I feel very old among these boys. "We went in to strafe the airfield near Gabes," he said. "I got a good hit on a Ju 88 [Junker 88] and we shot up some planes, gasoline bowsers [Bowser gasoline pump] and trucks. They shot a lot of stuff at us and then the ME's jumped us. Two of the boys didn't get back—Kimball and Sneed. Dammit, you feel like hell when that happens. They were good guys—all these boys are good guys, the best in the business as far as I'm concerned. They've got the fighting spirit. They love to fly and they like to fight. They know they're good and they're cocky. Not like the small town bully is cocky—but like any man is cocky when he knows he's good." Later I went over to the Black Scorpions' operations tent. The boys were coming back from another mission. They were being questioned by Capt. Carl A. Nelson of Los Angeles, intelligence officer. "How was visibility, Jerry?" "Good. A little hazy, but good!"—"What was your height?"—"Four or five thousand," Wm. S. Barnes of Glenspey N.Y. said. "They were scared. They didn't get their ships off the ground." "Did you bomb in pairs?" "Yeah. Glide bombing. The ackack was heavy, too. It was popping all around me. I looked down once and then I said 'uh-uh, I don't wanna see it!' So I didn't look again." Gradually the story of the mission took form, giving the tactics, the targets, the disposition of enemy antiaircraft guns and loading grounds.

Sunday February 28, 1943
Zuara

I spent most of the day going through the group's diary. Tonight there was an open-air movie. A cold wind was blowing but the attendance was good. There was a news reel and then a "community sing." The boys roared—and they sang in falsetto when the "girl's" part of the song was indicated. The picture was very good—Wallace Beery in "Jackass Mail."

Monday March 1, 1943
Zuara

Visited the US squadrons today.[11] They're a great bunch of kids, and its surprising how much pride they take in their own squadrons, whether they are Black Scorpions, Fighting Cocks or X-terminators. Each has a lounge tent or officer's club tent. They have neat carpets, easy chairs and divans, radio-victrola with late records, library, games, and as the center of attraction, a bar. The boys made the bars themselves out of aluminum from destroyed planes. On the front were swastikas, each representing an enemy plane shot down—with the pilots name and the date of the victory. Met R. E. Whittaker of Knoxville, Tenn., and Gil Wymond of Louisville, Ky., a brother SAE. They're fine boys and you had to be proud of them. They were swell to me.

Tuesday March 2, 1943
Eighth Army Hq.

Capt. Conan, 57th Medical Officer, and I came forward today in his jeep. The fighters are moving up to an advance field from which to bomb the Germans and strafe their MT [Military Transport] and guns. Conan dropped me at Warrener's trailer and I'm spending the night with him. The artillery is booming in the distance. I could see the hills in which the Germans are entrenched. A plane came over to drop flares. One bomb fell near. Montgomery issued an order of the day—and then withdrew it—in which he said the Eighth Army should be ready for an attack by the Germans. "Every man must stand his ground. When he attacks, we'll give him a bloody nose. We want him to attack for then we'll get to hit him—and after that we will attack and destroy him. We'll give him a bloody nose and that will be magnificent. We are ready." No one knows why the order was withdrawn. Perhaps Monty thinks there will be no attack and changed his mind about the order. I worked until midnight writing two stories, after Bill & I had several drinks of Bourbon. Then a Jerry began dropping flares and bombs near. "Turn out the light, Don," Bill said from his tent. "There may be some light showing." So I'm turning out the light and going to bed.

Four

VICTORY IN TUNISIA,
MARCH–APRIL 1943

Wednesday March 3, 1943
Medenine [Tunisia]

After today all copy will be routed to Algiers instead of Cairo. My first story via Algiers was about 12 American boys who joined the Canadian airforce in 1940 and fought with the RAF. Now they've transferred to the U.S. airforce. I stayed with Warrener until after lunch. Then Capt. Steve Gordon drove up. I packed my kit on the truck. Eric Bigio has returned to Cairo and Ronald Legge is ill, so I'm the only member of Gordon's party. We drove just outside Medenine and pitched camp in a palm grove, a clean, grassy spot. I spent the evening writing to Marie, then to bed at 10 P.M.

Thursday March 4, 1943
Medenine

I made my first tour of the front-line area. The place swarms with men, guns, tanks and trucks. Medenine is another deserted town lying white and quiet on a huge plain. To the west a few miles away are the Matmata hills. They rise black and forbidding, their steep sides barren of vegetation. That's where the Germans have their guns. They must know every move of this army for the heights overlook the plain where there can be no concealment. I don't think Rommel will attack in force. A few days ago he could have. Then the Eighth army was strung thinly from Tripoli. The tanks, guns, and trucks were badly battered from the desert trek. Now the vehicles and tanks have been overhauled. Monty has his army in the plain in position. He beat Rommel to the punch. So I just can't see an attack in force. Last night three companies of Italians followed by 30 tanks and lorried infantry attacked the Highlander's advance screen. The Jocks "mowed 'em down"—and didn't lose a man. The tanks and infantry scurried back to the safety of the hills. Half the Italians were killed. This afternoon six Stukas dived out of the sun to bomb our advance positions. The ackack knocked down one.

Friday March 5, 1943
Medenine

Dropped by to see Lait, Belden and Russell. Their utility is on the blink. O'Donovan, their conducting officer, isn't dry back of the ears. He passed someone on the road who told him the Jerries were going to attack and a flap was on. He came back and ordered the drivers to pack up for a move. The boys convinced him he was being hasty. Then he suggested they post a sentry for the night. I can imagine Lait doing sentry duty! Belden, Gordon and I visited the New Zealand div hq., the N.Z. 5th brigade hq., and the Grenadier Guards to get the dope. Late in the afternoon we went into Medenine to visit a club operated by Seventh Armored div—a frontline club where the boys come to read, listen to the radio and have sweets and tea.

The German air raid yesterday hit around the Grenadier Guards. One stick hit a light field-ambulance and killed five. Two others fell near the guards hq. apparently the bombs were intended for our advance gun positions. German planes, very high came over again today but I heard no bombs. Rumored there will be an attack by our troops tonight. Personally I think there's nothing to it. I'm sure it will be another ten days before we'll be ready to move.

Saturday March 6, 1943
Medenine

Rommel attacked at dawn. He brought 120 tanks out of the Matmata hills and down the coast road onto the Medenine plain. He came under cover of a moonless cloudy sky. An east wind kept the noise of the moves from the British. It was a perfect night for the move—which I never thought he'd make. For days the sun has shone and at night the sky has been clear and bright with stars. But Rommel took advantage of the weather. At dawn his tanks moved across the plain toward the British positions which bristle with anti-tank guns. Early morning mists, heavier than usual, cut visibility at least fifty percent. The Germans attacked along an eight mile front toward the city of Medenine. At some places they were within 200 yards before the British guns opened up. The first attack moved in on the Maoris of the Second New Zealand Division. The Maoris knocked out five. Then the attack swung north toward the Grenadier Guards and the Queens. The roar of the guns woke me. There could be no doubt something had broken when the guns kept at it. As soon as we had breakfast, Steve and I drove to New Zealand Div headquarters and got the dope. By 9:30 our guns had knocked out 16 tanks and the Panzers had failed to break through at any point. Nor had our tanks been forced into action. We drove through Medenine and turned north on the road to Seventh Armored Div. hq. The ugly crack of air bursts showering shrapnel followed us up the road. We talked to the intelligence officer. The guns were roaring. Shells were bursting nearby. A little man walked up with a small case under his arm. It was the field cashier. "Does anyone here want any money?" he said, as though he were standing in the quiet lobby of a bank at home. He was the field cashier. "I suggest you take it now because I won't be able to get back for two or three weeks." But none of the officers appeared in need of spending money. The little man hurried off. We started for the Grenadier Guards to see what they had been doing, traveling over a side road since the enemy had been shelling the main road. We drove down into a wadi and suddenly all hell broke loose. We'd blundered into a battery of medium artillery which opened up over our car. The ugly snouts of the guns seemed to be pointing straight at us. So we scrammed out of there fast, and finally arrived at the guards headquarters behind Elephant Hill. Elephant Hill rises from the plain of Medenine like a huge hump. Its peak is 800 feet above the plains and commands the entire countryside. Steve and I decided to climb it for a view of the battlefield. The slopes were steep and rocky. A sergeant warned us: "When you get to a little gap in the hill, get across in a hurry for Jerry has been putting some 88 shells through there." We climbed up the first slope and scurried through the gap. Then came the hard climb—almost straight up. We heard the shells coming and flattened ourselves behind a rock. Three shells burst on a slope some 100 feet beyond us. Steve & I smoked a cigaret and then hauled ourselves to the crest of Elephant Hill. You felt as though the whole German army could see you silhouetted on top of that bald knob. Sitting on the top was a New Zealand observation officer. He'd seen the Jerries put in their attack in the dawn and he'd helped direct the fire against them. He had no cover or dugout although his telephone operator was crouched between two protecting rocks. Then we heard the shells coming—that sighing moan like the wind vibrating the strings of a cello. We fell on our faces and pressed against the sharp rocks. The shell passed over and hit on the road below the hill. "I think they're trying to hit the top of this hill," the officer said dryly. I began to think so too after picking myself off the rocks a half dozen times. Two shells hit the ridge just above us. Below us stretched the battleground, hazy with smoke and dust. Columns of black smoke race from burning tanks. In the distance we could see the weary tanks maneuvering. Behind us our own guns thundered. Six Messerschmitt 109s came over and dropped their bombs on the forward gun positions of the Queens'. The anti-aircraft bursts blossomed around them in puffs of black smoke. From the hilltop the roar of guns was thunderous. The hill was a sounding board for the noise. I could see a cloud of dust, a puff of smoke, and then came the crack of the gun and the express train rush of the shell going over our heads toward the enemy line. This was a hot spot but a beautiful vantage point for us. After a while we bid the officer goodbye. I gave him a bar of chocolate figuring he needed it more than I did. We started down the steep slope. And then Steve and I dived for cover again. There was that moan of the shells. Both of us squeezed into a little cave which gave us protection for our heads, anyway. The shells passed over and fell on the road below. Each time we'd start to stick our heads out we'd have to duck back. Every few seconds the shells rushed over—close. Three burst on the shoulder of the hill just around the hill from us. Shrapnel and rock showered around us. More than 100 shells fell on the road and near the road below. Two hit on a hill near one of our guns. I couldn't tell whether it was put out of action. But during a lull Steve and I scrambled down the hill. We turned cross country and made our way back to Medenine. At the edge of town I saw Major Archie Knight and Capt. Conan in a jeep. They were watching a dog fight between two Kittyhawks and a Messerschmitt. The ME broke away and scrammed for home with the ackack pouring up at him. Knight & Conan came back to our camp for lunch. Knight was so excited by the planes in the sky he couldn't sit still. "Boy, this is a wonderful show. Watch those Kittys go. And look at those damned MEs, flying formation right along with them. Why those bastards. Did you see those Kittys pour the lead into that Messerschmitt? Did they make him run. Boy what a show. This is most fun I've had since I've been out here. Don, I'll trade jobs with you right now." I wrote my story and took it to the PR. Lait, Belden and Russell were there. "Where were you today?" Belden asked. I told him I was on Elephant Hill during the shelling. "I knew that's where you would be," Belden said. "I told the boys you'd be there. That's where we should have been." Tonight I'm worn out, and could kick myself. While at New Zealand hq. I left my camera on the trailer doorstep. I'll probably never see it again. And I had several pictures on the roll taken from the top of Elephant Hill.

The spring of 1943 was lovely in the desert near the coast where heavy dew gave moisture to the sands. Wild flowers bloomed in riotous confusion of color. I remember counting more than twenty varieties within a radius of six feet, delicate blossoms which scented the air and gave an illusion of tranquility belied by the occasional rumble of guns.

At dawn on the morning of March 6, the artillery fire swelled into a thunderous roar. Rommel was attacking the Eighth Army!

In the mists of early morning he sent 120 tanks driving out of his Matmata hills stronghold, supported by truckloads of infantry. The night had been perfect for preparation. There had been no moon and a strong wind from the east blew the noise of tanks and trucks away from the British lines. When daybreak came the British looked out across the Medenine Plain and saw the tanks approaching. Troops were leaping from vehicles and following the tanks into battle.

This was Rommel's gamble to smash Montgomery's Eighth Army. If the British could be given a crippling defeat, then Rommel would be free to turn all his strength against the Americans in the North and perhaps drive them from North Africa. Then he could deal with the Eighth Army without a threat to his rear.

But Montgomery was ready for battle. He had anticipated the move. His intelligence had forewarned him Rommel was preparing for offensive action. In forced night marches, Monty had brought up the New Zealanders from Tripoli and slipped them into the line. A Grenadier Guards Brigade had come all the way from Damascus and arrived in time to get into the line. Anti-tank guns were in position.

Sunday March 7, 1943
Medenine

The New Zealanders saved my camera for me, so I'm very pleased. Steve and I went out to look for the gunners who knocked out the first tanks. We found 'em, two English kids excited as hell over cracking the panzers. Two guns knocked out five tanks in ten minutes. A shell from one of the tanks knocked one gun and the crew out of their pit. The crew hauled the gun back into position and knocked out the tank. I went over to see the Maoris, to try and find a Luger. I got two from them, both taken from prisoners who escaped from the burning tanks knocked out by the two guns near the Maoris. Came back to camp to find Ronald Legge, Eric Bigio and Paul Bewsher, all British correspondents. They had tried to get here before the attack, but been a day late. I gave them a fill-in on the story I had.

Monday March 8, 1943
Medenine

A lazy day in camp with breakfast in bed, a bath, and spare time to clean my guns. Rommel lost 52 tanks in the battle Saturday, at least a third of his tank strength on this front. It was a hard blow and just what the British had hoped for.

Tuesday March 9, 1943
Medenine

Bigio and I went to N.Z. hq. to find no developments. Then we went to an advance blood bank for a feature on the bottled blood transfusions.

Wednesday March 10, 1943
Medenine

Another day of loafing about camp. Lait, Russell and I played rummy during the afternoon—to accompaniment of Lait's bawdy songs. Lost 15 piasters.

Friday March 12, 1943
Island of Djerba [Tunisia]

We broke camp yesterday morning and drove to the little Mediterranean town of Ad-jib which is the ferry point to the Island of Djerba, lying about a mile off the mainland. The port was nothing more than a small pier with a few buildings about. There was an empty Standard Oil gas pump at one building. Several Arabs huddled about it and lounged in the doorway. The ferry was a small gasoline launch. Boards were laid across it midship and the cars or trucks driven onto the boards with nothing to hold the vehicles except wooden blocks and rocks behind the wheels.

Bigio, Legge and I went over to the island in an old native sailboat and then came back on the launch. I was the first American the Djerbans had seen. They spoke French fluently and seemed a healthier, cleaner more intelligent group of Arabs than those on the mainland. We put our truck in a garage and then drove the car onto the boat. I could see the car rolling off the planks into the sea—and our trying to explain what in the hell we were doing with an automobile out at sea. But we made the ferry trip all right, and drove across the island to the main town, Houmt-Souk. The drive was beautiful, the road winding between groves of olive trees. There were scarlet fields of poppies splashed with vivid yellows of daisies. The fields of barley were green, the houses whiter than any I've ever seen. In all the countryside along the path of the war, the houses were daubed with dirty yellows and browns for camouflage. These houses gleamed in the greens and yellows and reds. We saw many flocks of sheep and herds of goats. Before we left the mainland we'd heard the steady roll of explosions from one of our bombing raids. Here there was a sense of serenity and utter peace so foreign to the fighting a few miles away that it might have been another world. Reaching town, the population crowded about our car. We found rooms at the Grand Hotel—a two-story hotel run by a French woman born on the island. We went into a little courtyard with a well in it, and into the hotel. My room was spotless. The sheets were clean and the mattress soft. I washed and then Steve, Bewsher and I took a stroll about town. Never have I seen a cleaner place. It looked as though every building had been freshly scrubbed. The white buildings glared in the sun. People walked about the streets and greeted us with "bon jour." I saw a woman pushing a baby carriage—the first I'd seen since leaving home. There were a few shops open but they had little of value, some of the lucky ones displaying small shelves of powder, perfume, lotions and beauty creams from France or Tunis. The Germans and Italians had left only three weeks ago. Since the island has a Jewish population of 5000, many we saw were delighted with the arrival of the British. A few days before they left, the Germans ordered the Jews to give them 100 pounds of gold or else they'd kill several hostages. They were given twelve hours to deliver the gold. After eleven hours in which women gave their wedding bands and men their gold watch cases and Davis, the dentist his gold for filling teeth, the Jews had only eighty pounds. So they went into their synagogue and stripped the gold from the sacred vessels and statuary—until they had 100 pounds of gold. Many refugees, about 200, had found refuge here after fleeing from Sousse,

Sfax and Tunis. They said the American and British bombing raids had done great damage. We had several bottles of wine when we got back to the hotel. And I got tight—but felt all right this morning. I did another tour of the city and went out to a sponge fisherman's house where I bought a big sponge for 60 francs. The same sponge in Cairo would cost at least two pounds—$8.00. If I had enough money with me I could buy 20 pounds worth of sponges, take them back to Cairo and make a net profit of about $200. But my funds are low at the moment so I'd better forget it. After dinner we went to Bewsher's room where he regaled us with stories, one of the funniest guys I've ever known. Then we got to figuring our bill. We found the total would run to 3200 francs or 16 pounds. We could barely scrape the money together. Bigio and Bewsher had no money and Bigio had spent four pounds of Legge's funds to buy laces and silks. I had five pounds, fifty piasters, Legge seven and a half pounds and Gordon three—just enough. We discovered we were paying 30 francs for breakfast, 40 for lunch and 60 for dinner—and we were furnishing the food.

Saturday March 13, 1943
Medenine

We returned to our wadi to find our campsite taken so we moved up the wadi to a new site. I had a note from the office saying my salary was increased as of Feb. 1 from $82.50 weekly to $400 per month, a result of Ed Kennedy's letter to New York last December. There was a letter from Marie, too. She was feeling so blue when she wrote it. And I can do nothing to help her. It's such a helpless feeling. All I can do is pray that this goddamned war will be over before many more months have passed.

Sunday March 14, 1943
Medenine

Not much activity on the front except for regrouping of brigades. The N.Z. div. has moved south, probably to do another flanking movement. The moon is half full. In seven more days it will be full and then the Eighth Army attack will probably go against the Mareth line. The line extends along the Zigzaou wadi into the Matwata hills at the southern perimeter of the Gabes oasis. It was built by the French as a defense against Italian invasion from Tripolitania, and was completed in 1939.

The line is composed of concrete pill boxes and gun emplacements in strategic mountain passes and heights. Once this line is smashed the Germans must fall back on the narrow Gabes Gap, an 18-mile wide bottleneck between the sea and impassable salt marshes.

On Feb. 9, 1943, at Tripoli, Montgomery told his officers: "I think I have better sources of information than some of you gentlemen. Field Marshal Rommel has a complete attack of jitters. I have only one fear, that Rommel will be removed—even Field Marshals can be removed."

A soldier wrote home saying Monty's "on to Tripoli" message was "rather cocky," and added: "Never has he told us nor will he ask us to do anything he knows we cannot perform. That he promised us."

Montgomery's personal message to his troops on the morning of the German attack 6/3/43: 1) The enemy is now advancing to attack us. This is because he is caught like a rat in a trap and he is hitting out in every direction trying to stave off the day of final defeat in North Africa. 2) This is the very opportunity we want. Not only are we well equipped with everything we need, but in addition the soldiers of the Eighth Army have a fighting spirit and morale which is right on top line. 3) We will stand and fight the enemy in our present positions. There must be no withdrawal anywhere and, of course, no surrender. The enemy has never yet succeeded in any attack against a coordinated defensive layout and he will not do so now. We have plenty of tanks and, provided defended localities hold firm, then we will smash the enemy attack and cause him such casualties that it will cripple him; we will in fact give him a very "bloody nose." 4) It will then be our turn to attack him. And having been crippled himself, he will be unable to stand up to our attack and we will smash right through him. 5) This attack of the enemy, therefore, is one step forward toward the end of war in North Africa. I did not expect for one moment the enemy would attack us; it seemed absurd. But he has done it and we must show our gratitude in no uncertain way. 6) Let us show him what the famous Eighth Army can do. 7) Good luck to each one of you and good hunting.

And good hunting it was. The New Zealanders, Indians, Guardsmen, Highlanders and home country troops had planned their defenses carefully. Rommel walked into a gigantic trap, figuratively speaking, and the Desert Fox did not look so crafty.

I found the two gun crews who had caught the spearhead of the attack near Medenine. Within ten minutes they had knocked out five German tanks.

The crews had set up a dummy minefield under cover of night at the approaches to a deep draw leading to the British lines and furnishing excellent cover for tanks. They hoped the fake minefield, marked by barbed wire and warning signs, would turn the tanks into the gully. The guns were placed in position to fire on the tanks as they emerged from the draw.

The German tank drivers fell for the ruse. They came to the dummy minefield and wheeled into the gully to push on toward Medenine. The tense gun crews heard the roar of the tanks and then saw them slowly nosing their way from the gully not more than 5o yards away, two Mark III's and three Mark IV's with swastikas painted on their black sides.

Simultaneously the British gunners opened fire and the tanks began bursting into flame. Hatches opened and tank crews scrambled out but most of them died in their burning iron chargers. One tank was badly crippled, but the gunner had seen the flash of the British guns. The turret swung and the German gun fired. The explosion of the shell blew the British gun crew out of their pit along with their weapon but miraculously none of them was killed. The Tommies frenziedly hauled their weapon into position and knocked out the enemy.

This was the story they told me as they sat beside their gun before Medenine, blackened by the sun and the grime of battle. But they were a happy lot.

After the fight, the Maoris came out of their trenches and swarmed down on the tanks to capture those who had lived. In the tanks they found American C rations, clothing and weapons taken from the Yanks in the Kasserine battle. Now the German command was shifting its tank forces from one front to the other.

Rommel had gambled heavily on this attack but Montgomery's defenses held all along the line. Not at a single point were enemy tanks able to penetrate Monty's anti-tank screen.

Within less than eight hours Rommel lost fifty-two tanks on the Medenine plain. He was forced to withdraw late in the day into the Mareth positions and leave the British victorious and unshaken.

Monday March 15, 1943
Medenine

Still nothing much happening although our push isn't far distant. Last nite Legge, Bewsher and I had a bull session in the car over a bottle of brandy (terrible) and a bottle of zabib. I felt fine today. Drove to 30 Corps to find nothing new. And returned to camp for a lazy day. Norman Swart replaced Bigio in our party.

Tuesday March 16, 1943
Medenine

The Jerries were over last night. The throb of the motors droning for hours. Across the wadis they dropped flares to light up the road. Apparently they were reconnoitering our night movements. The halfmoon cast a bright light over the desert. Bewsher, Legge, Swart, Gordon and I stood on a little rise above our camp and watched the flares drop around us. "Blyme, it's beautiful," Bewsher said. "We used to pay money at home to see sights like these. Funny but I'm always on the side of those blokes up there. When I was in London during the blitz I stood on the rooftops firewatching. I'd see the ack ack go up after them and I'd shout 'Turn around, you bleedin' fool. Dive. Climb. That's right. Get back across the channel. They're after you. Hurry! It was a lot of fun." You feel as though the planes are searching for you—that eyes are peering at you from the starry heavens. Then there was the whistle of a falling bomb. We fell flat on the sand. The bomb exploded in the next wadi. After we went to bed I could still hear the planes. I woke up once when a bomb fell near. Then there was the chatter of a machine gun. A plane passed over our tent very low. I heard it coming and my muscles contracted involuntarily. The roar came nearer and nearer. Then it thundered overhead. Nothing happened. I relaxed as the motor faded, and went back to sleep.

The time for the Eighth Army attack is drawing nearer. It may be the Germans will pull back from the Mareth line when our push starts. There have been signs of movement to the north toward Gabes.

Wednesday March 17, 1943
Medenine

God, what a day. I'm bone tired and my head is splitting. In a few minutes I'll take a couple of sleeping tablets and climb in bed. We were up early because we knew something was popping. Last night the German planes came over early, dropping flares which hung in the heavens like bright lanterns slowly being lowered by an unseen hand. The motors

droned in circles over us. Antiaircraft bursts popped in white splashes
and bombs burst with dull heavy crumps. Then the artillery opened up a
barrage, the flashes of the guns looking like lightening [sic] on a sultry
summer day at home. The rolling thunder of the guns continued for an
hour, two hours. The Grenadier and Coldstream Guards had put in an
attack with three battalions to take four ridges southeast of Arroni which
we needed as a jumping off place for the big attack on the Mareth line.
They stormed the hills to reach their objectives—and succeeded. But the
supporting guns being brought up ran into heavy enemy fire and were
caught in German mine fields. Mortars and 88's poured a heavy fire into
the vehicles. And so the 90th Light had time to reorganize. They overran
the Guards' positions. Few of the three battalions came out. And so the
Eighth Army lost a round to Rommel. We left camp early to get the
story and stopped by the Indian Ghurka encampment. They had sent out
a patrol last night which cleared out a German gun position in the Matmata hills without firing a shot. They did the job with bayonets and
Kukuris, a big handled knife with a curved blade. Then we set out to
find the Guards Brigade headquarters. We found a sergeant who had
been in the attack. He said the Germans were stronger than they had
expected. Then we drove over dusty bumpy roads to 7th Armored Div.
Hqts. for a conference with Capt. Wallace. By this time it was getting
well into the morning. We drove back to write our stories and give them
to the dispatch rider. Again we set out to find the Guards. We drove for
miles through clouds of dust, over rutted roads and down rocky wadis.
At last we found them and got their story. A young captain told us the
tragic story—and it is a tragedy. The Grenadier Guards came to this
front from Damascus—2400 miles. They performed magnificently in
stopping the German attack 6/3/43. But in their second engagement they
were virtually wiped out. We stood in a dusty wadi while the young
captain told us the story. "Twenty officers went out," he said, "and only
six got back. All of them were wounded. But our men got a lot of Germans before they were overrun. They went out to hold their objectives
at all costs and they did." We drove back to camp, packed hurriedly and
set out for Army hq. There I learned the big attack will open the night
of March 20–21 under the full moon. After finishing our business at hq
we drove back to camp for a quick supper in the twilight. All day our
car had been balky because of dirt in the fuel line. Twice we'd gotten
out and pushed. "And some people think being a war correspondent is
glamorous," Bewsher said. "If our offices could only see us now." We

were probably the most unglamorous collection of war correspondents in Africa—tired, dusty, and irritable. We pitched camp tonight by moonlight.

Thursday March 18, 1943
Medenine

Both 10 and 30 corps moves up tomorrow nearer the front. At 11 A.M. the Boston bombers came thundering over, majestic and powerful looking, with a swarm of fighters to protect them. There were 18 in the flight. A few minutes later 18 came back. And an hour later they came over again. I was glad they were our planes. It rained last night and my clothes were sopping. The wind is blowing today, flapping the tent like an old rag.

Friday March 19, 1943
Medenine

We broke camp today and moved to a new wadi nearer 30 corps.

Saturday March 20, 1943
Medenine

The battle begins tonight. This is Montgomery's personal message to the troops: 1) On 5th March Rommel addressed his troops in the mountains overlooking our positions and said that if they did not take Medenine and force the Eighth Army to withdraw, then the days of the Axis forces in North Africa were numbered. The next day, 6th March, he attacked the Eighth Army. He should have known that the Eighth Army never withdraws [underlined for emphasis]; therefore his attack could end only in failure—which it did. 2) We will now show Rommel that he was right in the statement he made to his troops. The days of the Axis forces in North Africa are indeed numbered. The Eighth Army and the Western Desert Air Force, together constituting one fighting machine, are ready to advance. We all know what that means; and so does the enemy. 3) In the battle that is now to start, the Eighth Army: a) Will destroy the enemy now facing us in the Mareth position, b) Will burst through the Gabes Gap, c) Will then drive northwards on Sfax, Sousse and finally Tunis. 4) We will not stop, or let up, till Tunis has been captured, and the enemy has either given up the struggle or been pushed into the sea. 5) The operations now about to begin will mark the close of the campaign in North Africa. Once the battle starts the eyes of the whole world will be on the Eighth Army, and millions of people will listen to the wireless every day—hoping anxiously for good news, and plenty of it, every day. If each one of us does his duty, and pulls his full weight, then nothing can stop the Eighth Army. And nothing will stop it. 6) With faith in God, and in the justice of our cause, let us go forward to victory. 7) Forward to Tunis! Drive the enemy into the sea!

We had an early supper and left for 50 division headquarters late in the afternoon. There was little traffic on the roads and the countryside was quiet and peaceful looking. A crowd of soldiers were kicking a soccer ball around. We passed a truck load of men. They were singing. A few fleecy clouds drifted in the sky. The field of wild flowers added color to the brown of the sand. We called at the camouflaged headquarters vehicle concealed in a ditch in the side of a sand hill. Across the plain we could see the outline of a little town. The attack was going in on a mile wide front near the sea, toward a house which a young captain pointed out to us in the distance. The sun was setting when I noticed a slight, dark man in civilian clothes sitting on a knoll staring out across the plain toward the Mareth line. He was a lonely strange little man, out of place so near the front. I went over and began talking to him. He was a Frenchman, Pierre Triolet. The house on the horizon was his home. He had built it 10 years ago, a chateau of arabesque architecture with eight bedrooms, a swimming pool and modern furnishings. He owned extensive olive groves, and had a wife and four children. His parents and a sister lived with him, also. But last January the Italians took him to Tripoli and put him in prison. The Arabs had accused him of being in radio communication with the English. When the British entered Tripoli he was freed. "Perhaps when I get back home I can find some trace of my family," he said. "I don't know where they are." I left him sitting on the knoll. A young British captain said to me: "The poor devil doesn't know we're going to blow his house to hell. It's being used by the Germans as a regimental headquarters." At 9:45 the guns opened up with a preliminary barrage. The flashes rippled along the gun line like lightning flashes. An officer invited us into his trailer. On the wall was a map of the attack plan. He explained the operation to us: "This is a preliminary barrage. The main barrage will open at 10:45. We'll concentrate 300 guns on this enemy position to the left and fire on it for 30 minutes. Then the infantry will go in. This will prevent the enemy from firing on us from the left flank. At 11:15 the guns will shift their fire along a line in front of our infantry. They will fire on the line for 18 minutes and then the barrage will creep forward 100 yards every three minutes to the Wadi Zigzaou, lift across the wadi, and concentrate on enemy strong points on the west side, part of the Mareth line." Shortly the main barrage opened. The earth shuddered with the concussion. Shells swished through the air continuously. The noise beat across the plain in waves. Red flares shot into the sky: "Those flares are the Italians calling for artillery support," an officer said dryly. German planes droned overhead dropping flares and the crack of bombs added to the noise. I walked down to our car to write some of my story. As I was coming back toward the hill a flare lit overhead, lighting up the plain around me like day. Then I heard the plane diving. I jumped into a ditch and buried my face in the sand. I could hear the bombs whistling. I held my breath and my muscles were tense. Then came a splitting crash, another and another. Dirt showered over me. And I could hear the plane's motor fading away. The flare had hit the ground about 50 yards away. I ran over and got the parachute, a big bag made of some sort of synthetic material resembling silk, or heavy rayon. I found all the others unhurt. More planes came over and we crawled into a slit trench, machine gun tracers poured out of the heavens in a stream while our gunners shot back at the ghostly plane no one could see. The bullets showered around our driver but he was unhurt. It's remarkable how little real damage is done in the desert by shelling and bombing when vehicles are dispersed 100–150 yards apart. And if you're in a slit trench, almost the only danger is from a direct hit. And one man in a vast desert is a small target—so the chances are small against being injured. Still, that bomb was too damned close. Capt. Forwood, former equerry of the Duke of Windsor, came up hunting for the members of his party, one of them a Russian correspondent, Solodovnik. He saw Solodovnik and rushed up to him. "My little chickabiddy!" Forwood exclaimed. "Where have you been? Have you been a naughty boy? I was afraid something had happened to you. Are all my chicks safe?" The Russian was baffled. "What do he mean by 'chickabiddy?'" Solodovnik said. "I look in dictionary. I no find any chickabiddy. No one can tell me what it mean. He ask if I'm naughty. I look up word naughty. It mean 'bad'. Why do he think I been bad?" The Russian wandered off shaking his head.

As Rommel retreated across Tripolitiania into Southern Tunisia to hole up in the Mareth line, the correspondents' corps was joined by an uninteresting visitor—comrade Solodovnik, representing the Russian News Agency, Tass.

Solodovnik was a lean, sandy-haired young man in his early thirties with a ready smile which flashed a solid row of gold teeth. In the Russian army, he said he held the rank of lieutenant colonel, but in the desert he wore the conventional British battle dress and correspondents' insignia. His arrival created quite a commotion for the British had assigned a special conducting officer to accompany him. And perhaps it was a touch of the subtle British humor that his conducting officer was Captain Dudley Forwood, former equerry of the Duke of Windsor after his abdication.

Solodovnik was the first Russian to be permitted the freedom of the Eighth Army front and this led us to speculate that perhaps the Soviet government was relaxing its policy of giving no foreign newsman freedom of travel in Russia. We reasoned, erroneously, that if the British were opening the door to a Russian on the Eighth Army front, then the Russians must be permitting the British access to the Russian front. This, we said, was good.

Although Solodovnik was accompanied by a conducting officer, he had complete freedom of movement. There were no strings on where he could go or what he could see. This freedom included also freedom of speech and Solodovnik never lost an opportunity to needle the British brass.

Arriving in Cairo, Solly, as we called him, was taken to see Colonel Philip Astley in the public relations section for a briefing on the military situation. Astley's chief claim to distinction with the Americans was that he formerly was married to Madeline Carroll, the beauteous actress.

One of Solodovnik's first questions was why the Americans in North Africa were not making greater progress.

"It is the weather and the difficulty of supplies," Astley said. "Winter rains have turned roads into quagmires. Supplies cannot be taken forward rapidly. Tanks get bogged down and our airforce has been unable to operate efficiently because of the weather and condition of the fields. Also, the Germans have been able to reinforce Von Arnim's army."

Solodovnik nodded and then said: "Ummm! In Russia we call these . . . excuses!"

On another occasion, an officer was explaining the El Agheila operation in which the New Zealand division swung around Rommel's flank while the Highland division moved head-on for battle—the maneuver that sent Rommel retreating toward Tripoli.

Solly listened to the explanation of the employment of these two divisions in spearheading Montgomery's drive.

"Ah, yes," he nodded. "As we say in Russia, a patrol action!"

In February Solly was flown to the American front in Tunisia for a look-see. Things were fairly chaotic in the American command at that time for the Germans had given the Yanks a bad beating at Kasserine Pass where our forces were spread too thinly over a wide front.

He returned to the Eighth Army front and prepared to file his dispatches of what he had seen. He promptly was called to headquarters for an argument with the censor who had read his copy, and it was quite a scene according to one of Monty's staff officers.

"Mister Solodovnik," an officer said sternly, "You cannot say the things you have written in this dispatch. We cannot permit it. You were in North Africa only two weeks and had only a superficial look at the front and the operations there."

"You simply cannot say that General Eisenhower should be removed!"

I never knew whether Solodovnik got his dispatch through as he had written it. But it was evident Solodovnik did not want anyone to think he was impressed by the Allied contribution on the "second front."

Neither could he understand what was meant by a human interest story or why the American and British correspondents wasted their time with them.

One dull day a reporter started to leave camp and Solly asked where he was going.

"I'm going out to try and get a good human interest piece for my Sunday edition," the reporter said.

"What is a human interest piece?" Solly asked.

The reporter explained he intended to get a story from a desert veteran about his hopes and fears and little personal struggles.

Solodovnik lost interest. "I do not understand your human interest story," he said. "I am interested in how many guns you have and what kind, how many planes, how many men are fighting. That is what is important."

Later in the campaign after Solodovnik had left us presumably to return to Russia, we often wondered what had happened to the gold-toothed little soldier-correspondent and if his dispatches had been received favorably by his superiors.

I got the answer almost a year later in Italy while standing at the airport in Naples waiting to board a plane for Algiers. A slim figure entered the building, resplendent in blue uniform with crimson stripes down the trouser legs. On his breast were many medals and he wore the insignia of a major general. He was Solodovnik, member of a Russian mission to the Italian front.

And when the war in Europe had ended and General Bradley was invited to be the guest of Marshal Zhukov at a victory celebration near the Elbe, there was Solly among the Russian brass hats.

Sunday March 21, 1943
Medenine

It was cold at midnight as the guns still roared and they continued their pounding. We sat at the edge of a slit trench, Bewsher, Legge and Dick Hughes, a big Australian who looks like Jim Farley.[1] There was no news from the front yet. We didn't know whether the attack was a failure or success as the hours dragged by. Legge went to sleep on the bank but we didn't notice him. At 3:30 we decided to return to camp. Legge, who has been ill, was chilled through. Forwood gave him—and the rest of us, a slug of gin. When we got in the car Legge passed out as though drugged. We put him to bed and I got in the cab to write. I was dead tired but had too much copy to wait. Then I got in bed for an hour's sleep—with my clothes on. We were up at 6 A.M. and drove back to 50 div. to learn that we'd breached the Mareth line with a wedge, troops taking three enemy strong points after crossing the wadi under heavy enemy fire. After that we came back and wrote our stories. Then we drove to a medical dressing station where we found a young Major Warrell of Taunton [England]. He had led the party which captured the first strongpoint in the Mareth line. A bullet had drilled a hole through his arm and into his side just an inch from his heart. I wrote the story when I got back to camp, and then piled into bed. There were German planes about but I was too tired to worry about them.

Monday March 22, 1943
Medenine

We were up again at 6 A.M. The fighting is still raging in the bridgehead we hold in the Mareth line. Our troops have taken six strongpoints. But the Germans are counterattacking this afternoon with infantry and tanks—and our men must be tired out. We have a few antitank guns across the wadi and a few light tanks. Getting stuff across the wadi is hell as the enemy has it taped and is shooting into it with machine guns,

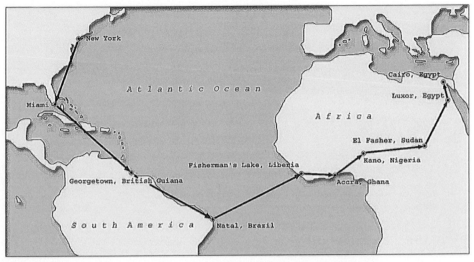

Whitehead's New York–to-Cairo Itinerary, September 29–October 9, 1942.
Map by Thomas Ingram

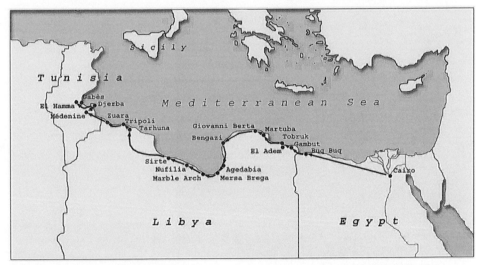

Whitehead's Trek from Cairo to Tunisia in Pursuit of the Desert Fox, November 15, 1942–
April 1943. Map by Thomas Ingram

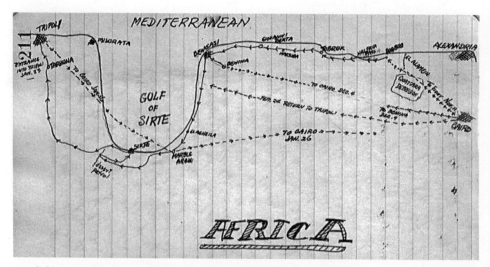

Hand-drawn map by Don Whitehead in diary section for March 1943. The map illustrates his many treks through Egypt, Libya, and Tunisia over a five-month span.

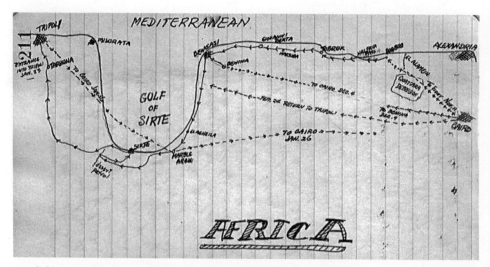

Second hand-drawn diary map by Whitehead, illustrating the fighting around the Mareth Line in southern Tunisia in late March 1943.

During the invasion of Sicily, an American cargo ship is hit by a bomb from a German plane, and its cargo of munitions explodes off Gela, Sicily, July 11, 1943. (National Archives)

A U.S. reconnaissance unit searches for enemy snipers in Messina, Sicily, August 1943. (Courtesy of the Associated Press)

British General Bernard L. Montgomery, commander of the Eighth Army, congratulates British and New Zealand armored troops, who with the British Eighth Army made the flanking attack around the lower end of the Mareth Line, in North Africa, March 1943. (Courtesy of the Associated Press)

Nick Parrino, Don Whitehead's friend and Office of War Information photographer. This picture was taken in 1943 in Iran "somewhere in the Persian corridor in the Jeep in which he rode to make a photographic record of the first run by an all American United States Army convoy carrying supplies for Russia," according to OWI records. (Library of Congress)

One American soldier who found his relatives in Sicily was Vincent J. Orivello of Milwaukee, Wisconsin, eating ice cream at a sidewalk cafe in Palermo, Sicily, with three of his cousins. (Photographer: Nick Parrino, Library of Congress)

A cheering crowd welcomes Allied troops as they enter Tunis, Tunisia, May 1943. (Photographer: Nick Parrino, Library of Congress)

General Erwin Rommel with the Fifteenth Panzer Division between Tobruk and Sidi Omar, 1941. (National Archives)

President Franklin D. Roosevelt, General Dwight D. Eisenhower, and General George S. Patton, Castelvetrano, Sicily, December 8, 1943. (National Archives)

Don Whitehead, *right*, with two unidentified soldiers in August 1943. He is holding a 155-mm "Long Tom" artillery shell, the first to be fired from Sicily across the Straits of Messina onto the Italian mainland. (Courtesy of the Associated Press)

Near the town of Cerami, Sicily, August 4, 1943, Major General Terry Allen, commanding general of the First Infantry Division, and Brigadier General Theodore Roosevelt, assistant commanding general, explain the tactical situation to American newsmen. *Left to right*, Major General Allen; Clark Lee, International News Service; Don Whitehead, Associated Press; Milton Lehman, *Stars and Stripes*; and Brigadier General Roosevelt (leaning against building). (Courtesy of the First Division Museum at Cantigny)

Don Whitehead pounds out a story on his portable typewriter. This newsprint-style photo accompanied an ad ("Reporting the Truth Like It Is") for the Associated Press in *Editor & Publisher* magazine (March 11, 1944). The story profiled in the background is from his reporting on the Anzio landings in late January 1944.

mortars and 88s. We have one road across the marshy ravine. During last night the Germans replaced Italians in the Mareth line. Many Italians surrendered—but the Germans turned machine guns and artillery fire on some who tried to quit the fight. This is the map of the strongholds we are fighting around in the Mareth Line.

[Map sketched on the page; see second page of illustrations]

We seized the three main center positions the first night of the attack, and the others Sunday nite, breaching the Mareth line in 30 hours of fighting, but some enemy points are still held in KSIBA [the town of Ksiba] west and the two rear positions, although we control them.

Tuesday March 23, 1943

We've lost ground in the bridgehead across the Wadi Ziggaou and hold only KSIBA East and the road across the wadi. The Indians are going in today & tonight to relieve the men holding and to try to clean out the enemy points. Somebody made a boner of our crossing of the wadi. The tanks were supposed to tow six-pound guns behind them but they went across without the guns. And so there were not enough antitank guns when the Germans attacked with 30 tanks backing up the infantry. Someone made a monumental blunder, a blunder that will cost many lives. Later: We've been driven from the Mareth Line. Three days and nights of bitter fighting, magnificent fighting by troops who cracked and then broke the Mareth Line—all lost because someone forgot to send the guns across.

Wednesday March 24, 1943
Medenine

We decided today to go around the flank of the Matmata hills to follow General Freyberg's New Zealanders. That appears to be where the big story will break. Tuck sent up cigarets and chocolate bars. The chocolate was marvelous—and the cigarets like a Christmas gift. Now I have 5 cartons of Camels, Chesterfields & Old Golds. Capt. Dudley Forwood, former equerry for the Prince of Wales, came by the camp. He was telling us about Solodovnik, the Russian correspondent who is a lieutenant colonel of artillery. When in Cairo Solodovnik was asking Col. Philip Astley why it was the Americans and British could not advance in Northern Tunis. "Because," said Astley, "this is the rainy season. The roads are muddy. We cannot get airdromes near the front and the line of communication is long." Solodovnik thought it over. "In Russia," he said, "we call these things excuses." Astley later said to a friend: "What can you say to a chap who talks like that—when it's the truth." When S. heard about the failure to get the guns up, he said, "You have shot the brigadier, of course?" When Churchill was in Moscow, the story goes, he said to Stalin: "Mr. Premier, there is one thing which worries us very much. We are afraid, frankly, that you have liquidated your best generals." And Stalin replied: "What you do not realize, Mr. Prime Minister, is that we have no war office to send them to."

We went to a little oasis near our camp for a hot shower. In a square tent under the palms was a bath tent. Naked soldiers many of them just back from battle, stood in line. We undressed at the car and joined the line. In a few minutes a shower was vacant. The spray of the warm water was delicious, soothing. There were about 20 under the showers. The bath could handle 240 men an hour, and did a rush business daily. It was the first bath I'd had in exactly one month. It was good to feel clean again. Received a package from Tuck—chocolate and two cartons of Camels. He sent up three cartons yesterday and a letter from Marie—the first in more than a month. God but it was good to get it.

Since I've been in the desert I've had hours to think of the past and the future. Somehow I can't make any clear plans or chart any sort of course for the future. Everything is too confused and uncertain. I don't know whether I want to stay in foreign service or whether I want to go back home. It may be I'll get a chance at a bureau chief's job. There isn't much use to try to make plans until the war is ended. Most of my thoughts of the future revolve around one person—and that is Marie. God, how I want her—how I long to hold her in my arms—that will do it. But I can see us in each others arms without actually feeling ourselves together—but we'll be in a heaven of our own—a timeless boundless space beyond understanding. That time will come because of our love— and then there can be no loneliness or heartaches or pain.

Thursday March 25, 1943
Medenine

We left Medenine this morning heading for the Melab gap west of Gabes. The point where the Eighth Army is striking after being pushed out of the Mareth line. We drove to Foum Tatahouine, south of Medenine, but had to be towed part of the way as the carburetor was out of order. Foum Tatahouine was a picturesque little Arab French town hugging a barren hill. There were more natives there than in any village I'd seen. Camels and heavily laden donkeys trawled the road with processions of Arabs going in and out of the town. An old crone picked up faggots and put them in a huge bag on her back. Most of the natives were ragged and dirty—but three Arabs passed us on beautiful horses. The saddles were silver inlaid. The robes were snowy white and looked as though spun of pure wool. One of them obviously was a sheik. Behind the trotting horses ran a servant. I watched the horses trot over a hill two miles away. The servant still ran at the heels of the horses. I wondered how far the servant had to run that day in the tireless jog with his masters paying not the slightest heed to him. We stopped under a tree for lunch at the edge of town near an oasis. Natives crowded about to watch us. They offered us eggs, but wanted a package of cigarets for one egg. South of Foum Tata-houine we turned into the desert—heading along the fringe of the Sahara. We didn't know how long it would be before we could reach a water point so we were rationed at three cups of tea a day and half a cup for shaving and washing. We knew we were taking a big risk for if the army failed to push through we would be in a precarious position. When we got into the desert the Khamseen began to blow—a steady south wind which blows for days without stopping. The dust swirled across the tracks, a brown mist obscuring the horizon. When we passed a truck the dust billowed up in a choking blinding cloud. The fine dust scoured your eyeballs and gritted on your teeth. Our faces were powdered masks. Late in the afternoon we camped in a gully. The wind still blew as we went to bed.

Friday March 26, 1943

We awoke this morning with sand silt covering our beds, heads, faces, and clothes. The wind is still blowing, a nerve rasping wind that never stops. A few miles on the road we ran into our worst dust storm—and lost our truck. We retraced our route thinking it had stuck in the sand, but then we realized it was ahead of us. There was no way to tell whether we'd find it for days—and all our water, food and bedding was aboard. One small truck is hard to find in an army on the move. So we went forward. We passed more than 70 truckloads of German and Italian prisoners. Our thirst became a burning craving for water. We had no lunch for the little food in the car might have to last us for an indefinite time. We could hardly borrow or beg water or food unless it was a last resort—for everyone was traveling on short rations and a minimum of water. Then our car bogged in soft sand. We exhausted ourselves trying to push it out—and the thirst became worse. I don't believe my spirits were ever at lower ebb. Finally we got a tow behind a big truck and went jerking over the desert. Trying to get out of the sand we'd stripped the reverse gears. At last we went on under our own steam and were resigned to sleeping out with no bedding and little food for supper. But then we saw our truck ahead waiting. I don't think I ever saw a more beautiful sight. We rejoiced by having an extra ration of water. The tea tasted better than anything I ever drank—but I couldn't help but conjure up visions of ice cold coca-colas stacked in a refrigerator. With the truck was a young American pilot who'd been shot down a few minutes before. He was Dale R. Deniston of Akron, O. [Ohio], a blond handsome kid. His plane had been hit by ackack as he was bombing and strafing enemy positions west of Gabes. We divided our blankets and he spent the night with us.

Saturday March 27, 1943
Melab Gap

I'm tired tonight, almost exhausted by the hard desert trip, the wind, sand, and then having to write a story. We traveled at the end of a tow rope, and the spine-cracking jerks jarred and shook us up. Legge was in bad shape at the end of the day, but none of us were exactly healthy looking specimens. And the thirst never is quenched because our water is brackish and salty. How the army made that 200 mile desert trip so fast and then went into battle is a mystery. British armor & troops, after failing to crack the Mareth line, were shifted (part of them) to reinforce the New Zealanders. They left Medenine on the night of 23/3 and went into the attack on this front last night. The fight is going well, but we didn't capture El Hamma as the Germans are strongly entrenched. During the night under cover of a dust storm our armor moved on El Hamma. The tanks bypassed some German tanks and then had to turn and fight them, meantime the Germans had time to get more guns into El Hamma. But Monty's quick move has put R. [Rommel] in a hole, forcing him to divide his army on this front and the Mareth line. If R. doesn't move fast his forces at Mareth may be cut off.[2]

Sunday March 28, 1943
West of Gabes

We're in no worse condition with our transport than other parties. All the correspondents are limping about in vehicles which are worn to clanking wrecks by the desert campaign. We find we can use our car some by careful driving although the sheared gears thump and knock at times. We slept in the open last night and were up at 5:45 A.M. I worked until midnight last night and I'm still tired from the grind. Chet Morrison came up yesterday to join Lait's party. We drove forward today to see some knocked out German gun positions. Clothes, bedding, and personal effects littered the ground. Some of our tanks had been knocked out in the fighting and everywhere there were signs of a bitter struggle. I picked up two Mauser rifles and a case of ammo at an infantry trench we'd overrun. Guns littered the ground. At corps conference we learned the Germans had left the Mareth line and were racing north to escape being cut off at Gabes by this push. The Highlanders are reported to have pushed through the Mareth line in pursuit. And there wasn't a correspondent on that front when the Mareth line finally fell into our hands. But then R. is making another magnificent retreat and it looks as though he'll get most of his army out of the trap. We may be able to get into Gabes tomorrow. But I've yet to watch the junction of the Eighth Army with the Americans coming down from the north toward Gabes. That is a big story—but with our car in such a state I may get my tail whipped on the story. I gotta watch that story, and get to it some way.

Monday March 29, 1943
El Hamma

The crack Second Armored Brigade put in the first night tank attack in history to break through the Melab gap and flank the Mareth line. The attack caught the enemy by surprise. The tanks burst through the defenses in dim moonlight, roaring by many anti-tank guns before they could get into action. We drove into El Hamma this morning. Arabs crowded the streets to gape at the tanks roaring through. In the main square two soldiers were having their hair cut at an open air barber shop.

Soldiers were brewing tea on the side streets. Outside the town was a small stream. We parked on the bank and wrote our stories. Then I went to take a bath and get rid of some of the accumulated grime of the desert trip. I had to walk upstream for half a mile to get above a great bloated corpse lying in the stream. A German soldier had been bathing and apparently was hit by a shell fragment. Then we learned Gabes had fallen but we couldn't go on because the road outside El Hamma was being shelled and the sappers hadn't cleared all the mines. We camped outside the town. As we went out, the antiaircraft guns around us began to roar. We jumped out of the car into a ditch as German planes came over. The ackack bursts were thick as tracers poured into the sky. But the planes dropped no bombs.

Tuesday March 30, 1943
Gabes

Once upon a time this town was a beautiful little place. Now it's battered and pocked by bombs dropped from American & British planes. Entering town we stopped and bargained for eggs with the natives, getting two dozen for some tea. We walked through the town. It was badly torn. The parks had been gouged and ripped to build air raid shelters. Many gardens were turned into shelters. Still, there was a holiday spirit. The soldiers were happy to be out of the desert. The people, most of them French, seemed glad to have the British instead of the Italians and Germans. The soldiers rode children on their motorcycles and crowded into jeeps. We stopped for lunch and a crowd of men, women and children gathered. A little red-haired, chubby faced tyke came and crawled onto my knee. She chewed hungrily on a piece of bread I gave her. Her name was Claudette, and everytime I asked her anything, she would say "Oui". We had a half-gallon tin of plum jam open, and gave the children pieces of bread & jam. They squealed with delight. Then the adults looked so longingly at the food we gave them bread and jam, too. It was a regular jam party. I passed out cigarets. These people hadn't seen a cigaret in four months. They gabbled excitedly in French and I could catch only a few words now and then. But nobody seemed to mind. On the long white beach hundreds of soldiers bathed and had sun baths. It resembled a resort playground. Officers lost no time in making a play for the girls, many of them quite attractive. In the afternoon we drove outside town and made camp in a palm grove near Cocklin's post. He had a batch of letters for me, one from Marie. The mosquitoes are bad tonight and I'll sleep under a net.

Wednesday March 31, 1943
Gabes

Our car is being repaired so Legge, Bewsher and I rode in the back of the truck on a fruitless attempt to get an interview with General Eisenhower who is visiting Montgomery. I spent the afternoon writing letters—got another letter from Marie—a V-letter written March 9. There must be a dozen letters from Marie I've never received. Perhaps they'll catch up with me soon.

Thursday April 1, 1943
Gabes

The Highlanders and New Zealanders and Indians are going to put in an attack soon to drive the enemy out of the Wadi Akarit north of Gabes. Our camp is next to an airdrome which is being cleared of mines. Once the planes come in we'll have to move because Jerry likes to bomb airdromes. Legge, Doug Brass, Clifford Webb, Capt. Crighton and I went souvenir hunting in Gabes. I tried to buy an Arab Burnoose [Burnous] for Ruth—but the Jew whom we bargained with wanted 3000 francs—$60—for the cloth. The burnooses a few months ago were selling for 175 francs. The price of everything in the town has gone up with the arrival of the British. The Germans would have taken the stuff if it hadn't been hidden from them. We come in, offer to pay, and the merchants ask robbery prices. Sometimes I think the German methods are good enough for these profiteers. Tonight an argument with Legge and Bewsher who see this war leading to a brave new world—a world federation in which all men have equality and capitalism does not control men's destinies. It's a beautiful idealistic dream—but I can't see it being achieved.

[Editor's note: The Germans and Italians did not surrender to the Allies until May 11. However, with the campaign against Rommel winding down, in April 1943, Whitehead was reassigned from Cairo, Egypt, to the Associated Press desk in Algiers, Algeria, to join with U.S. General Mark Clark's

forces in Oujda, Algeria, where they were training troops for the invasion of Sicily. Whitehead witnessed the training for the amphibious storming of the Sicilian beaches. During these operations, he met General George Patton for the first time, a man he later called "a very imperious figure, perfectly played by George C. Scott in the movie Patton."]

Five

SICILY,
JULY–AUGUST 1943

During the war there always were lively discussions among the correspondents concerning the fundamental differences between the American soldier and the soldier of other nations, particularly the British.

In some ways, the Tommy was a more desirable soldier—from the military point of view—than the American. Centuries of fighting for Empire had taught him to accept personal responsibility without question. He was more amenable to discipline. He knew the people at home were not living in comfort or piling up fat war profits. He knew they were little better off than he and perhaps in greater danger. The Tommy was more self-contained and politically more mature and thus he could endure the hardships of war with less complaining.

On the other hand the American was stronger physically, better fed, better equipped; and had far better mechanical training than his British counterpart. He had a saving sense of humor and could jeer at himself but he felt he was a victim of a raw deal which permitted others to strike and make fat wages on a plushy, safe war job while he stuck out his neck in combat. He wanted appreciation for the job he was doing, and wasn't much impressed by the "sacrifices" made at home.

In action, there was no greater soldier than the American. His courage and stamina and initiative were inspiring. But it was interesting to make comparisons between the nationalities.

Turner Catledge of the *New York Times* and several colleagues once collaborated on a little story to satirize some differences between the British and American soldier.

The British soldier: A German machinegun was holding up the advance of a Guards brigade. It was imperative the enemy position be wiped out. A Guards Major sent for Sergeant Smythe who entered the headquarters tent a few minutes later, clicked his heels sharply, saluted smartly and said: "Sergeant Smythe reporting, sir."

The Major pointed to the map on the table. "Sergeant," he said, "we're being delayed by a Jerry machinegun at this position. It's bloody important to silence that gun. I've got a few men waiting. I want you to take care of this. Do you understand?"

The Sergeant studied the map for a moment. "Yes, sir! Very good, sir!" He saluted and left the tent.

Four hours later the Sergeant re-entered the headquarters tent, saluted and said: "Sergeant Smythe reporting, sir. Mission accomplished."

"Bloody good work, Sergeant!" the Major exclaimed. "How was it?"

"Not too bad, sir."

"Now! Now! There must have been more to the job than that, Sergeant. Let's hear what happened."

"Well, sir, I took the men you gave me. A very good lot they were, too, if I may say so, sir. Stout fellows. We walked to the foot of the hill in front of the machinegun position and then crawled to the top to avoid detection. Unfortunately, one of my men lifted his head when we reached the top and a shell . . . well, sir, I lost one man.

"We crawled over the top of the hill and the Jerries must have seen us coming, sir. They laid down a rather sticky barrage but we worked our way into position from which we could throw grenades into the Jerry position. We silenced the gun, sir, and came back. That was all. A bit of a go, but not too bad, sir."

"Very good, Sergeant. I'll remember this. You may go now."

The American soldier: A German machinegun was holding up the advance of an infantry battalion. A Major called for Sergeant Smith who entered the headquarters tent a few minutes later. "You lookin' for me, Major?"

"Yes, Bill. I've got a job for you." He explained the situation. "We've got to kick those bastards out of that position. I've got men waiting outside. I want you to take care of this. Do you understand?"

"Okay, Major." Smith saluted with a wave of his hand and left the tent.

Three hours later Sergeant Smith burst into the headquarters tent, his hair hanging over his eyes. "It's me, Major," he gasped. "But I don't see why. Anybody got a drink?"

"What hap . . ."

"Sit down, Major, and let me tell you all about it. It was awful. You know that bunch of knotheads you gave me? Where in hell did you ever find 'em?

"Anyway, I got 'em together and we went to the foot of the hill just in front of the machinegun position. Then we crawled on our hands and knees all the way to the top—I mean all the way, Major. It must have been three miles, or two, anyway.

"When we got to the top, one of them dumb guys stuck his head up and a shell took it off right clean smack-dab with his shoulders. Major, you ever see a man with his head knocked off at the shoulders? Hell of a sight.

"The boys wanted to stop right there, but I told 'em to hell with that—the Major give us a job to do and we're goin' to do it, see? And any sonuvabitch who started back would get a slug in his tail!

"Well, we started crawlin' toward that machinegun. The Krauts seen us coming and I never went through such a barrage in all my life, Major. It was awful the stuff they dumped on us. But we kept goin' and pretty soon we was in throwin' distance and we let 'em have grenades.

"Boy, oh boy! You never seen such a beautiful sight. Blood! Guts! Chitlins! All over the place. We sure knocked hell outa that machinegun nest.

"And Major! Don't you think that's worth a little home leave?"

There were weaknesses in leadership, discipline and physical fitness in many of our divisions sent overseas. Discipline was a recurrent problem because America as a nation is undisciplined and unregimented in the military sense, for which state we should give humble thanks.

Lieut. Gen. Mark Clark was discussing this point one day before the invasion of Sicily. He said: "We have been undisciplined because we have not been a military people. We do not like to have anyone tell us to do things we do not like to do. This is easily understood. Parents love their children and want them to be happy. We give them all the comforts we can afford without enforcing discipline. Now we must teach discipline to our soldiers. For the undisciplined soldier is likely to be the first killed, and his lack of discipline endangers the lives of others."

This, of course, is not the whole solution. Much of the answer lies in the army providing the intelligent leadership which is the key to discipline. Much of the lack of discipline in the American army usually could be traced to fumbling, incompetent leadership. The much discussed American soldier does not make a good follower unless he has a leader who commands respect and admiration. And it can't be done merely with a little brass and loud orders.

A "good division" always meant the division had a competent commander and good regimental and battalion commanders. Discipline and morale stemmed from the top. It never grew from the bottom of the ranks. And I never saw the formula vary.

Any general who complained of a poor division had only to look in his shaving mirror for the reason. The raw material with which he worked—the troops—were basically the same in every division. Each had the same equipment, the same food, the same ammunition, the same basic training. The troops were a cross-section of the people of the United States. And if the commander didn't get the desired results, it was because the men did not get the desired leadership.

Strangely enough, the greatest bitterness among troops resulted not from combat duty—but from seeing officers in the rear echelons abuse their rank and uniform. The American soldier can endure hardships without more than ordinary amount of bitching until he begins to think he is getting the short end of a bad deal—and then all hell pops.

The army must accept a big hunk of responsibility for the great demobilization panic which swept the army after the war ended in the Pacific. This does not include merely the regular army but also the reserves who abused their privileges as much if not more than the regulars.

War is cynical enough in itself and you can not talk to troops about his ideals and loyalty to duty when those cherished things are being sneered at by officers setting themselves up with luxuries they never could enjoy in civilian life.

There was, and still is, a double standard in the army and navy for officers and enlisted men. An offense, such as drunkenness, which will get an enlisted man tossed into the guardhouse or the brig, will only bring a reprimand to a man wearing the officer's insignia. The "peons" simply can not observe such obviously unfair treatment and not become disgusted.

If the army and navy are unable in war and peace to correct inequities which exist, then Congress should set up committees to police the service and demand the elimination of abuse by those who use their position as a "gravy train".

To the everlasting credit of General Eisenhower and General Bradley, they always were on the side of the troops in permitting as much freedom from restrictions as possible and easing the burden the men had to carry. Had this attitude extended throughout all the commands there probably would never have been a demobilization panic.

Even though the soldier wears a dog-tag with a serial number, he still is an individual and the army must never forget it for the dignity of the individual will not be submerged without dire results.

But we did not know so much about soldiers and soldier reaction back in 1943 when our troops in North Africa were undergoing intensive invasion training to prepare them for Sicily. At that time we had two armored divisions and four infantry divisions in North Africa, reinforced by other smaller units. They were the First and Second Armored divisions and the First, Third, Ninth and Thirty-fourth Infantry division. Later they were joined by the Eighty-second Airborne division.

While millions of men were engaged on the Russian front, this could hardly be called an overwhelming concentration of strength—but it was a beginning and these divisions were to form the hard core of other armies of the future.

The invasion of North Africa and the fighting in Tunisia had proved the basic training of our troops was inadequate for the tasks ahead. The training at home was not sufficiently realistic to condition the troops either physical[ly] or mentally for actual warfare. Few of them knew the strange and terrifying sounds of battle, how to handle live land mines, how to attack a pillbox, how to take care of themselves in combat and on amphibious operations—until they learned the hard way.

General Eisenhower recognized the deficiencies and long before the fall of Tunis he authorized an invasion training center at the little Mediterranean village of Arzew. In total secrecy, the troops who had won their battle scars in Tunisia were trained for their second task, the conquest of Sicily.

General Clark had his headquarters in the sunbaked village of Oujda where I was assigned in the interval between the conquest of Tunisia and the invasion of Sicily. Clark commanded the Fifth Army but the Sicily invasion was to be made by the Seventh Army under the command of the fiery tank warrior, Lt. Gen. George Patton. Actually Patton's army was to be made up of Fifth Army divisions plus the Forty-fifth Infantry division which was to join the invasion fresh from the States.

This juggling of troops may have given the illusion to the enemy, as well as the people at home, that we had two armies in the Mediterranean theater. In reality, once the Seventh Army became operative, Clark was left commanding only his headquarters, the First Armored division, and a lone infantry division (the 34th) until new divisions arrived from the States to prepare for the Italian campaign.

Grizzled Brigadier General Mike O'Daniel was selected to direct the Invasion Training Center. While the high command plotted the invasion of Sicily, O'Daniel and his staff of combat veterans put division after division through obstacle course training to toughen them up. They schooled the troops in street fighting and house-to-house fighting in a little shantytown built for the purpose. They rehearsed them in amphibious landings under fire and reviewed the lessons learned during the winter fighting in Tunisia.

O'Daniel never got enough credit for the job he did there in his secret training ground. I was one of the correspondents permitted to visit the center, and it was not until after the invasion of Sicily began that I could write the story. By that time any mention of the training was buried in the crush of battle reports.

The ITC [Invasion Training Center] was laid out along 100 miles of coastline west of Algiers, a setting for a summer idyll rather than the rattle of machineguns and the crash of shells. Training was based on the lessons learned at Dieppe, in the amphibious operations of the North African invasion, and battle-front experience in Tunisia. The army had learned that essential to an efficient operation was close coordination of land, sea and air forces in amphibious operations.

Here at Arzew, the army and navy began to learn the basic lessons of cooperation. Each began to study and appreciate the other's problems. The navy was conscious of its limitations, and it came as quite a shock to the army, I know, to see how much dependence they had to place on the navy in amphibious warfare. Troop commanders realized how utterly helpless they were until they were placed ashore at the proper place with their troops and guns and supplies. While at sea the army was not an army at all—merely cargo with no fighting ability, a liability in case of attack.

Thus the services were forced into the healthy position of having to recognize the other's problems and to solve them on a mutually agreeable basis. They were pioneering in amphibious warfare—literally writing the book page by page with scanty past experience to guide them in the hazardous business.

The irony of all this effort and study is that the lessons learned already are obsolete. The book now has to be rewritten in the light of the lessons at Bikini, where the atomic explosions opened up a whole new field of fantastic problems for the military mind.

In North Africa, as at Bikini, the goat was an experimental animal. On one occasion, I accompanied General Clark from Oujda to the Fifth Army's tank-destroyer demonstration center near Arzew where troops were learning the art of fighting tanks with flame-throwers, bazookas and rifle grenades.

My friend, Lieut. Co. John W. Casey of Chicago, had selected a particularly stubborn old goat to place inside a demonstration tank as the guinea pig of the day. Presumably what happened to the goat, Oscar, would happen to a tankman inside the tank.

The goat was placed inside the tank in the driver's seat and the tank was set in motion by radio control. As it rolled across the field a bazooka gunner fired rockets until a hit stopped the tank.

Casey opened the hatch and soon came out hauling the struggling goat which was baa-a-aing defiantly.

"He's just lucky," Casey said.

Once again Oscar was put into the tank which was pounded by rifle grenades. When the hatch was opened Oscar gave out with another belligerent "Baa-a-a!"

He was shoved back into the tank. This time a GI arose from a foxhole and shot a stream of blazing liquid from a flame-thrower. The tank was enveloped in flames and its steel sides were blistered and blackened before a firefighting team subdued the fire with chemicals.

Casey climbed up and opened the hatch . . . "Baa-a-a!" . . . Oscar, not a hair singed, was hauled out. He trotted off disdainfully into the Moroccan hills and I'm sure he'll still be there today.

"Anyway," said Casey, "we proved a goat is a hardy animal."

But there was little levity in the preparations for invasion. The training was grimly serious and time was short. It seemed there was more of everything than time.

Early in July I was recalled to Algiers and went aboard the Coast Guard ship, *Samuel Chase*, which was headquarters ship for Vice Admiral John Hall and Major Gen. Terry Allen of the First Infantry Division. My assignment was to go ashore on Sicily with the First Division and follow the American troops to the final conquest.

In those early days of July (1943) Algiers harbor was filled with ships and amphibious craft leading for the invasion of Sicily. A bomb dropped in the harbor could scarcely have missed hitting a ship, but the Germans missed an opportunity to disrupt the invasion schedule or at least complicate it by heavy air raids.

H. R. Knickerbocker, then of the *Chicago Sun*, and I were aboard the *Chase* as our convoy steamed out of the harbor and turned eastward along the coast. The other correspondents were scattered throughout the fleet.

The Mediterranean along the coast of Africa literally was swarming with troop transports, LST's, LCI's, and all the other strange craft of an invasion fleet. Convoys were moving with apparent aimlessness in all directions, to confuse the enemy as to the direction of the attack. Our convoy steamed almost to Tripoli, and then turned. On the ninth day of July we were heading for Sicily. Other convoys were joining us or maneuvering to meet us after nightfall. Like pieces of a puzzle, the convoys were falling into pattern for invasion.

And then the Mediterranean began to kick up as though protesting the armada disturbing her calm. The skies were dirty gray. Leaden, wind-whipped waves rose higher and higher to toss the little invasion craft about. Troops became deathly sick and weak from retching. It became obvious if the storm continued with such fury the invasion was headed into disaster. Small landing craft could not possibly carry troops and equipment through a stormy surf. They were certain to be capsized or strewn along the beaches in wild disorder.

Knickerbocker and I went up to the skipper cabin where Admiral Hall and Terry Allen were discussing the situation. Terry was disturbed and his face reflected his anxiety. I never knew a commander more sensitive to the comfort and welfare of his men than Terry Allen. He was suffering because his men were suffering in their storm-tossed craft.

Throughout the convoy were many officers who were convinced disaster would result if the invasion continued on schedule. And later we learned the high command in Algiers at that moment was discussing the possibility of delaying the invasion even though the delay might give the enemy time to reinforce his defenses with all the advantages of surprise lost.

At dusk the waves still were heavy, but the invasion was to continue on schedule. And then God took mercy on the warriors. The winds quieted and the seas began to calm. Spirits soared as the change of weather was accepted as an omen of good luck.

In the darkness the ships arrayed themselves in line and moved slowly toward the Sicilian shore. Guns flashed and flares arched into the sky. Searchlights along the shore suddenly threw long blades of light across the waters and our ship was stabbed by the glare. We felt exposed and vulnerable to the shore batteries, certain the enemy could see every move made on the deck of the *Chase*.

"Shoot the goddamned lights out!" an officer implored.

But Admiral Hall waited to see what the enemy would do. The searchlights continued to sweep the waters. The surprise of attack was gone but strangely there was no bombardment from the shore batteries near the town of Gela, where we were to land.

During the night the paratroopers from the 82nd Airborne division opened the invasion by dropping out of the skies onto the enemy's soil. Their mission was to disorganize the enemy's defenses and wipe out certain strongpoints before the infantry reached the beaches.

Strong winds blew most of the troops-carrying planes off their course. The paratroopers were scattered miles from their objectives in some cases. They fought singly and in pairs and in isolated groups wherever they met the enemy. Many objectives assigned to them were not attacked but the paratroopers achieved their mission of confusing the enemy and disorganizing his defenses.

The infantry climbed over the side of the transports and into assault craft. The sea grew calmer with each passing minute. On our left the Third Infantry division was landing at Licata. The Rangers, led by Lieut. Col. Bill Darby of Fort Smith, Ark., were attacking the town of Gela and a battery of enemy guns near the town. The First division was landing just east of Gela. To our right, the 45th Infantry division was attacking, and further east the British and Canadians under Montgomery were swarming ashore.

The sun slowly stripped away the protective blanket of night and revealed the great armada standing off the smoke-shrouded shore. Small craft were shuttling back and forth from the beach and big navy guns were pounding enemy strongpoints. The initial assault was going well. The First division's mission was to rush the enemy's beach defenses and seize the Pointe Oliva airfield as a fighter base from which our air force could give close support to the ground forces.

Soon after daylight I joined a small group led by Capt. Paul Gale of Cornwall-on-Hudson, N.Y. We climbed down the landing net into the assault boat. I tried to appear calm and indifferent to the sounds of battle before these veterans of Tunisia, but my heart was pounding with excitement.

I had wrapped my typewriter in a piece of rubberized material to protect it from the sea spray. I discovered along with the troops that the handiest items issued by the army were rubber contraceptives. The troops stretched them over the ends of their carbines and rifles to keep moisture out of the barrels. They were good for waterproofing money, cigarets, pictures and letters. I found the number of contraceptives issued by the army to the troops had no relation to morals.

Our LCVP grounded on a sand bar a few feet from shore. We waded through the surf to the beach where engineers were working to construct roads by laying metal mats on the sand. There was a terrible sense of urgency—of time slipping by with too little accomplished. This always was the feeling during an invasion. Actually the landing was proceeding smoothly. But we knew the real fight would come when the Germans made their counterattack against the beachhead.

Lieut. Col. Robert Porter, First Division G-2, predicted: "The danger period is not in the landing. We will get ashore all right. The critical time will come when the Germans size up the situation and throw their counterattack to break the beachhead. I believe it will come within forty-eight hours after we land."

Back in the hills, the enemy's artillery found the range of the beach. Shells crashed into the water sending up ugly geysers or landed on the beach exploding showers of sand and chunks of steel. Panting and sweating, I followed Captain Gale across the dunes into a little lemon grove where Brig. Gen. Theodore Roosevelt, Jr., the First division's assistant commander, was setting up the advance command post. A small sign said: "Danger Forward" and I thought someone was trying to be funny until I realized that "Danger" was the code name for the First division and this spot near the beach was the forward command post.

We stretched out next to a low stone wall while the radio operators dug deep foxholes to accommodate both themselves and their radios. The artillery fire grew heavier. The Luftwaffe appeared over the scene and planes dived through a thunder of anti-aircraft fire to blast at the ships and at the beach.

The Fighting First was having a tough battle. It always seemed the First hit the hard spots. And wherever they were there was "Danger forward."

Soon General Allen joined us in the lemon grove. He could not bear to remain aboard ships while his men were in a hard fight. He was accompanied by his executive officer, Colonel Stan Mason, one of the best soldiers I ever knew—hard-boiled and tough on his men but fair and honest and with a great love for the First division that kept him driving others as hard as he drove himself.

The command post began to take form. Reports began to come in from all units as the communications improved. The picture of the battle began to take form and substance. We learned the paratroopers had failed to take out a strongpoint assigned to them and the First was having to do the job itself in the Sixteenth regiment's sector. Teddy Roosevelt was pushing himself unmercifully, going from unit to unit getting first-hand information, completely ignoring his own safety.

Watching Allen and Roosevelt at work, along with their staff, I began to understand why the First was recognized as the greatest fighting outfit in the American army at the time. These men formed an inspired team and they had the trick of inspiring those who fought with them. The men of the First were intensely proud of their division and loyal to it. They simply refused to recognize another division might be as good as the First.

While the command post was being organized, Knickerbocker and I hitched our way into Gela where Bill Darby and his Rangers had beaten off an Italian tank attack. The civilians had swarmed out of their hiding places when the first wave of fighting ended. They cheered and wept and surged through the smashed streets in a frenzy of welcome.

The American boys were bewildered. They did not understand at first these people were tired of fascism, tired of war, tired of giving their food and money and sons to the Italian army for a war for which they had little stomach. The Rangers knew how to slit a man's throat in the darkness, how to break a man's neck with a quick shove of the knee, how to wipe out a machinegun nest—but this joy-filled mob was too much for them. They did not know how to cope with the laughter and happiness of an enemy.

In the tumult, a few men and women stood silently in the background or stared from windows. A crone leaned from a balcony and mouthed curses. The laughing crowd booed, drowning out her curses with shouts of "Viva America!"

Then the Italians attacked. Eight light tanks broke into the town and ran through the streets spraying machinegun bullets. The frightened crowds scattered for shelter. From windows, doorways and rooftops the Rangers fought the tanks. Darby wheeled a lone anti-tank gun into position, aided by Capt. Charles Shunstrum of Radburn-Fairlawn, N.J. and fired point-blank at one tank. The recoil knocked them both down but the tank was destroyed.

Running down another street, Darby slipped to the side of a tank, climbed on top and laid an incendiary grenade on the turret. Soon the metal was red hot and the crew scrambled out screaming in surrender. The tank attack was broken.

On D plus one, the sun spilled hot rays across the Gela plain and the barren ridges where the First division was fighting to deepen its bridgehead. They dissolved the gray mists over the sea and warmed the chill wind which blew across the knoll where Jack Belden of *Time*, Knickerbocker and I were lying on flea-infested mattresses salvaged from an abandoned Italian beach barracks.

I looked on the scene below us and shivered when I thought that the morning might bring a counterattack. Belden mumbled curses sleepily. He kicked off the blanket covering him and sat up rubbing his eyes. Knick just grunted and pulled the blanket higher over his red head.

"Jeezus," Belden growled. "What am I doing here? I could have gone home for the first time in eight years—and I turned down the chance."

I tossed him a cigaret. Belden never had cigarets or matches.

"Why didn't you go home?" I asked.

"Well, I saw the Chinese being beaten by the Japs and I was with Stilwell on his retreat from Burma. I figured I'd like to be with the winner for a change. You get awfully tired writing about retreats."

Knick roused himself and yawned. "Quit your beefing, Shanghai," he said. "You are lucky to be alive."

Belden grinned. "Maybe, but it would help to see a good looking dame occasionally."

We pulled on our shoes and sat smoking. The sun splashed on the grayish countryside, shone on the ragged peaks of the hills behind us and sparkled on the blue sea. Directly below was the lemon grove sheltering Danger Forward. Beyond was the beach on which he had landed.

A haze of smoke and dust hung over the beachhead and tinted everything a dirty gray. Sicily had a gray look to it. Even the people had a gray, worn appearance. Their towns perched on hilltops like ragged caps stuck on the hoary heads of gray old men.

Artillery rumbled behind us. Occasionally a shell from an enemy battery whined over and exploded near the beach. The invasion fleet of warships, transports, supply ships and amphibious craft was spread before us. A streamer of black, oily smoke curled up lazily from a burning tanker, which had been hit by a bomb.

Across the beach through the soft sand came a steady procession of jeeps, trucks and ducks, flinging up clouds of dust. Sweating, weary, dust-caked drivers had been at their jobs through the night without rest and they had many more hours of work ahead before they could afford to close their red-rimmed eyes for a few hours sleep. Everything seemed to move so slowly, like a movie thrown into slow motion. You wanted to yell at them "Hurry! Hurry!" but you knew they were straining to the breaking point to get men and equipment ashore.

A jeep bounced up the slope. We piled on our bedding and typewriters and walked down the hill to the First division mess for breakfast. Afterward we went to a little house that had been a barracks, and began writing.

The shelling increased. A major looked into our crude little newsroom, more startled by the sound of typewriters than shells.

"What are you doing?" he asked.

I explained we were correspondents in the process of writing our dispatches.

"That's wonderful," he said, "but by God you may have to swim back to Algiers with your stories. Right now the Germans are less than a mile away."

It was 8 A.M. The Germans were attacking with about 100 tanks from the north at a time when the First division had only three tanks ashore and only part of the artillery and anti-tank weapons.

The Second battalion of the Sixteenth regiment was one of the first to be hit—doughboys against tanks.

"I never saw anything like it," Capt. Robert Irvine of Framingham, Mass., said later. "I saw men stand up in their slit trenches and shoot pistols and throw grenades at them. One man even threw an antitank rifle grenade at a tank from close range and he set it afire."

One of the heroes of that fight was Capt. Edward F. Wozenski of Terryville, Conn.

"A tank ran over my foxhole," Wozenski said. "But then it seemed to me tanks went over almost everyone's foxhole. Once there were eight tanks within twenty-five yards of me. The boys were shooting pistols, rifles, tommyguns and bazookas and throwing grenades. Some of the men ran off when the tanks came in. I wanted to take off, too, but then my men were looking at me and I couldn't run."

The Germans never did knock the Second battalion off Hill 41, but while this battle raged, another tank column moved down the Gela plain toward our beach headquarters.

Lieut. Col. Bob Porter took the news of the northern attack to General Allen. The tanks were coming close now and were within sight of the sand dunes behind which the command post was hidden.

A few minutes later Porter received additional messages and went to see Allen again.

"Don't tell me," the general said. "I can guess. They've attacked from the east and the west."

Porter merely nodded. Couriers dashed in and out of the grove. Field telephones rang and men shouted instructions into radios. Shells whined over in increasing numbers and out of the sun came a flight of Fochwulfs, diving on the beach and transports. The Germans were throwing everything at once at the Fighting First, to smash the center of the American beachhead and divide the Forty-fifth and Third divisions.

Anti-aircraft guns aboard the ships and along the beach hurled up tons of steel and ackack bursts riveted the pale blue sky with dark bursts. A Messerschmitt 109 dived on an LCI and a bomb hit the ship. The pilot pulled out of his dive strafing the beach with his guns. He pulled into a climb and turned the white belly of his plane broadside to the gunners. An almost solid stream of tracers streamed into the fuselage and cockpit. The plane burst into flames, made a graceful arc and crashed beyond the sand dunes.

Halftracks from a cannon company churned by on the dusty beach road to meet a reported attack by Tiger tanks. Allen was doing a juggling act with what artillery and antitank guns he had available. The tanks were coming nearer, shooting up trucks, supplies and ducks and rolling down the plain as though nothing could stop them.

When the lead tanks were less than two thousand yards from the beach, Brig. Gen. Cliff Andrus, First Division artillery officer, opened up on them with every gun he had. Big 105 howitzers designed for long-range barrage were trained on the tanks at point-blank range. The gunners fired over open sights. Antitank guns were depressed in the sand and held in readiness in case the tanks came over the tops of the sand dunes.

And then the navy guns joined in the bombardment. Ships at sea were in their first tank battle!

On the beach, troops were digging in for a last-ditch stand. Officers from Allen's headquarters staff were on the beach rushing up guns and ammunition as they were landed. There could be no retreat because there was no place to go except into the sea.

Back from a look at the battlefield—which meant climbing a few yards to the top of the dunes—Allen listened to a report from all sectors and checked positions on his maps. He must have been thinking of the battle his division fought at El Guettar in Tunisia where the German panzers almost ran through his division.

"Hell!" he snorted. "We haven't begun to fight. They haven't overrun our artillery yet!"

And then Terry gave an amazing command. "Send out an order," he said. "We attack tonight at ten o'clock!"

The First division was hanging on the ropes to all appearances. The center of the line was bent back almost to the sea and the men were fighting tanks with everything but slingshots—and Terry Allen orders an attack! He must have noticed our surprise when we heard his order.

"It's like this," he explained, like a schoolmaster lecturing a group of none-too-bright students. "We'll stop this attack. We'll break it up, and that will be the psychological time to attack. It's good tactics."

Even as he talked the guns on the dunes a few yards from us were pounding away. It was a dramatic piece of showmanship and Terry wasn't even conscious he was playing one of the greatest roles of his career. Terry was magnificent and none of us could dream then that a few weeks later he would be relieved of his command because superior officers considered him "too temperamental," too unstable in action and his troops not properly disciplined! But more about that later.

While the General directed the close-range battle, Captain Paul Gale assembled a task force of engineers, cooks, drivers, and clerks and led them off to the right flank to meet a growing threat there. He came back late in the afternoon and jumped from his jeep laughing. "I got three Ities myself," he laughed. "We broke up the counterattack. Slipped in on 'em before they knew we were there."

As the sun slid behind the hills, the counterattack was broken. More than a score of tanks had been knocked out and the others had withdrawn.

"You might say," Terry grinned, "the situation could have been critical. As it was, it was merely embarrassing."

And at 10 P.M., the First division attacked.

* * *

That night Knick, Belden and I sat on the hillside above the beach and talked of the day's action. And we listened for the drone of planes—paratroopers were scheduled to fly over at 11 P.M. and drop on the beachhead to support the advance of the First division. This time they were not to drop behind enemy's line. They were to jump inside our own lines.

Shortly after 10 o'clock, the planes came. But they were not our planes—they were enemy bombers. Chandelier flares hung in the heavens like great ballroom lights illuminating the sea and the invasion fleet. The navy's guns thundered as bombs burst. Ackack tracers were strung into the sky like multicolored baubles. Every gun aboard the ships was firing at the unseen enemy.

The enemy's attack was short and vicious. But their flares had hardly sputtered out before our troop-carrying planes came over in tight formations like low-flying fat ducks—some of them no more than five hundred feet above the fleet.

We sat there and witnessed one of the most blood chilling sights I have ever seen. The navy's guns opened fire on our own planes. They were flying so low we could see the lights winding on their wing tips. I knew that in each plane the paratroopers were standing up now with their ripcords hooked for the jump. The jumpmaster was at the open doorway peering into the darkness and waiting for the pilot's signal that would send the men stampeding from the plane yelling their battle cry "Geronimo!"

An awful hail of steel rolled up from the fleet to meet the paratroopers. The green, trigger-nervous young navy gunners thought it was another enemy attack. A plane burst into flames and fell in a long glide into the sea. Another went down in flames and then another.

"Oh, God, No! No! Stop, you bastards, stop! Stop shooting!"

Belden was screaming at the top of his voice. All of us were yelling as though the gunners out there could hear our voices above the roar. But still the planes came and still the guns hammered out their thunder of death. And shattered planes fell into the sea or crashed on the beachhead.

Miraculously, some planes flew through the hail of fire. Some crash landed safely and others flew around the fleet to escape the fire. But more than twenty-five of our own planes were shot down that bloody night of death.

* * *

Ernie Pyle's Captain Waskow, whose body was brought down the mountainside on mule back that dark night in Italy, was an officer beloved by the men who fought beside him. Another of that select group was Lt. Colonel Bill Darby of Fort Smith, Ark.

And Bill Darby loved his men—his hell-raising, commando-trained Rangers. Twice he was offered a promotion to the rank of "chicken colonel" and twice he refused because it would have meant leaving the Rangers. I never met another quite like Bill Darby. He didn't believe in spit and polish. He treated his men as equals and yet he maintained iron discipline. He was all man and a soldier's soldier.

On the fifth day of the Sicily invasion, Darby's Rangers were given the mission of capturing the town of Butera which sat on a high hill overlooking the route of the march toward Caltanisetta.

At his command post on a hill overlooking the Gela plain, Darby picked up a field telephone, and cranked the handle.

"Jim," he said, "we're going to attack. We're going into a deep inland town.

"Now listen. I'm sending up some assault guns. I'm going to put four self-propelled 75's in your position. So reconnoiter a spot for them.

"I'm sending in one company. If they are fired on we'll blast the hell out of the enemy. I want you to shoot anything that moves while we're getting our stuff up. Okay?"

"Roger," replied Captain Jim Lyle of San Antonio, Texas.

Darby replaced the phone and looked around.

"Chuck!" he called.

Captain Charles Shunstrum of Radburn-Fairlawn, N.J., stepped from the group of Rangers lounging near the command post.

"Chuck, you're the lead-off man. I know your boys are tired. They've fought hard and they need a rest. But they are the best for this job. You understand?"

"Yes, sir," Chuck said. He moved off down the hill.

Darby pulled out a bottle of cognac from a bag.

"I found this after we drove the Italians off this hill," he said. "That's when I knew they left in a hurry. You don't leave good cognac behind unless you're in a hurry."

There was only a swallow around—a toast to the success of the night's operation.

Below us lay the plain of Gela. The town itself looked like a toy village in the distance—not a place where men fought savagely and bodies lay sprawled on the bloodstained pavements. Beyond the village the invasion transports lay in the harbor with small craft shuttling their cargoes to the bench.

This was an excellent observation post. Nothing could move on the plain without being seen from this half-cave gouged in the side of the hill. This was where Italian observers sat on the morning of the invasion to direct artillery fire at our troops.

"This was one tough position to take," Darby said. "If we hadn't had help from a cruiser we couldn't have taken it. The cruiser put salvo after salvo on this position. We had to knock out some machineguns but the shelling did the trick."

He walked to the crest of the hill and looked at the road. Twisting up the valley toward Butera, it climbed the side of a ridge and disappeared through a gap which would be Darby's command post for the operation.

The valley was darkening with shadows. Our artillery opened up, registering on their targets. Along the road marched the first company of Rangers getting up to the starting line.

Second Lieut. Clifton Roe of South Portland, Me., reported to Darby.

"I want you to put your tanks by that stone house you see on the ridge," Darby said. "I may use you as supporting artillery. We are going into something we know nothing about. We've got to face it out. We may take this place without a fight. We may walk into a trap. We can't tell. So get into position."

There were no written orders and no paperwork for this attack. The orders were simple and direct.

"Here comes Sammy," someone said. A slight blond young captain with a long handlebar mustache walked up. He seemed too small to be carrying that upswept mustache which belonged in the Gay Nineties.

Sammy grinned at Darby and said: "I've lifted 19 German teller mines out of the road myself. I went over every yard probing with a bayonet before darkness got me, but I'm positive there are no more mines. I'll drive over the road first if anyone feels bashful."

"No one doubts you Sammy," Darby said. "You've done a good job."

"Well," said Sammy, "I reached down once and shook hands with a dead German. I saw three bodies out there on the road where the mines were. They were killed by their own mines."

"Sammy, your mustache is drooping," Darby chuckled. "You better get going, and good luck!"

It was 10:30 P.M. We climbed into jeeps and drove down the hill onto the road where troops were marching to their assembly points. Near the gap in the ridge we pulled off the road under a grove of trees. Darby and his company commanders huddled over maps and studied them by the faint glow of a covered flashlight. Their faces were blurred and indistinct patches of gray.

"You'll move in exactly twenty minutes," Darby said. "If you are not fired on, do not fire. One mile from the town, Shunstrum, hold your men until I give the word. If you get in trouble, fire a steady stream of red rockets. That will be the signal for our artillery. If you are successful, shoot two green flares. That will be the signal for all the Rangers to move on the town.

He straightened up. "Gentlemen, the best of luck. We'll see you tomorrow morning."

The little group of conspirators broke up. The men walked off into the night. Jack Belden and I joined Shunstrum's company and he called his platoon leaders around him.

"I want fifteen yards interval between each man. March at a slow pace. We go in alone and with fixed bayonets. Be sure to keep plenty of distance. We don't want to be caught bunched up in an ambush."

None of us knew what to expect, but intelligence reported a garrison of about four hundred enemy troops in the town. We marched in single file strung in a long, wavering line along the roadside. There was no sound except the crunch of boots on gravel, the creaking of harness and the singing of crickets as our platoon walked through the moonlight.

It was 12:40 when we reached the top of a ridge and looked across a dark valley to see Butera capping the hill ahead. It was dark and forbidding against the starlit sky.

Shunstrum picked up the radio transmitter and spoke into it. "We are going to move in a few minutes for the attack."

We walked down the ridge road winding into a deep gorge. Each shadow was menacing, a potential enemy crouching in ambush. In the road lay the bodies of six men. A shell had landed near two enemy vehicles and blown the bodies into the roadway. The clothes of one had been blown off and his white body sprawled obscenely in the night.

The road began winding upward toward Butera which now was above us. The column halted and the men crouched in the shadows of the embankment at the roadside. It was 3:30.

Shunstrum said: "Kendrick (First Lieut. Collins Kendrick, Macon, Ga.) will lead the first platoon along the side of the road. The second platoon will go up the hill and cover his flank. Let's go!"

It was slow, hard climbing. The men clutched at bushes and rocks and tufts of grass to pull themselves up the steep slope which seemed to rise straight up. Our hearts were pounding and we gasped for breath. We were almost to the top when machinegun and rifle fire blazed on our right. The Rangers hugged the hillside searching the darkness for sight of the enemy.

"Shunstrum to Kendrick . . . Shunstrum to Kendrick . . . what has happened?"

The radio crackled. "Kendrick has been wounded. We ran into trouble."

"Pull your men out," Shunstrum said. "We'll shell the damned place."

"You mean you don't want us to go on?"

"Do you think you can?"

"We'd like to try."

"Okay, but don't stick your neck out."

Our platoon was ordered to withdraw to the road below. The men scrambled and slid down the hill cursing. But we no sooner reached the bottom than the order came to move again to the crest.

"God damn it," a soldier said. "We can't go on all night climbing up and down this hill."

We toiled back up the slope to a little shelf below the town.

"Something's moving out there," the platoon leader said. "Open fire!"

Tommyguns and carbines poured fire ahead of us. The crash of gunfire echoed against the hills, and darts of flame sped from the muzzles of the guns along the edge of the shelf. We waited for a return blast of fire, but the darkness was solid and unbroken. We moved ahead to the road which curved around the hill, and followed it toward the town. On the road were two antitank guns and around them lay the bodies of ten Italian soldiers, mowed down by the Rangers' fire. The crews were killed before they could fire their guns.

As we neared the entrance to Butera two green victory flares arched into the sky. The town had fallen to two platoons of Rangers, a fortress that might have been held against a division.

The Rangers filed through the dark cobbled streets. Dawn was beginning to soften the shadows. The houses were barred and shuttered. No one moved in the night except the Rangers. Shunstrum selected a small courtyard near the center of town as a command post. It was well-protected from snipers and the one entrance was guarded.

Kendrick lay on a pile of blankets, smoking and talking to the men. His wound wasn't serious. He said the Italians killed on the road had been commanded by two German officers who escaped into the town.

Shunstrum said: "I'll try to find them." He called two riflemen and prepared to go man-hunting. Belden and I said we would like to go along. "Okay," said Shunstrum. He shoved a .45 automatic pistol into my hand and gave Belden another.

"We're not supposed to be armed," I said, feeling slightly foolish with the heavy automatic in my hand.

"To hell with that," Shunstrum snapped. "If there is any shooting I want everybody with me to shoot back."

We walked through the dark streets, slipping along the buildings and peering into doorways and down alleys. I felt like a kid in a game of cops and robbers. I looked around and Belden grinned at me sheepishly. We were a couple of Boy Scouts playing at war in the moonlight.

Suddenly Shunstrum stopped beside a window. "Something moved in there," he whispered. He pulled a grenade from his belt, jerked the pin and tossed the grenade through the window. And there was silence. I wondered if a mother and her children were in that room.

A scared old man ran from a doorway down the street and Shunstrum yelled for him to halt. The old fellow cringed in terror before the young Americans, babbling incoherently. Shunstrum ordered him to go to his home and stay there.

The search was futile. So we returned to the courtyard where the others waited and after Shunstrum had posted security guards, some of us went to the home of a Sicilian baron which had been chosen as a command post. The baron and his lady had fled, the neighbors said, a few hours before the Rangers reached the town.

Tired, dirty Rangers filed into the house. Some of them threw themselves on beds covered with bedspreads of fine Brussels lace. They pillowed their heads on soft down pillows and slept as dawn touched the windows. Their mission was accomplished.

Often I wondered what had become of the handsome, fierce young Captain Shunstrum. He distinguished himself in the fighting at Salerno and he was known as "The Wild Man of the Anzio Beachhead" where he was one of a handful of Rangers who escaped a German trap, which wiped out most of his comrades.

A few months ago news dispatches carried the tragic sequel to this war story. Shunstrum was brought before a Superior Court judge in Los Angeles, and he pleaded not guilty and not guilty by reason of insanity to ten counts of armed robbery.

"I find," said the judge, "he changed from the daring, reckless young officer that his comrades knew, to a man filled with discouragement, disillusionment and even hatred for people who he thought would not allow him to earn a livelihood.

"A nation cannot train a man to kill his fellow men without developing dangerous tendencies which often break out after he has returned from the combat areas. The passion to kill, rob or plunder, when developed, cannot shut off like a faucet. This man . . . is free to begin life anew."

Charles Shunstrum, hero of Sicily, Salerno and Anzio, deserved a new life in payment for the one he lost when his best friends died around him in battle.

From the beaches, Patton's Seventh Army fought its way inland on Sicily. Montgomery was halted before Catania and was behind schedule but the Yank drive gained momentum day by day and it became apparent Patton's strategy was to cut the island in half and then turn his divisions westward to wipe out the enemy resistance.

I traveled with the First Infantry division and on the eighth day of invasion my jeep bounced over the cobbled streets of Mazzarino and turned down a steep road into the valley stretching beyond. For a moment the grandeur of the scene made one forget the wretched poverty of the people on this island and the dull, pleading look in their eyes. One forgot for a moment about the war, the sight of blood spilled on streets, the bullet-punctured bodies lying in the hot sun, and the stench of death that clings to a land corrupted by war.

This plain below was a lovely landscape, rolling to the hills beyond. The fields were tinted with that peculiar yellow brightness which the late afternoon sun sometimes daubs over the landscape. The white, dusty road wound lazily through the valley and disappeared into the purple hills.

The illusion of a peaceful countryside lasted only a moment. There was the thunder of cannon and clouds of smoke puffed up where the shells exploded and left dark patches in the fields. A few hours earlier the valley had been a battlefield. The enemy had been repulsed and now it was our turn to attack.

Attack . . . counterattack . . . attack! It seemed this had been going on for weeks instead of days. But then time had become meaningless except to the generals poring over timetables back at headquarters. They could play with time, but for the men in combat the hours ran on endlessly and time was lost in a vast weariness.

Outlined against the sky on the ridge across the valley was the next town, Barrafranca, and still further across those ridges was Caltanisetta, one of the key inland cities of Sicily, dominating the island's central road network. Caltanisetta was a major objective.

In the valley, my driver turned off the main road and the jeep came to a stop under a grove of trees gray with the dust which billowed up from each passing vehicle.

"Where is the Major?" someone asked.

"He's getting things lined up. He'll be here soon."

A jeep rolled up and a young officer with lines of worry and fatigue in his face walked over. He introduced himself—Major Charles Horner of Doylestown, Pa. But he was off again in a few minutes.

"Chuck is wearing himself out," an officer said. "He won't stop long enough to get any rest."

"Rest?" someone said. "How do you spell it? I've forgotten."

We followed Horner across the fields to the foot of a slope where he gathered the company commanders of his battalion around him to review the night's operations. The objective was the high ground around Barrafranca.

"We've got to watch our left flank," Chuck said. "It's wide open. Everything will be all right if we can get on the high ground of Cozza Di Manganaro." He pointed to a goose egg on his map.

"Yeah," said Capt. Kimball Richmond of Windsor, Vt., "But if there is anyone on that hill we're going to get hell shot out of us."

Horner shrugged. "The heavy weapons and mortars will follow behind us. They can't fire at night. We'll start moving about 7:30." The men checked their watches with Horner's.

Across the wheat fields came the troops, getting into line for the attack. They had the heavy springless tread of old men. Their woolen uniforms were dark with perspiration.

"They're tired," Horner said. "They marched all last night after a fight and they couldn't sleep much today because of the heat."

"What about rations?" asked Capt. Albert H. Smith of Baltimore, Md.

"We will have to go without rations until they catch up with us," Horner said. He watched the troops slogging up the slopes toward their assembly points.

A jeep drove up and Col. George Taylor, commanding the Sixteenth Regiment, stepped out.

"The tanks already are in Barrafranca," he said. "The enemy has withdrawn from the town. We'll go beyond to the high ground but let's have a reconnaissance."

The prospect of an immediate fight had passed but the men showed no elation. They knew if the enemy was not on this ridge he would be on the next, so there was no reason to be jubilant. They calmly began planning their next move while the troops settled down to get some sleep.

I selected a soft-looking spot, moved a few rocks and fell asleep. Sometime during the night someone spread a blanket over me. I awoke shortly before 3 A.M. Soldiers were swarming out of the fields and off the slopes where they had been sleeping. The columns began moving at dawn. The few hours of rest had helped the men. They walked with vigor and were in good spirits.

"We don't have to walk so damned fast," complained one soldier.

"Sooner we get there the quicker the fight will be over," another reasoned briefly.

And so the infantry marched in the hot sun toward their next battle, slogged along with their carbines and tommyguns and mortars and shells, and heavy machineguns and automatic rifles. Each thinking his own thoughts but bound to the man in front of him and behind him by the strange bonds forged in war.

Why did they fight? What force impelled them to walk toward death, to punish their bodies and souls in a business they hated? Was it hatred of Nazism and Fascism? Was it love of freedom or a burning desire to liberate millions enslaved in Europe?

I thought of what General Terry Allen had said during the battle of the beach.

"Those boys fight because they have to," he said bluntly. "They don't fight because they hate the Germans. If I ordered them to attack the British tomorrow, they would fight just as hard as they are fighting now."

I was appalled when I heard that statement and there will be many now who will be appalled to think such a thing could happen. But as time went by I began to understand what Terry Allen had meant and to realize he was right. And men who fought will tell you the same.

Some say the trouble was that our soldiers were politically adolescent and never did know what they were fighting for. The advertisements said it was chocolate malteds, the corner drug store, a ride with the gang in a jalopy, mom and pop, and a seat on the fifty-yard line.

Maybe that's one way of saying the soldiers were fighting for liberty and the dignity of the individual, the right to be an individual and choose the manner of living they wished. But few soldiers consciously fought to crush a vile system that had enslaved millions and threatened to enslave millions more. They were on no crusade.

There always were exceptions, of course, but American soldiers for the most part fought with no hatred in their hearts for the enemy or his ideology. They were unwilling pawns in the bloody game of war. They hate it. But they had no power to resist the forces which had caught them up. They fought with a terrible, impersonal and cynical determination.

And this is a frightening thing.

The fault does not lie with the soldier. The fault lies in history, in our long isolation from the rest of the world, in our schools and homes and in our Congress. We have been a politically immature nation.

And in our isolation the thing that Abraham Lincoln once warned against became a tangible threat. That was the "silent artillery of time" crumbling the fierce love for liberty borne by our forefathers. And let no one confuse liberty with the "Rugged individualism" of a dead era just past.

We simply had accepted freedom as a constitutional right and then gone on about our business.

We know now the world has not been saved for democracy and there can be no war to end all wars. For violence only breeds violence. We know now if a strong nation is not willing to compromise, if a nation is greedy for world power and its leaders lust for new territory—then the road leads to war.

There is a dream that some day the little people of the world will stage a sit-down strike against the war. They will just refuse to take up arms against a neighbor or refuse to permit their leaders to force their will on a neighbor. And then the world will live in peace and everlasting happiness.

It is a beautiful dream—but the dream is not to be confused with the realities. And if the call to arms should come some future day, there will be millions who will answer. They will be like the youngster who came to my home recently to jitterbug with my 15-year-old daughter. "You know," he said, "I realize war is horrible but I'll always be sorry I did not get into the last war."

The world still is an armed camp. Billions are being spent for arms. A titanic struggle is on between Russia and the United States and we only delude ourselves ignoring the possibility of another world conflict. The time has not yet come when nations are accepting the simple injunction: "Do unto others . . ."

I remember one day in France standing by a roadside with Lieut. Gen. Lawton Collins, watching the infantry march into combat.

"If we don't win the peace for these men," Collins said suddenly, "then we are not fit to wipe the mud from their boots."

And the General was right.

But there was little time in Sicily to analyze the reasons why men fight as the infantry moved across the gray land. The Germans were falling back onto the key defenses of Troina.

At this point Patton decided to make a bold drive for the capital city of Palermo by turning the Second Armored division loose in the first full scale armored attack of invasion.

I learned of the attack while at Caltanisetta and raced in pursuit of the columns in a requisitioned Fiat. Along the way I picked up Clark Lee of INS and a couple of other correspondents for a wild ride through the columns of tanks churning up a heavy dust. We reached the head of the column as it was entering the city and drove slowly down the dark, winding road into Palermo.

The tank drive had been spectacular but actually there were only three anti-tank guns along the way to contest the attack. And Patton was irked by the fact the doughboys of the Third Infantry division had outsprinted his tanks to reach Palermo first. Patton wanted the glory reserved for his tankmen.

"This was the greatest armored blitz in history," Patton boasted, but the old tankman wasn't quite convincing in trying to sell that story to the correspondents.

The official surrender of Palermo was one of those comedies which frequently relieve the grimness of war.

Major Gen. Geoffrey Keyes, provisional corps commander, reached the outskirts of Palermo at 7:24 P.M. on July 22, just ahead of Patton and his heavily guarded armored car.

A car full of Italian officers was waiting for Keyes. Among them was the Italian General Molinero, who had tried without success to surrender to advance patrols at dusk. But nobody would listen to him. By the time Keyes arrived, Molinero was sweating with frustration and confusion and ready to burst into tears. His dignity and pride were rubbed raw by these Americans who would not wait until the city surrendered before entering.

Keyes' arrival created additional confusion until an interpreter was found to untangle the international snarl of language difficulties.

"General Molinero says he is through and will fight no more," the interpreter said. "He says there will be no resistance from the troops under his command."

However, Molinero could not speak for the Italian General Mario Arisio, who also commanded troops in Palermo. Immediately an expedition party was organized to find Arisio and obtain his official surrender. A pillowcase was borrowed from a Sicilian housewife and tied to the radio mast of the jeep. But the pillowcase hung limply and would not flap in the breeze. It was such a disappointingly inconspicuous flag of truce that a bed sheet was borrowed from a Sicilian who had been waving it from a fishing pole in frantic personal surrender.

The crowd cheered as the truce jeep moved into the city. Arisio was located. He was amenable to unconditional surrender. And at 8 P.M. official orders were signed for the troops to march into the city although they already had entered hours before.

Next morning the citizens of Palermo swarmed into the streets to welcome the Americans. Even Patton was slightly bewildered by the enthusiasm of the reception. The conquered people were acting like liberated people.

"They even threw flowers, lemons and watermelons," Patton chuckled. "But it should be emphasized all the fruit was tossed at us in a spirit of friendliness."

One of the incongruous sights was to see Italian soldiers still in uniform standing on the curb and cheering the Yanks as wildly as the civilians. Some of the soldiers were so overjoyed to be out of the war they ran into the streets and kissed the hands of the embarrassed Americans.

All of us felt much like the battered American soldier who fought his way through an enthusiastic throng of the enemy and exclaimed: "Who's nuts in this crowd? I'm beginning to be afraid it's me!"

* * *

After the fall of Palermo I rejoined the First division and was invited by Brig. Gen. Theodore Roosevelt to join him on a trip to the front. We piled into a jeep with his aide, Lt. Marcus O. Stevens of San Antonio, Texas, at the wheel, and burly Corp. Bill Donley of Lebanon, Pa., acting as the General's guard.

Roosevelt was in high spirits. He sang loudly, waved at his troops along the way who grinned and waved back when they recognized the doughty little warrior. They liked Roosevelt. And he knew scores of them by their first names.

We drove down into a dry creek-bed which the engineers were bridging and Roosevelt asked Stevens to stop the jeep.

"Hello, Jim," he said to a captain standing nearby. "You've done a fine job here." They chatted a few minutes and we drove on.

All along the way he had a cheerful word for the men we passed. They always recognized Roosevelt quickly because he was turning up suddenly at unexpected times and places where the action was heaviest. He drove himself harder than he drove any of the men under him.

He wanted to visit an advance artillery observation post, so Stevens stopped the jeep on the roadside and we began climbing a hill that only billy goats should climb. I marveled at Roosevelt's stamina and his eagerness to get close to the fighting where he could see for himself what was going on.

In the shade of trees near the top of the hill, soldiers were gathered in small groups. Some were sleeping, some were rubbing their aching feet. Night attacks, day marches, always keeping pressure on the enemy.

On the crest of the hill, we looked down on a little town where our advance troops were fighting an enemy rearguard. But the artillery observers were watching enemy concentrations beyond the town. The artillery was pointing at the retreating Germans.

"Let's go down and see what's going on in that town." Roosevelt said after a while. We hurried back down the steep slope.

Donley jerked his thumb toward Roosevelt and said: "If you stay with this guy you'll have some fun. He always goes where things are happening. Just the other day he was knocked down by the concussion from a mortar burst but he wasn't hurt."

We drove slowly into the town. Gunfire rattled in the narrow streets. At the northern edge of the town where a causeway crossed a dry streambed, Capt. Charles E. Murphy of Knoxville, Tenn., crouched behind a low brick wall while machinegun bullets snapped overhead. Other soldiers crouched behind walls and behind a road scraper which the engineers had brought up to clear a bypass around a blown bridge.

"He's behind that ridge across the way," Murphy said. "Let him have that .50-caliber." A machinegun opened up answering the enemy fire which was holding up the advance of the column across the causeway.

"Bring up a mortar," Roosevelt ordered.

In a few minutes three soldiers came running forward with a 60mm mortar. They dropped three shells around the machinegun position and the firing stopped.

"That clears up the situation very nicely," Roosevelt grinned.

We climbed into our jeep and headed back toward the command post. We passed a group of soldiers and Roosevelt said:

"Where are you boys from?"

"Massachusetts," said a private.

"Everything all right?"

"Yes, sir. But when are we going home?"

"Going home?" Roosevelt exclaimed. "Why, the First division never goes home until the battle is over. We're the first in and the last out. So let's finish this job in a hurry and we'll all go home."

A year later Teddy Roosevelt went "home". He literally wore himself out in the crucial early days of the European invasion. One night his tired old fighting heart quit.

Teddy Roosevelt was buried in a Normandy cemetery with his "doughs," as he called the infantrymen. That's the way he wanted it.

The battle which broke the German hold on Sicily developed with a startling suddenness which caught General Omar Bradley, then commanding the American Second Corps, and his staff by surprise.

Our intelligence figured the Germans would make their big fight at the base of Mount Etna near the little town of Randazzo which was situated in a good defensive area but the enemy chose to make his stand at Troina. We soon learned the reason. Troina was one of the greatest natural defensive positions on all of Sicily.

On August 1, the 24th day of invasion, the tired First division began pulling out of the line for a much needed rest. The men of the Red One had fought day and night and the 39th Regimental Combat Team of the Ninth Infantry division was going into the line.

The command post of the 39th consisted of a few tents under the deep shade of gnarled olive trees, a couple of battered tables with water cans for seats, and a radio jeep.

Lt. Col. Jack Toffey, Jr., his woolen shirt dark with perspiration, paced nervously about, his feet scuffing up little puffs of dust. The tension which goes with sending troops into the line to relieve another outfit was not helped any by the crashing fire of nearby 105mm Long Tom rifles. Their roars echoed and re-echoed in the little valley behind the ancient hilltop town of Cerami.

Toffey strode to the jeep and picked up the radio transmitter.

"Ray from First! Ray from First! Come in Ray."

"First from Ray! Go ahead First!" came the reply.

"Ray from First," Toffey repeated. "What in the hell are you doing to help Bond? He's under small arms and mortar fire and being counterattacked. Can you put mortar fire in the vicinity of 492-140?"

"Roger."

"I want you to get every goddamned weapon you've got and put them on 492-140! Do you understand?"

"Roger."

"Okay. Get going!"

Toffey turned to one of his officers. "We're getting guns on 'Whistlin' Willie,' that damned German contraption that shoots six mortar shells at once and sounds like a lion screaming."

Toffey and his men studied the maps on the tables. "Who is going in here?" someone asked, pointing to a spot on the map.

Toffey grinned. "I'm sending in Company B. They are our bums, AWOLs and bare knuckle fighters. They're just the boys we need for this job and they are coming around the left flank."

Major General Manton Eddy, commanding the Ninth, rode up in his staff car and stepped out.

"How is the counterattack going?" he asked.

Capt. Wayne Corpening, Waynesville, N.C., saluted. "We're taking care of it, sir."

"Well," said Eddy, "I don't know of any better way for the bastards to kill themselves than to counterattack."

But it quickly became evident the 39th regiment could not carry the burden of attack alone. The Germans were dug in in force. The 39th fought to the crest of Hill 1209 above the road to Troina but the enemy counterattacked and drove them back again.

The First division was pulled back into the line again for a full scale assault on Troina, their left flank to be protected by the 29th and the fierce, brown-skinned Boumiers of North Africa who collect enemy ears as trophies of victory.

On the third day of the battle, Jack Belden and I joined Chuck Horner's battalion for the final drive on Troina. It was dusk when we anted to the top of a ridge and found his command post at the end of a road culvert. His men were preparing for another night attack.

"Jeeezus!" a soldier said. "Will there ever be a night when we are not attacking? What day is this? I wonder if the Krauts are as tired as I am."

"Sure they are," another said. "Sure they are tired. You just better be glad you are on this team. Look at that!"

A flight of eighteen Mitchell bombers roared majestically overhead and dumped their tons of death on Troina. The gray city was lost in clouds of smoke.

"Yeah," the first soldier said. "Yeah. I guess we're pretty lucky at that." He picked up his kit and tommygun and trudged slowly around the ridge to join his platoon.

On the opposite side of the culvert, Lt. Col. John Matthews of Bridgeport, Conn., had his battalion command post. He sat whittling on a stick, jabbing the wood in short, vicious stabs.

"Chuck's going to attack," he said. "I'm here just to hold the position. There is not much else we can do. We've only got about fifty per cent of our frontline troops left."

Matthews gouged a chunk from the stick and then stood up. "Come over here." We walked around the ridge.

"See that ridge over there? We came up last night. They were looking down our throats with machineguns. They drove us back. Then we had to flank their positions to drive them off."

He shaved a thin sliver from the stick and snapped shut his knife and shrugged. "Some of our boys didn't come back with us."

We walked back and sat down on the roadside. Lieut. Melvin Groves of Lawrence, Kans., joined our group, grunting as he sat down.

"What's the matter?" someone asked.

"Hell, I went through all the shooting this morning and then fell down and sprained my back."

"How are things going?"

"The dirty bastards won't let me get our wounded off the field. When we go out after a wounded man they shoot at us. If a wounded man wiggles, they shoot him again. We never had that trouble in Tunisia. These guys must be getting jumpy."

Up the hill came a pack train of mules carrying ammunition, food and water. The army had requisitioned the long-eared transports from Sicilian farmers to carry supplies where the jeeps couldn't go.

Groves grinned. "These are smart mules. On that last ridge we were bringing up mortar ammunition when a shell burst nearby. One of the mules fell down as though pole-axed. We thought he was dead but after a while he got up and began grazing. That mule just naturally has learned to take cover when a shell bursts near him."

It was dark now, with only a thin sliver of moon in the star-spangled heavens. Someone passed around cans of C rations and from somewhere came a water can filled with hot coffee. We ate and listened to the ghostly whisper of shells passing overhead, the eerie swishing of death hurtling toward the enemy.

Capt. Alan Moorehouse of Providence, R.I., trudged along the ridge road at the head of his company, leading them into position for attack. Other companies from Horner's battalion were turning off the road below us. Dark forms moved silently through the night. No one said anything. The men plodded along slowly as though carrying a great weight on their young shoulders. They were as tired as death.

Each time I have watched troops plod into battle, I have choked back a desire to sob. There is no sadder sight. The weight that burdens them is more than guns, mortars and ammunition slung over their shoulders. But they march on with amazing endurance of body and spirit.

I thought of an ad I had seen in a slick magazine from home. There was a bright-faced young soldier with a toothpaste smile, a tommygun in his manicured fingers, his shoes polished, his trousers creased, his pockets smooth and flat, buttons buttoned. The caption said: "Scared, son, going into battle?" And the kid's reply was "Hell, no! They can't scare me!"

And I looked at the real soldiers brushing by me in the pale moonlight. I knew their faces were caked with sweat and dust, unshaven and marked by lines of fatigue. Their trousers bagged from days of fighting and sleeping in them. Their pockets bulged with toilet paper, boxes of K rations, tins of cheese, cans of C rations, and the things a soldier carries for his personal comfort.

If I had asked any one of them if he were scared, he would have looked at me and said: "Hell, yes, I'm scared. So what?" Fear is no badge of disgrace among soldiers. They talk to each other of their fear openly and without shame. The mark that brands a man is cowardice—not fear.

The troops walked on across the ridge, a ghostly legion marching into eternity, silhouetted for a moment against the stars and then vanishing.

Before long there was the slow pounding of American machineguns and the quick "brr-rr-rtt" of bursts from German burp-guns. Flares shot into the sky. Behind Troina a great fire blazed, probably a munitions or gasoline dump hit by our artillery fire.

The night attack was stopped. Heavy enemy fire pinned down the troops and the battalion was unable to make any progress. We wrapped ourselves in blankets and lay down by the roadside to wait for dawn.

Just before the stars scurried into hiding, Horner called for Moore-house on the walkie-talkie. "Al, goddamn it, we've got to get that ridge. It'll be too late when they can see you. Let's get moving!"

At first light we walked to the crest of the ridge. On the next ridge the enemy were dug in in a vineyard and wheat field and were using a concrete house as a strongpoint. Machinegun tracers raked the ridgetop. Figures dashed from hiding and ran behind the ridge.

"Get McCarthy up here!" Horner ordered. Then he explained "He is the best damned mortar man in this man's army. He'll clean off that ridge."

The order went back for Second Lt. John E. McCarthy of New York City to get to work. "That guy," said Horner, "can take six mortars and get 60 shots into the air before the first shell lands. He can drop them in a rain barrel."

In our excitement, we edged too far beyond a protecting embankment and an enemy tank-gunner spotted us. A shell whacked into the hillside nearby and shrapnel buzzed around us. We ran for cover and circled around the ridge, crawling to a new vantage point.

McCarthy already was at work. His men were pouring mortar bursts into the enemy positions. Machineguns chattered. And then the Germans cracked. They threw down their weapons and came running across the fields with their hands up shouting in surrender. They popped out of trenches and from behind rocks by scores.

The defenses of Troina had begun to crack.

It was 8 A.M. Overhead a formation of American bombers roared across the sky. It was the beginning of an all-day bomber shuttle.

We went back to Horner's new command post and pressed against a bank while enemy mortar bursts seared the ridgetop above. A slender lad in blood-stained fatigues slid down beside us. He had been helping evacuate wounded from the battlefield on doors and tabletops and anything else that would hold a wounded man. The soldier was Second Lieut. Claus Anderson of Kenosha, Wis.

He said suddenly: "You know, I believe it's true there are no atheists in foxholes. I found that out yesterday over there." He jerked his head toward the battlefield.

Anderson and Corp. Wayne Palmer, Ladysmith, Wis., had gone to the aid of a wounded comrade and were machine-gunned as they dressed his wounds in a gully. They picked up the wounded man and ran with him into a stone house nearby.

"There were five wounded men in the room," Anderson said. "Palmer kept going out and bringing more in even when he was wounded. Sometimes we couldn't get to the wounded. The machineguns would drive us back. We couldn't move out of the house for ten hours to evacuate the casualties. But they never complained. Nobody's got more guts than a wounded man."

One of the men had a walkie-talkie. They tuned in on a German officer giving commands to his troops and then by some strange freak of reception the little shack suddenly was filled with American swing music, probably from Algiers.

"One boy was in bad shape. Everybody thought he was going to die. And so each of us said a prayer for him. There were a couple of Catholics with us. They read a prayer from a book. I don't think the wounded man was a Catholic but nobody cared what his religion was. It didn't matter, did it?"

No, we said, it didn't matter.

After a while Anderson climbed back over the bank to help with the wounded.

Our rations, one can of cold stew per man, arrived at noon and we wolfed it down as the Germans began shelling our ridge again. Machinegun bullets whined over. Around us soldiers lay in slit trenches, too tired even to move the rocks from under their bodies. You marveled how they endured attacks night after night, the never-ending marches across the valleys and the steep rocky ridges, the continual pounding of artillery and machinegun fire.

One soldier said he had not had his shoes off in 21 days. "I'm afraid if I take 'em off," he smiled ruefully, "I'll never get 'em back on."

Belden and I climbed into a rocky shelter as shells began falling nearer. There were voices talking around us as the shelling continued.

"When this is over, I won't mind going back to Wisconsin and looking at cows the rest of my life . . ."

"If I could just get into a bath tub and soak for hours and hours . . ."

"Remember that last town? I went to a farmhouse and the woman locked the gates. She had her kids bring water in a big wooden tub while I scrubbed . . ."

"Tell you what I'd like. A thick chocolate malted, sort of icy, with plenty of ice cream . . ."

"Aw! Why don't you guys quit sluggin' yourselves with that kind of talk?"

Captain Albert H. Smith of Baltimore, Md., reported by radio a German column approaching from Troina.

"Get some mortar and machinegun fire on them," Horner ordered.

A machinegun began its heavy fire on the crest of our ridge.

"That's Kelly," someone said. "You can always tell when Kelly puts his finger on the trigger. Listen to him!" The gun spit short, angry bursts.

Another machinegun squad went by to the edge of the ridge. "Crawl out there on your bellies and give 'em hell!" Chuck called.

The second gun began firing and the mortars thumped. We could see the enemy troops scattering and running for cover.

"They're running around completely disorganized," Smith reported. "We've knocked hell out of them."

Late in the afternoon a formation of Mitchells thundered over, made a wide sweep and came back over Troina. Great columns of gray smoke mushroomed up and obscured the town. Dive bombers roared in and lanced out of the sky in screaming dives.

The war came to a halt. Soldiers climbed out of their holes and stood open-mouthed watching the battering of the enemy fortress.

The sun was falling behind the dark Sicilian hills when Horner decided to send a patrol to try to get into Troina. Slim Lieut. Stan Mastyl of Philadelphia gathered seven men in a vineyard at the edge of this no-man's-land.

"What arms are you taking?" the Major asked.

"Each man has a tommygun, a bandoleer of ammunition and hand grenades. Do you want us to fight if we run into trouble?"

"No. Try to avoid a fight. There are too few of you."

"All right, sir. Goodbye."

Mastyl and his patrol filed across the ridge. They were silhouetted for a moment against the sky and then they were gone. A chill wind blew across the ridge. Troops lay in slit trenches trying to get some rest before the next move forward. Some had blankets. Others huddled together for warmth. Overhead the shells from our artillery moaned across and crashed into the valley beyond where Mastyl and his men were headed.

Belden and I wrapped ourselves in blankets and lay down in a slit trench to rest. I pulled the blanket over my head to light a cigaret and then cupped the glow in my hands.

I wondered if Troina would be like all the other shell-pocked towns we had passed through . . . dead, stinking, depressing. I wondered if there would be old women sitting in doorways and peering out of dark rooms. Always it seems the first living things you see in any wrecked city are old women. Old women and cats. They either are very brave . . . or forgotten.

That's the way it was in Cerami. Everyone had fled in terror to caves in the hills to escape danger except four old women and the village priest. And on Sunday morning after the American troops occupied the village, the four old women attended mass as usual, sitting stiffly in their accustomed places.

The priest conducted the services and then he told them the Americans had come as liberators of the people, that they must not be frightened. He read the military proclamation prohibiting possession of firearms, ordering curfew, outlining penalties for those conspiring against the army.

The four old women sat and solemnly nodded their heads.

It was near midnight when Mastyl brought his patrol back. "We got about half way when they opened up on us with machineguns," he reported to Horner. "I tried to work around to the right but we ran into rifle fire and I figured we had better get out."

"Good work, Mastyl," Horner patted his shoulder. "We'll just sit tight tonight and see what happens."

We were up at dawn for a can of cold C rations and chocolate dissolved in a cup of cold water.

"We're going into Troina," Horner said to Captain Smith. "Order all companies to move."

With the sun throwing long shadows into the valley below we filed down the ridge and onto a gravel road winding toward Troina. No shots came from the enemy. Belden and I joined Lieut. Everett Booth of East Chicago whose platoon was scheduled to enter the city first.

Along the road were burned out German halftracks, trucks and mobile guns smashed by shellfire and bombs. Every culvert had been a strong point as well as every ledge and protecting bank.

It was 7:30. Our column was about a mile from Troina when dive-bombers roared out of the sun to dump bombs on the town. Again the town on the high cliff before us was washed out in smoke and dust.

Around a curve in the road machinegun bullets snapped over our heads. We dived for cover behind a bank.

"Where is that machinegun?" Booth cried.

"Over there!" A soldier pointed toward a vineyard below Troina.

"All right, I'll work around the right flank."

We crawled along the bank and ran across an exposed stretch into a gully through which ran a shallow irrigation ditch.

At 7:40 our dive bombers hammered Troina again and ten minutes later another flight dropped its bombs. Then another flight dived in, screaming down in echelon, but this time they came hurtling toward our position. We watched the planes roaring toward us.

"Oh, God! No!" a soldier whispered.

Fascinated, we saw the bombs hurtle from the belly of the plane. The fins caught the air and the bombs arched downward. The earth shook and the air was filled with dust. Another plane dived in and then another. We lay in the shallow ditch holding onto the earth.

"For God's sake, don't move!" Booth cried.

A plane's machineguns chattered as the pilot strafed the road above us. A vehicle burst into flame. And our own planes raced away to report this movement of an "enemy" column.

"Every man take off his undershirt," Booth ordered. "We'll lay them on the bank above us. And dammit, hurry!"

We stripped off our undershirts, most of them grimy from days of wear with no chance to wash them. We handed them to Sergeant Vincent Burns of Woodhaven, N.Y., and he spread them on top of the embankment. For some reason, the pilots were supposed to recognize those shirts as those of friendly troops. By the laundry mark, I suppose. Anyway, it seemed reasonable at the time.

We crawled back into the trench when we heard the planes coming back. "My friends, and I mean my friends," a voice intoned, "I hate war!"

"Burns," said Booth, "When we push on be sure and pick up all those undershirts."

"I want mine back," said a muffled voice. "I just washed it."

"Oh, you'll get it back," Booth snapped. "You'll get it back. We'll send them all to the laundry and have them ready for the next dance."

The planes were overhead. They dived again but this time the bombs crashed into Troina.

"Now that is great goin', guys," someone said. "Thanks."

The enemy machinegunner was silenced. We worked our way around the vineyard until we stood below the city. Civilians stood on balconies and ledges waving white flags. Sheets were draped from windows.

We climbed the steep slope into the bomb-wrecked streets. Bombs had hurled great blocks of stone and debris into the streets, choking them. Over everything was a pall of gray dust and the smell of destruction.

And then down the cobbled street came two old women, arm in arm, picking their way slowly through the wreckage, mumbling wordlessly to themselves. They seemed to have materialized out of the debris.

The soldiers stopped and the two women walked by as though there was no one in all Troina but themselves. They spoke to no one and no one spoke to them. If they noticed the troops, they gave no sign. They walked on and disappeared into the wreckage. And a gray cat stalked after them.

We climbed over the debris and up the winding, narrow streets to the town's main square. A few people had come out of their bombed homes to cheer the doughboys and to give them wine.

Someone touched my arm and I looked down to see a soft, white hand. I never can forget the sight of that dainty hand after so many days of dirt and filth. It was lovely.

I looked around to find a young, black-haired girl beside me.

"We are so happy the Americans have come," she said simply. There were tears in her brown eyes. "We've been miserable but now everything is changed."

I touched her hand to see if she were real. He skin was soft and warm. And she laughed at my surprise.

"Who are you?" I asked.

"My name is Mildred." I realized she was speaking English. "I'm an American, too. Come over here and meet my mother and twin sister."

I followed her into a building where a prim, gray-haired woman and a carbon copy of Mildred sat on a wooden bench looking as though they would both burst into tears any minute despite the happiness shining in their faces.

"Thank God you are here," the mother said as though they had been waiting for me personally. "We've been waiting for you for days. It has been horrible."

She explained that she was Mrs. Rose Pennisi and these were her daughters, Mildred and Santa. She and her husband, Angelo, had operated a millinery shop in New York City until 1929 and Angelo decided he wanted to return to his native Sicily. Mrs. Pennisi and the girls came with him and opened another shop in Catania. When the invasion started, the Pennisis fled from Catania to escape the bombing and shelling. They arrived in Troina a few days before the Americans attacked.

"The Germans wouldn't let us leave," Mrs. Pennisi explained. "They made everyone stay in the city and even took shoes away from some who tried to escape.

"Yes," said Mildred bitterly, "except the rich and the fascists. They went away. They didn't care about anyone else."

When the battle began to rage before Troina, the people crowded into the dark, cavernous vault of a 600-year-old cathedral. They brought their food and wine and water with them and jammed every nook.

"We lived like . . . like . . . beasts!" Mildred burst out. "Come, I'll show you how we lived."

We walked into a sun-washed square and across to the cathedral. We went down a dark passageway and pushed open a great oak door. The stench of human excrement and hundreds of sweating bodies was sickening.

Inside the great, low-ceilinged room only feeble shafts of light filtered in from dingy windows. Men, women and children crouched like animals over their little hordes of food and piles of belongings. They still could not realize that danger had passed, that now they could come into the clean air without fear. They had found at least safety in this refuge and they clung to it.

Over the babble of voices rose the thin wail of hungry children. There had been no milk for the babies for days and most of them lay listlessly in their mother's arms. A little girl slept at the feet of an image of a crucified Christ.

Mildred closed her eyes and shuddered.

"At night," she said, "it was very dark until a monk came in with one candle for prayer."

In the flickering light illuminating the gaunt face of the monk, the people knelt in prayer. Mothers hushed the fretful wails of the children and a moment of peace fell over the miserable people trapped by the battle for Troina.

We climbed a winding stairway into the main part of the Cathedral. A shell or bomb had blasted a hole at the side of the altar, scattering debris about the image of Saint Sylvester, patron saint of Troina. On the floor directly above the refuge of the townspeople lay a 500 pound unexploded bomb.

Our prayers must have been answered," Mildred whispered in wide-eyed wonder. And then she said "Look!"

At the end of the cathedral, a shaft of sunlight fell through the hole in the roof and illuminated the altar. It shone like a spotlight on the lone figure of a doughboy, his helmet and tommygun beside him, kneeling in prayer.

We turned and tiptoed out of the shadows of the cathedral and left the doughboy to his solitary communion.

When the First division completed the capture of Troina, Terry Allen turned over his command to Major General Clarence Huebner, who had begun his army career as an enlisted man in the First division.

This was a galling, bitter blow for Terry, to lose his beloved Fighting First. He had trained the division, led his men through the Tunisian campaign and directed a spectacular campaign on Sicily from the beaches to Troina. Unconsciously dashing and colorful, he had the knack of inspiring the men who worked with him.

Most of us thought Terry was returning home as a hero to take over the command of a corps as a reward for his division's performance in two campaigns. Certainly it seemed Allen was one of the few American generals equipped by combat experience to handle a corps.

But Terry Allen in effect was being demoted, being brushed off, getting the old heave-ho from upstairs. Instead of being promoted to command a corps, he was going home to train a green division—the 104th Timberwolf division.

The blow would have broken a lesser man—but not Terry Allen. He vowed he would come back to the war with another great division and make some of his superiors eat humble pie. And he did.

Allen's troubles sprung from the fact his ideas of discipline differed sharply with those at Eisenhower's headquarters.

After the First division returned from Tunisia, the boys that had met the Germans at Kasserine and battled their way up Hill 609 thought they were entitled to a round of whoopee. They felt they had a right to relax the shackles of discipline and slap a little red paint around town. Unofficially, Terry Allen thought the same thing. He was proud of his men and considered they had earned a night off.

But the MP's and rear echelon troops in Algiers had little sympathy with the tough Mauldin-like characters who barged into town ignoring off-limits signs and curfews dearly beloved by base commanders. There were a lot of brawls and somewhere in the fight there generally was a soldier wearing the First division shoulder patch. They were cocky with the cockiness of combat men who look down their noses at the base section troops who have never been shot at. And they never sidestepped trouble.

Somehow, too, the story started among the First division troops they were going home to march down Fifth Avenue. The we-are-going-home talk spread false hope in a division which had many more months of fighting ahead before anyone could dream of returning without a purple heart.

Unfortunately, Terry Allen's deep sympathy for his men, his sensitiveness to their suffering, and his efforts to avoid casualties were interpreted by some as a weakness. He liked a drink along with his fighting—but so did a guy named Grant.

At any rate, the high command became alarmed at the reports and rumors which drifted back to headquarters and there was fear that a crack combat division was becoming frayed at the edges for lack of sterner discipline.

Actually, Allen had excellent combat discipline and his men admired him. Few foot soldiers ever know the name of their commanding general—he is a shadowy figure too far above their lowly foxhole life. But the men of the First knew Terry Allen was their general.

And so in the gray dust of Sicily, Allen and Teddy Roosevelt were relieved of their commands. The order hit Roosevelt as hard as it did Allen. All of us knew this little warrior's fondest hope was to lead the First division into combat as its commanding general. He never realized his ambition.

The division's headquarters staff and line officers were bitterly disappointed to see Allen and Roosevelt leave. Most of them resented the arrival of Huebner who immediately began putting the troops through intensive training exercises—and marksmanship practice!

"Hell's bells!" one of the men said in disgust. "We've been killing Germans for months and now they are teaching us how to shoot a rifle. It doesn't make sense."

As a matter of fact it made a great deal of sense. Huebner found that in months of combat the soldiers had slipped into faults in their technique. He wanted the sharpshootingest division in the army. And I suspect he also wanted to impress on the men the fact that they had a new commanding general.

The story of Terry Allen losing the First division and then building a green division into one of the finest in the whole army as a sort of personal triumph—and the story of General Huebner's winning over the First division to his side—were two of the great human dramas of the war.

Allen and Huebner were strikingly different in appearance and personality. Allen was a dark, slender, intense man with a natural flair for showmanship. He made friends easily. He liked to have people around him. He played as hard as he fought.

Huebner was older, quieter, more reserved. Beside Allen one would at first think him almost stolid. But he had a gentle warmth which won people to him, and when he talked you found yourself drawn to this big, slow-speaking man.

During the Sicilian and European campaigns, I formed a great affection for both Huebner and Allen. Both of them, in their own ways, proved themselves magnificent soldiers and leaders.

Huebner had one of the toughest jobs any man ever had—to win the affection and esteem of his division when its heart had belonged to his predecessor. Huebner had had nothing whatever to do with Allen's transfer, but this did not make his job any easier.

The loyal First did not drop its reserves until Huebner proved in combat he knew his job. It wasn't until the invasion of France that many officers began to lose their resentment and to accept Huebner for the exceptional leader he was. Little by little he won their respect and affection by his courage, sincerity and genuine ability.

Terry Allen came back to the war months later and outside Aachen his 104th Timberwolf division joined the First army to fight beside the First division!

* * *

The northern coastline of Sicily is the kind of country described in tourist literature as picturesque. Quaint little fishing villages are tucked away in incredibly lovely coves. Lemon groves and vineyards break into the ruggedness with unexpected beauty. Mountains dip down to meet the blue sea in a wild tumult of rocks and foamy surf. The winding road is chiseled into the mountainsides. It is a tourist's dream but a soldier's hell.

After the Fighting First broke the German hold at Troina, the enemy fell back toward Messina fighting a savage rearguard action and the Third Infantry division took over the burden of the battle.

Each rocky ridge ahead of the Third division was an ideal defensive position. The Germans blasted the road from the cliff-sides and kept our engineers busy bridging gaps so that guns, trucks and supplies could roll across in a creeping advance. And at each hogback ridge, the doughboys were forced to leave the road and climb into the mountains to outflank the enemy. It was punishing, slow, heartbreaking warfare. Patton prodded Major Gen. Lucian Truscott to move his division faster and Truscott called on his regimental commanders for greater effort. The regimental commanders urged the battalion commanders forward. They passed the word down to the company commanders who pressed the platoon leaders, who sent the infantry head-on into the German fire.

Truscott finally conceived a plan of landing a battalion behind the enemy's lines near San Agata to break up the stubborn defense and speed the drive on Messina. On August 8, the Second battalion of the Thirtieth regiment landed at night from the sea—behind the German lines. The maneuver shook the enemy's defenses and drove them back a few miles, but still the Krauts fought for every yard.

Truscott decided to try the same maneuver again, this time landing a battalion at Brolo near Cape Orlando. But as he studied the situation he decided the time would be bad and the maneuver would not accomplish its purpose of breaking the enemy's stand.

But Georgie [*sic*] Patton was impatient to bring the campaign to a close. He overrode Truscott's objections and ordered him to make the second amphibious landing. The commander of the Third division reluctantly ordered the move only after a sharp and spirited dispute over tactics.

Officers of the Third division headquarters said later there were angry words exchanged that day in Truscott's command post but Truscott could not disobey a direct order. Had I known of the disagreement and Truscott's forebodings I probably never would have accompanied the little convoy which steamed from shore at dusk on August 11 for a rendezvous with tragedy behind the enemy's lines.

The battered Second battalion, commanded by Lt. Col. Lyle Bernard of Highland Falls, N.Y., again was chosen for the mission. This same battalion had made the previous behind-the-lines landing and the men barely had time to fight their way to safety before they were called upon again.

I found Bernard on the deck of our LST looking at the dark mountains on our starboard side. He sucked at a dead pipe.

"Brolo is our objective," he said in answer to my question. "The town is about twelve kilometers behind the enemy's front line. We've got to cut the coast road and dig in on Mount Brolo. Then we'll beat hell out of anything that comes our way."

"The men haven't had much rest."

"No, they haven't had enough rest." He knocked the ashes from the pipe. "They were tired, but before long you will see some of the best damned soldiers in the American army."

I liked this lean, square-jawed soldier who growled at his men one minute and spoke with unexpected gentleness the next.

"Come on," he said, "let's get some coffee."

We went to the wardroom and sipped scalding coffee. After a while a young lieutenant came in breathless. "Colonel, all the ducks are loaded with ammunition. Somebody forgot the rations and the water!"

Second Lt. Herbert Stranahan of Brookline, Mass., shook his head.

"It's all screwed up, isn't it?"

"Yeah," said Major Lynn Fargo of Ripon, Wis., "but when you start out with soup you wind up with ice cream, kid. That's the way these things go."

We went to deck to hear Bernard talk to his men. It was almost dark. The ship rolled gently.

"I know you men are worried as hell . . . worried whether the enemy will be sitting there waiting for us . . . if he isn't it won't be long until he knows we are around and you know it will be tough. No use kidding ourselves . . .

"When we land we'll have an olive grove and a railroad bank to give us cover . . . we can give 'em quite a fight on the beach if we have to . . . then we have a cliff ahead of us . . . I think you men could go up it if it were vertical, from what I've seen of you . . . We're going to knock the sonsabitches off if they are up there . . . And if you do your job we'll be in Messina in a week."

Jack Belden and I went below to try to get a few hours rest before the landing. Our quarters were hot and stifling but I slept until the ship's bell roused me. It was the signal to load the assault waves.

The ship's engines were quiet and the LST wallowed in an easy swell. A cheese-yellow half-moon was sliding below the horizon when we went on deck. A cool breeze felt good after the heat inside the ship. The dim outline of Mount Brolo loomed against the sky.

Troops came filing across the deck from below, their boots falling heavily on the steel deck. They clambered over the side and climbed down the rope nets into assault boats bobbing in the swells below.

"Hurry it up, you guys," a voice said urgently.

"Don't get your bowels in an uproar!" a soldier growled. "We'll get there soon enough."

"Who said that?" an officer demanded. A voice laughed mockingly in the darkness. A few hours rest had helped the men. They could bitch, laugh and joke even at a time like this.

Soon the boats were full and they moved off behind the shadow of a guiding patrol craft like black ducklings paddling after their mother. The boats dissolved in the darkness. The first wave of the assault was to hit the beach at 2:30 and we were to follow in thirty minutes.

We went back to the wardroom to fill our canteens with water and drink all we could hold. At 2 A.M. Major Fargo led us down a hatchway into the dark hold where ducks, loaded with ammunition and supplies, were waiting.

The hold was hot and clammy. Dim green lights cast a faint, eerie glow across the blunt-nosed amphibious vehicles looking like monsters crouching in a prehistoric cave. We clambered over the tops of the ducks to our place in the first vehicle and sat smoking, waiting for the hands of our watches to move around to the half hour.

"Why don't we do this more often . . ." hummed Fargo, but no one laughed.

Then from out of the gloom came the thin, sweet notes of a harmonica pouring out a love song, a poignant melody that was almost a sob . . . "Night and day, you are the one . . ."

To a girl somewhere, a soldier was playing a love song with unutterable longing in every phrase. The single little instrument's tones seemed to fill the darkness with pulsing sound that rose and fell with the rocking of the ship. But then the song ended on an unfinished note. The great ramp in the bow of the ship began to lower. A faint sliver of sky appeared and widened. We stared at the dropping ramp in fascination as it swung open and disclosed the dark water ahead.

Major Fargo broke the silence. "Start your motors!"

Starters whirred and motors roared. Our duck moved slowly down the ramp into the water and headed for shore with the others trailing. We crouched on ammunition boxes and watched the shore—that blackness ahead unbroken except for two winking lights set up by the engineers to guide the troops to the right spot on the beach.

Our duck rolled out of the water onto soft sand and the others rolled in behind us. Tanks were being landed and driven toward the main road. We wanted surprise, but to our supersensitive nerves it seemed that there was bedlam that could be heard for miles. Voices shouted in the night.

"Hill! Godammit, where are you, Hill!"

"Company F! This way!"

"Damn! Watching the f——g barbed wire! Keep your heads down!"

"Oh, if my mammy could see her sonny boy now!"

Belden and I fell in with a column. Crouching low we passed through a gap in barbed wire, climbed across a railroad and scrambled down an embankment, across a ditch and into a lemon grove blacker than the night. Shadows milled about everywhere and there was that sense of absolute confusion that falls over every amphibious landing.

Actually, there was an orderly movement among all the milling columns, lost troops searching for their units, weapons squads going to their positions. Then I realized there was no one in front of me. I stopped and the soldier behind asked what was wrong.

"Hell," I said, "I'm not supposed to be leading this column. All I've got is a typewriter."

The soldier cursed. "Well, goddam! I thought you were leading us."

Finally a guide came along and we made our way through the grove to a high stone wall. There was a sound of vehicles on the road above us. Machineguns, rifles and grenades exploded and we fell flat. There was a sharp flash on the road and an explosion. A fire glowed and wounded enemy troops caught in the surprise fire groaned in the night. Machinegun tracers streamed across the grove.

The surprise of the landing had been complete, but it was ended now. We heard a motorcycle race down the road and knew the messenger would spread the alarm. There was no time to lose.

The plan of defense was this: F and G companies were to hold Mount Brolo overlooking the town and coast road while E company was to hold the beachhead below with the support of five tanks and seven 105mm howitzers mounted on halftracks.

We ran across the road, skirted the edge of the dark town and began climbing the steep slope of Mount Brolo. The sky was graying in the east and officers urged the men to climb faster, to reach the hilltop before dawn when the enemy could spot them on the hillside.

Private Dan Dix of McRae, Ga., panted along behind me. "I reckon," he observed, "these mountains are worse than anything we got down in Georgia."

Below us machine gun tracers laced bright ribbons in the darkness. We could still hear the groans of the wounded on the road. Our first aid men were busy caring for our own wounded, getting them to places of comparative safety.

The sun was touching the mountain peaks when the two companies, F and G, reached the top of Mount Brolo and began digging slit trenches in the hard earth. I borrowed a small shovel and began hacking a trench. Within a few minutes my hands were blistered and the trench was barely six inches deep. Belden took the shovel and did no better except for the blisters.

"Look!" someone shouted. "Germans!"

A column of enemy troops came filing down a pathway, obviously unaware of our position on the hill above them. One of our machineguns opened up and the tracers ripped into the column. The surprised Germans raced madly for cover. But we knew the battle of Brolo would develop fast.

Two infantrymen came around the ridge guarding eight German prisoners, one a great hulking figure with arms as thick as an ordinary man's thighs.

"We caught 'em asleep in a gully," laughed Private Raymond Cummings, Norwich, N.Y. "We dammed near stepped on 'em. You never saw eight more surprised Germans."

Belden and I looked at the arms of the German. We looked at each other with the same thought. And soon, in exchange for cigarets, our reluctant guest was digging a wide, nice, deep slit trench that would accommodate two adequately if not comfortably.

Nearby, Homer Bigart of the *New York Herald Tribune* and Tom Treanor of the *Los Angeles Times* had purchased enemy labor to dig slit trenches.

"This guy says that before the day is over, I'll be digging a slit trench for him," Treanor laughed.

"Don't laugh," said a soldier. "He may be right."

And before the day was ended we were about ready to agree with the German.

At 8 A.M., only five and a half hours after the first wave of troops had landed, the enemy was preparing for attack. Our observers reported troops being unloaded from trucks east of Brolo, and small units were slipping into the town on the flank of our beachhead.

"Have the naval observer get some fire on the town from the destroyers," Bernard said. Our convoy had been escorted by destroyers which now were lying offshore to give the battalion fire support.

Our mortar squads were looping shells into Brolo when dive-bombers roared in to strafe and bomb the town. A haze of dirty smoke began to drift across the beachhead and then the navy guns opened fire. Lordy, they sounded good.

We kept listening for sounds of gunfire to the west. Two regiments of the Third division were attacking toward us to smash the rearguard resistance and relieve our battalion. We thought we heard artillery fire, but it was a long, long way off. Occasional machinegun and sniper fire sent us into our slit trenches. The artillery on the beach, the destroyers' guns at sea and our mortars on the hill kept pounding the road along the coast, trying to break up the enemy concentrations which were growing heavier and more menacing.

A private walked up to Bernard's command post—a slit trench with a field telephone and a field radio.

"What is it, son?"

"Sir, we are out of mortar ammunition. Can you help us?"

"Did you do any good with what you had?"

"I guess so. There were about 300 Germans in a draw and we put a lot of stuff on them."

"I'll see what I can do." Bernard called the beach ammunition dump and ordered mortar shells sent to Mount Brolo as quickly as possible. The ammunition situation was becoming serious for snipers were killing the mules which we had brought in to carry supplies from the beach.

"We'll catch hell this afternoon," the colonel predicted. "They are going to attack."

As the hours passed enemy fire on the beach and Mount Brolo increased in intensity. The sun was almost unbearable. The heat pressed on the men like a solid and perspiration poured from their bodies. They had drunk the water from their canteens by midmorning and they were beginning to suffer from thirst. No breeze stirred to temper the heat. Olive trees on the hillside gave only an illusion of shade.

Belden and I cut fir boughs from a scrub and laid them across the slit trench to shield our faces from the sun. But they didn't help much and only seemed to make the hole hotter. Tracer bullets had set dry leaves and weeds afire on Brolo. We were ringed by brush fires and the valley was a cauldron of smoke and flame.

Major Fargo returned from a reconnaissance with the report enemy tanks had slipped into town from the east.

"We've got to have air support, colonel," he said, "and have the navy blast hell out of them."

Bernard called the navy liaison officer. "You've got to give us fire into the town and I mean now!" he roared.

"It's going to be rugged," Fargo said.

A runner came panting from the beach, "We can't last five more minutes without fire support, sir," he said.

The expected German attack was under way. The enemy was driving in from the east with tank support for infantry. They were threatening to overrun the beach defenders. The sound of battle grew heavier and shells ripped into Mount Brolo.

The navy's guns opened up. Salvo after salvo poured into Brolo and the enemy concentrations on the road. The destroyers were hidden in the mists offshore but their gunnery was perfect. They broke up the attack.

By midafternoon the torturing desire for water was almost unbearable. Belden and I had shared the last of our water with a gaunt soldier shot through the shoulder by a sniper. I walked around the slope of the ridge to the only waterhole on the mountain. Dozens of solders with hundreds of canteens sat waiting for their turn. Some of the men had been there for five hours already waiting for water for themselves and for their friends. I timed the flow. It took four and a half minutes to fill one canteen. The men sat in the sun watching the water run from an improvised spout. They stared silently at the pitifully small stream as if their concentration would make it gush forth in cool torrents.

I looked at all those men in front of me. If I waited until some four hundred canteens were filled, I would have to wait 1800 minutes or thirty hours. I brushed the green scum from a stagnant filthy mudhole and filled my canteens into which I dropped halizone tablets. The water was stale and sour but at least it was wet.

An officer hurried down the path. "Back to your positions, men! The enemy is attacking!"

Reluctantly, the soldiers left the waterhole, the empty canteens clattering as they began hurrying back to their positions.

The battalion landing had snapped the enemy's line of communication and supply. They were fighting desperately to get out of the trap, throwing everything available against our beach defenses to smash an avenue of escape.

When I returned to our slit trench, the Germans were slamming 88mm shells against the crest and shrapnel was buzzing viciously. The wounded soldier sipped from the canteen of water and mumbled gratefully. Sweating, miserable, feeling like trapped rats, Belden, the soldier and I huddled in the refuge.

"I wonder," said the soldier in delirium, "what kind of corn crop the folks back home had this year."

It didn't make sense. Nothing made sense in this hell of sun and thirst and fire and smoke and fear. I looked at my watch and saw it was only 3:30. It seemed we had been on the hilltop for days playing a senseless game in which men tried to kill each other.

Nobody will believe this, I thought. A lost battalion fighting for its life behind the enemy lines, the hillsides blazing with fire. A colonel who acted like something out of a novel, no water, ammunition running low and a wounded soldier who mumbled about the corn crop in Indiana. I suppressed a crazy desire to laugh.

The fog of confusion was growing and rumors ran from trench to trench . . . "The Germans have wiped out the beach defenses" . . . "The 15th and 7th regiments haven't even begun their attack" . . . "We can't expect relief for two more days."

The situation was getting worse and Colonel Bernard ordered Company F to the beach to support Company E. Then our communications began to go. The brush and weed fires around the mountain burned through the telephone wires to the beach. Enemy artillery and machine-gun fire smashed the radios. The battalion was cut off completely with no way to reach the warships and ask for fire support. But Bernard gave no outward sign of nervousness as he leaned back in his slit trench smiling, puffing at his dead pipe as though this were a Sunday afternoon picnic and he was enjoying the antics of a playful group of children.

A young soldier edged up nervously. "Excuse me, sir. But have you heard anything from the other regiments? The boys are asking."

"Sure," smiled the colonel. "Sure. See that ridge over there? One regiment is in the valley just beyond that and coming fast. All we've got to do is hold on."

"Gee, thanks!" the soldier grinned, and went to his slit trench.

Bernard looked at me and shrugged as though to say "What else could I do?"

An exhausted runner who had slipped up the mountainside reported that German tanks and self-propelled guns had knocked out all our artillery and most of the tanks and were driving on the beach. The defense below was being overwhelmed by superior numbers and heavy fire.

Bernard considered the situation for a moment. "Order E and F companies to abandon the beach," he snapped. "Tell the men to make their way up here."

There was no alternative. It would have been suicidal to have left the troops on the beach with no artillery or tank protection. And an attack from Mount Brolo was out of the question.

The German tanks broke through to the beach. They shelled the ammunition dump and growled through the lemon grove where our infantry had dug in.

And then our hearts leaped joyfully. From the sea roared American dive bombers. They strafed and bombed the beach and hurtled toward Mount Brolo, where some troops stood beside their slit trenches cheering and waving.

I dived for a slit trench as the first bomb whistled down. An ear-splitting crash made the earth shudder. Smoke, dirt and acrid fumes of cordite rolled over the hilltop. Behind the first plane came another. Another whistle . . . another blast . . . and screams of wounded men. A soldier had jumped into the trench on top of me. I could feel his heart pounding against my back.

When he climbed out he said "I'm sorry I had to jump on top of you." I don't think he knew what he was saying. He was staring at the frightful scene around us. On the ridge a few feet above us one of the German prisoners stood whimpering a foolish chirping noise, a look of horror on his face. His left arm dangled by a shred from his shoulder. On the ground were five still lumps of flesh, the men who had been cheering the sight of our bombers.

A young soldier came walking toward me. There was a strange expression of small child wonder in his blue eyes. He stopped and looked at me inquiringly as though he wanted me to explain something to him. And then he fell to the ground. His carbine clattered beside him and his helmet rolled slowly down the hill. Great choking sobs shook his body.

"My head!" he cried. "My head. It hurts so terribly."

I held him in my arms as you would an unhappy little boy. He looked so very young. I heard the planes again and pulled him into my slit trench. But the planes went away.

A first aid man came by and gave the shocked boy a hypodermic. Gradually his sobs quieted to soft moans and he slept, but his face twitched and his muscles jerked in spasms.

Nearby a padre knelt in prayer by the dead. Some of them had caught the full blast of the bombs and there wasn't much recognizable. One man didn't have a mark on him. It was concussion. Beside him I found a charred bit of paper with a woman's delicate handwriting on it which said ". . . could ever ask would be peace and happiness—with you, dear. The ache grows a little every day in the place where my heart used to be. Always yours, Beth."

I tucked the paper into the soldier's pocket.

The sun was setting when Major Fargo came up the ridge and sank wearily beside the slit trench where the young soldier slept, drugged by the morphine. His face had stopped twitching now.

Fargo said: "I'm so goddamned tired my legs feel like they're off at the hips. E company is pretty badly shot up. I was there. I was on the beach when the tanks came down shooting up everything. But they didn't see me."

We walked to Bernard's command post. Fargo reported the companies on the beach had received the orders to retreat to the hilltop and the men were trying to make their way up the side of Mount Brolo to dig in with G company in a tight defensive circle.

"We'll keep packing away and give them more hell than they are looking for," Bernard boasted. But his was strictly for the benefit of any of the soldiers who might be listening. There wasn't much left to give anybody hell with.

Second Lt. Eric Tatlock of Gardiner, Me., came up from the beach. "We beat off two attacks on the ammunition dump," he said. "Engineers, artillerymen and every man who could handle a gun were fighting. We were cut off twice but they didn't get through until we got the order to evacuate."

Bernard nodded. "We had the bastards bottled up but they blew out the stopper."

Just as General Truscott feared, the battalion had not been able to close a trap even though they had shaken the enemy badly.

"Let's go take a peek at the situation," Bernard said to Fargo.

"If you don't mind, sir, I think I'll sit right here and think of cold malted milks."

"Son, you've got more guts than a sausage mill," the colonel said softly, looking down at Fargo.

Up the slope came two mortar squads with all the ammunition they had left—22 rounds.

"Good boys," exclaimed Bernard. "Just put them inside our little old last stand circle and then knock hell out of that bridge to the west. We won't be able to knock it out but we can keep them from bringing anything down the road."

The mortars were set up and began firing at the bridge. Fargo checked off each round as it was shot.

"Lordy that's a pleasant whistle," he said.

In the growing darkness was a sound of men digging slit trenches, men who had escaped from the broken beachhead. The dull sound of digging sounded through the night broken by the rattle of machineguns and rifle fire.

Soon after dawn a runner came to Bernard's command post. "There are troops and vehicles on the road, sir," he said. "Those damned vehicles look like jeeps to me."

"Tell the men not to fire and keep under cover," Bernard said. "I'm going down to see."

We worked our way down the mountainside to a ledge overlooking the road—and there were American troops!

We reached the road and Bernard's regimental commander wrung his hands. "You did a great job," he said. "You had us plenty worried but the boys fought like hell to get to you. They are so tired they can hardly walk."

"I knew you would get to us," Bernard lied.

"Well," said the regimental commander, "we've got plenty of rations and plenty of water. Get your men off the hill and we'll feed them. We'll take care of your wounded. If you will go back to the bridge you will find food and water. I know you are hungry."

"If you don't mind, colonel," said Bernard, "I'd like to look after my men first."

A short time later General Patton came riding up in his command car. His varnished helmet shone in the sun and the famous pearl-handled revolver glinted at his side. He was accompanied by young Senator Lodge of Massachusetts.

The command car stopped at the base of the hill where the tired, filthy infantrymen were filing down from fire-blackened Mount Brolo, dragging their feet like gaunt zombies. Along the roadway and on the sides of the mountain lay the bodies of scores of Americans cut down in the bloody twenty-four hour battle. There were more bodies in the lemon grove below the road but we couldn't see them.

"All you men from Massachusetts fall our over here!" Patton ordered.

A few weary doughboys trudged over to the roadside and stood listlessly waiting. The senator from Massachusetts walked over to them and made a little speech. Lodge may have delivered an excellent talk there among the dead on the slopes of Brolo. But for the life of me I cannot remember what he said. All I recall now is Patton standing tall and straight in his command car.

"The American soldier is the greatest soldier in all the world," the general said. And then he pointed to the mountains. "Only American soldiers can climb mountains like those."

All at once the whole little tableau sickened me. I wanted to get away from the voices of the general and the senator. The dead scattered on the hillside and in the lemon grove spoke eloquently enough.

Six days later Messina fell and the conquest of Sicily was complete.

[Editor's note: Most of the Germans escaped from Sicily despite Allied control of the sea and air. Many historians consider the Sicilian campaign to have been among the worst, if not the worst, of the war, owing to poor planning and lack of cooperation between Patton and Montgomery.]

Afterword

COMMAND SERGEANT MAJOR BENJAMIN FRANKLIN, SIXTEENTH
REGIMENT, FIRST INFANTRY DIVISION

I T is important to explain the frontline soldier's attitude toward the newspaper correspondent. I distinctly remember bitterly resenting the fact that they were able to come to the front at their discretion and then return to headquarters, where warm food, warm beds, and warm tents were available. We soldiers were not afforded those luxuries.

I carried this attitude with me throughout the war, and even meeting with Don Whitehead in 1963 or 1964 didn't soften my attitude. It was only sixty years after the war, when I read his diary, that I realized that he did not return to HQ every night for steak and wine; he endured hardships equivalent to those of the frontline soldier.

I am now aware of the fact that the newspaper correspondent also spent much time on the frontline. Back then, every time I saw a correspondent it was with a general, coming up to a very quiet sector at a very quiet time on an uneventful occasion to observe the fight when nothing was going on. My attitude regarding correspondents was shaped by these facts. Perhaps it was not fair. I'm glad to have realized that they struggled along with us. Certainly Ernie Pyle and Don Whitehead were on the frontline. Perhaps they endured the hardship from a different angle, but I'm sure they suffered just as much as we did.

At one event, before we jumped off into the attack on a little town called Gafsa, Ernie Pyle came and talked to a group of us young soldiers. We were just beginning to learn how to hate, which is a natural fact of life for the frontline infantry soldier—to hate everyone, even those on our team who are not subjected to the same hardships, which was basically anyone to the rear of us: generals, correspondents, and others. I distinctly remember it was in Gafsa, making it probably March, 1943, and I remember my resentment toward him and his ability to come and go as he wished. I was not permitted that freedom of mobility. I was restricted to where I was supposed to be, and I resented it.

I think Don Whitehead described the hardship of the infantry soldier—both British and American—as well as it could be articulated. When he was with my regiment in Sicily, he heaped praise on the Sixteenth Infantry. And on D-Day at Omaha Beach he was with my regiment. It's strange. Only with the passage of time and softening of memories is one willing to forgive to those who were not exposed to the same hardships as he was.

For years I suffered under the illusion that only two correspondents represented the frontline soldier—Ernie Pyle and Don Whitehead—and Ernie Pyle more so than Don Whitehead until I heard the story of Whitehead covering for Ernie Pyle.[1] Still, the resentment was there—the fact that they could go back and have dinner with the general. I never had dinner with a general. They had an overall picture of what was going on, and my scope of the war was a hundred yards to the right and a hundred yards to the left. They knew more than I did, yet I was doing the fighting, and that bothered me—again, until I was enlightened by the diary.

Don Whitehead was at his best in his graphic description of the hardships of the frontline soldier. We were hungry, we were cold, we were tired, we were wet, we were hot—every extreme that the human body can endure we experienced and he articulated, far better than I ever could have. Yet, he was a very simple person to talk to. When I had lunch with him, he gave me the impression that I thought he was going to have to pay the bill. He was little standoffish, a little reserved. He indirectly said, "I've talked to generals, and now I'm talking to a sergeant." But I could tell he was a thinker and a deep thinker at that. He was quite down to earth in his directness of speech.

Whitehead made some interesting observations on the differences between the British and American frontline soldier. In every occasion in the history of Britain, the leaders of soldiers in combat were members of the British aristocracy. In contrast to this, the American "aristocracy" are the people who avoid the draft. So we come to the army with a different set of values, in that the British royalty is willing to risk their lives for their position in society, while the American "royalty" uses their position to avoid risking their lives to protect the system. The American soldier inherently—all American soldiers invariably—dislikes those who are placed over him. He questions their authority, their ability, their reasoning. He questions everything. It's hard to convince an American soldier that he is to do anything. I know from experience. You've got to lay it out plain to him, how it's going to be advantageous to him to do a certain thing. Whereas the British soldier just accepts the fact that people are in control and you are to follow blindly what they say.

As for Don Whitehead's favorable view of Field Marshal Montgomery, I happen to agree with Montgomery's philosophy of war because I later had the privilege—and thank God I did—of having an army commander by the name of General Courtney Hodges, who shared his philosophy: Do not risk the life of one of your soldiers unless it is absolutely necessary. In other words, if the Germans will fire one round to kill one of your soldiers, then I will fire twenty rounds to protect that soldier. This was Montgomery's philosophy—never attack until you are absolutely sure that you have more artillery, more infantry, more gasoline, more supplies, more everything. In other words, don't attack as General George Patton was prone to do, on impulse. Montgomery was not that way. He was cautious and so was Hodges. When we took Aachen, the orders were that if the Germans fired one round to stop us, we'd fire twenty rounds to advance us. That was Hodges.

The big decisions are made by people who go down in history "protecting" history. The people who actually get killed have little effect on world history. Some people have the ability to explain their actions. Patton died in early 1946; Montgomery lived until well into his seventies. He had the time write a book to explain his policy; Patton never had the chance to write his memoirs. From a personal point of view, Patton could not say why he did this or that. Knowing what Patton did in North Africa and in Sicily, particularly with the Fifteenth Infantry Regiment of the Third Division, when he tried to land an amphibious operation behind the German lines, an event vividly described by Don Whitehead, it is clear that Patton was not the tactician that Montgomery was.[2] Montgomery was a cautious, deliberate student of war. Patton was an impetuous publicity hound, and this put his frontline soldiers in jeopardy. We resented bitterly his willingness to risk our lives for his name in the headlines.

Don Whitehead and I shared the same opinion of Patton. I was under Patton at El Guettar, Gafsa, Hill 523, Hill 609, Gela, and Troina. Don Whitehead was under Patton when he was with the battalion of the Third

Infantry Division, Fifteenth Infantry Regiment, which, on Patton's orders, pulled an amphibious assault behind the German lines. The consequences of his ambitious endeavor on the northern coast of Sicily going toward Messina were disastrous.

When I read Don Whitehead's diary, I was absolutely amazed at his grasp of the love of his soldiers for Terry Allen, our division commander. We knew without a doubt that our wellbeing was paramount in General Allen's mind. He defended us—for example, in the invasion of Africa, we took Oran, then we went to Tunisia for nine months, then we came back to Oran. It was described well in Whitehead's accounts. The rear-echelon soldiers controlled Oran. They lived in hotels and had a very soft life. So we came back to Oran in our OD (olive drab) uniforms. The distinction between a frontline soldier and rear-echelon soldier was that the rear echelon soldiers had suntans. Frontline soldiers wore OD uniforms. It was very easy to tell the two apart. The rear-echelon soldiers had taken our town, which we had taken in the war, and they wouldn't let us in. They had the best bars, the best cigarettes, and, of course, the best women, and we came back and they started putting us in jail. Then General Allen put out the order. If the First Infantry Division suffered three hundred casualties taking Oran from the French, we were willing to suffer twice that amount of casualties to take it from the rear-echelon troops. That was why Allen was relieved of his duty; he thought that everything we did was legal. If General Allen had said, "OK, turn around, we're going to fight General Patton back at Casablanca," the First Division would have turned around and fought Patton. If we were fighting for Terry Allen, and, of course, Teddy Roosevelt Jr., we didn't give a hell who we fought—that's how much we loved those two people.

Later in 1961, General Allen's son was the G-3 of my division. General Allen came from Texas to Germany to visit his son and come and have lunch with me (I was a Sergeant Major, Twenty-sixth Infantry then) and all the other people who had fought with him in Africa and Sicily. He confirmed that the reason he was relieved of his command was because he stood up for the men and did not take the bullshit from higher-ups.

The man who took over, Clarence Huebner, began his career as an enlisted man in the Eighteenth Infantry in World War I. He started out as a supply sergeant, then became a frontline platoon sergeant, got a commission and was decorated with the Distinguished Service Cross, eventually holding every position and every grade in the First Division you could have—from private to major. Of course, that impressed us.

He was one of us, and he was quite different from Roosevelt and Allen. Roosevelt was like a grandfather to us, and Allen was the good uncle. For example, Roosevelt would come to the frontline and would never talk to a private. I remember seeing him in Sicily. We were in a defiladed position, and a jeep drove up with "Rough Rider" aboard—General Roosevelt, bald headed, no helmet, no weapon. He got out of the jeep. We all stood up and saluted him, and he said, "Sit down boys, sit down boys." Whenever he visited the front, he would always find an old sergeant, take him aside, pull out a bottle, and they would have a little nip together. That sergeant would come back and say, "OK boys, we're gonna do so and so." Roosevelt was extremely fond of soldiers, and we were fond of him. Allen was the same way. Huebner was different. He was spit and polish and discipline.

There were times under Allen when the situation was hard to cope with. For example, when they would take one battalion of our division and attach it to the British First Army or the French Nineteenth Corps. We knew without being told that our division commander resented that. It did not happen under Huebner, because we were organized as an American army. In Africa when things were first developing, we were just learning how to hate. It's a process. You just don't go up and say, "We hate you." You've got to have some friends killed and go through hardship to start hating the enemy. Once you start hating the enemy you start hating your own people, like the officers who put you in this position. The more you hate, the better soldier you become. Love is completely absent in the heart of a rifleman. We don't love our country, we're not patriotic, we're not seeking glory or decorations, we live only on hate and without it we could not exist. It's a terrible thing to say, but it's true.

There's an unspoken bond between you and all the other line-combat troops, but you know that you cannot show any outward bond or affection, because he may get killed. That creates a void that cannot be filled. The paramount emotion for all rifle troops is hate. We love our battalion commander, regimental commander, and division commander, but we hate the sons of bitches at the same time. We know that without them we would be lost and that they are trying in their own way to protect us. At the same time, they are the ones who are putting us in the face of danger. It's a complex thing. It was only after the war that I understood why I felt certain ways.

When we first went in to the Ousseltia River valley in Tunisia, in the hills behind us was part of the French Nineteenth Corps. We would patrol across the valley at night and attack and harass the Germans. It was kind of a static, sporting thing. When we captured Germans, we treated them properly, and when they captured one of ours, they treated us right also. The attitude was, "We're here and you're there, and that's the ways things are."

Then in Kasserine when there was the brutality of tanks running over troops and vicious firefights, of being completely overrun by the Germans and trying to escape, we realized we had do something more than be sportsmen. We had to hate. That is the progression in combat.

When we went into combat in Africa, if you fired a machinegun, each round or burst of six you fired kicked up a little dust, which an enemy observer could pick up. At the time we had smokeless powder and so did the Germans. Still, from that little puff of dust you could pick it up. I remember the first position we overcame that was defended by the Germans. They had a wet rag lying on the ground in front of the machinegun. I thought, "why would they have a wet rag lying here in front of the machinegun?" That wet rag prevented the dust from kicking up. Therefore, we could not see where the machinegun was firing from. We learned this little combat trick, which is not mentioned in any manual or in anyone's war diaries. It's a little thing you pick up as a combat soldier.

Whitehead vividly describes the sights and sounds of the North African campaign. He talks about the bodies of soldiers blackened by the sun. I was on a burial detail after the Sixteenth Infantry Regiment had taken Hill 523. I remember coming across a German soldier with his helmet tipped down over his face and holding a rifle. He was in a rock crevice. As soon as I saw him, I started firing away with my tommygun. When I got up closer, I saw that his face was completely black. In Africa, you get killed and in three days your face turns black. My buddies kidded me after that. They said Franklin was great at killing dead people.

When Whitehead writes about the throb of the motors of the German planes flying over his camp and how he reacted, it reminds me of how different the German planes sounded from the Allied planes. The German motors were not synchronized, so they produced the kind of throbbing sound Whitehead mentions. Allied planes had a smoother sound, a kind of continuous roar.

As Don Whitehead points out so correctly, Africa was our weeding ground. We had some leaders who were incapable of sending men to die.

These people generally break up psychologically. They might be good, educated people, but they are not suited for combat. It takes about six months to a year to weed out the sergeants, the corporals, the lieutenants, and the captains who are incapable of combat. They're replaced by sergeants who've become lieutenants and captains and who've demonstrated their ability to withstand the rigors of combat. This is my objection to Stephen Ambrose, who called the 101st Airborne Division an elite outfit, even though they'd never been in combat. There is no way you can be elite until you've been in the frontline for six months to a year and the deadbeats have been weeded out. This is what we learned to do in North Africa and Sicily.

Appendix

EDITOR'S note: *Don Whitehead and Thoburn Wiant, formerly members of the Associated Press staff in New York, joined the AP staff of war correspondents in the Middle East in October 1942. The first two stories that follow were cowritten and carried both bylines.*

CAIRO, October 12—America's armed forces are shoving aside the twin barriers of time and distance to pour a rising tide of men and materials into four vital fronts of the second world war: the Middle East, Russia, India, and China. America is on the move in Africa.

That's what we saw on a 10,000-mile journey by air from the United States to this city in the Valley of the Nile, about 150 miles from the Egyptian desert battlement. Tough, tanned Americans, fresh from battle training and technical schooling back home, are ripping apart jungles and establishing new bases in the blazing heat of the desert in preparation for the day when the United Nations forces will move to drive Marshal Rommel's armies from North Africa.

The movement of men, munitions, tanks, and planes by land, sea, and air has not yet reached flood tide. The desert front is the immediate scene of action, nevertheless United Nations forces are keeping a wary eye cocked on relations between Berlin and Vichy, since there is more than academic interest in Vichy's attitude.

Speed has been the keynote of the American move into Africa. There are many little Americas in Africa—places which have conveniences such as electric lights, running water, showers, ice, and cold beer. These things might be classed by some as unnecessary luxuries, but they are permanent fixtures which demonstrate that the Americans have arrived.

At one stop we looked with amazement upon what might have been an encampment somewhere in the United States, yet we were told that its site was wild and totally undeveloped only a few months ago. There were rows of modern barracks, each with electric lights, running water, showers, and good beds, reminding us of college dormitories.

Winding through jungles were miles of paved roads. Desks, chairs, tables, and even wastepaper baskets were made of solid mahogany—so plentiful that it was used also in floors, walls, and rafters.

The men smoked American cigarettes and there was plenty of American food. The Army does everything to feed the men well, and it is a bit surprising to sit at a mess in a remote camp and be served a good steak, baked beans, green salad, coffee, and cake.

We were impressed by the morale of men everywhere we went. We heard occasional griping, but the gripes mostly were those you would hear anywhere along main streets back home. What they want most is action.

We found health conditions excellent, every safeguard having been taken on a past, present, and future basis. Before troops moved into any camp, medical officers surveyed the area for miles around and took every known precaution against malaria and other prevalent diseases.

Long before a spade was turned, plans for encampments were blueprinted in the United States, but engineers often came up against problems not solved by blueprints. That is where ingenuity played a big part and when necessary they improvised, often using native methods such as constructing light, airy buildings of native materials which required no priorities.

Not a nail was used in some of these structures. Sidewalls, supports, and roof poles were lashed with strong fibers obtained from the jungle. Roofs were thatched. But while they have Americanized their bases as much as possible, with movies for entertainment, most lads still look on Africa as a strange and awesome continent. They were hungry for news from home.

These Americans are in Africa to do a job—but they want to get it finished. As one soldier put it, "I want to stick my feet under Mom's table as soon as possible and have a mess of fried chicken, hot biscuits, country ham, four eggs sunny side up, and some of her good freckleface gravy. So let's get going."

CAIRO, October 13—Incredible Cairo is living in the valley of the shadow of war, trying desperately to be gay and normal, succeeding only in being gay.

There's a note of hysteria in the babble of voices, the constant blatting of automobile horns, the restless surge of humanity through the streets.

We arrived in this ancient city after a 10,000-mile trip from New York expecting to find a grim, gloomy citadel bristling with guns and subdued by the nearness of Rommel's armies.

Instead, we found a never-never land of confused unreality where most of the people are trying to forget or ignore the war—and doing very well except for the suppressed excitement which can be felt with electric awareness.

The strange contrasts of Cairo are confusing to the newcomer. The skyline is western, but the heart of Cairo is of the east. And the growing population of British and Americans doesn't alter the fact that Cairo belongs to Egypt.

We are only minutes by air from the desert battleground, and yet we have no feeling of being close to the actual fighting. There is little to remind us that a war is near.

That's because the people seem so unconcerned. They don't talk much about the war. They don't rush to buy newspapers containing the latest communiques. They appear more interested in the boom that has swept Cairo.

Cabarets and bars are crowded, mostly with uniformed men celebrating a few hours' leave or just celebrating. They have to drink fast for alcoholic beverages are served only from 12:30 to 2 P.M. and from 6 to 10. You're fortunate to find a seat in a bar.

Movie houses are packed. One theater showing "The Man Who Came to Dinner" was sold out the other night long before the picture was scheduled to begin.

Hotels are crammed with lucky people of many nationalities—lucky because they were able to find a room. It takes pull to get a room on short notice. Apartments are out of reach of persons of ordinary means, and profiteers are having a field day.

Since the war began, Cairo's population has doubled. Living costs have soared and still are going up. Simple meals cost $1.50. Beer is 35 cents a bottle and whisky at least 40 cents a drink. Soft drinks cost as much as beer and whisky. American cigarettes sell for 50 cents a pack.

There are shortages of rice, corn, and wheat. No meat can be bought three days a week. Kerosene and gasoline are rationed, and automobile tires are as scarce as they are in the United States. A black market, where virtually everything can be bought by paying a premium, is beginning to flourish.

At night, it's an adventure in the realm of involuntary manslaughter to ride through Cairo's blackout. Dim blue lights cast an eerie glow through which the taxis plunge without slackening speed. Every minute you expect to see pedestrians bowled over, but somehow they escape with a last-minute leap for safety.

Thick cement barricades five to ten feet high have been built before some store and cafe entrances to protect customers from flying debris or shell fragments, should Jerry bomb Cairo seriously.

Cairo is both primitive and modern. Horse-drawn cabs, taxis of forgotten vintage, military motor lorries, sleek limousines, and ass-drawn carts flow through the streets in strange procession. Robed Arabs and veiled Moslem women walk side by side with creations that might have come from Bond Street and Fifth Avenue.

From one doorway comes the quavering wail of Egyptian music and from another the hot rhythm of American jive. On the edge of the desert, a motor caravan whirls in a cloud of dust past a camel caravan. There is dirt, ugliness, and poverty alongside cleanliness, beauty, and wealth.

There still is a brisk business in tourist trade even if most of the tourists are in uniform. Soldiers on leave from the desert wander through the bazaars and haggle over prices.

At the edge of the city where the desert meets the green of the Nile Valley, children clamber about the bases of the pyramids. Only a few of Cairo's modern buildings have sandbags for bomb protection, but the Sphinx is up to its ear in them.

CAIRO, November 10—Given bases along the entire coast of North Africa, United Nations air forces could control the Mediterranean and reopen shorter supply lines to Allied shipping, Air Chief Marshal Sir Arthur William Tedder, commander in chief of the R.A.F. Middle East command, said today. The air chief said land-based planes could throw a protective umbrella over shipping along the southern Mediterranean once bases were seized. And that day, it was indicated, may not be far distant. Sir Arthur paid tribute to the Americans fighting in the Middle East. "American bombers have an improved batting average," he chuckled. "I told them they would when they were more experienced."

He disclosed that the Allies did not have air superiority when the battle of Egypt reopened, but gained it with paralyzing blows beginning

October 9, from which Field Marshal Rommel's air force never recovered. "The enemy was knocked off his stride at the very beginning," Tedder declared, adding that this was a major factor in the Eighth Army's victory, "since a land battle really depends on air superiority."

Rommel was not given a chance to recover, although apparently he made a desperate effort to strengthen his air force by bringing planes from Russia. The Allied air forces also played an important role in smashing Rommel's supply convoys on sea and land and in hunting down enemy shipping in Italian, Greek, and North African ports. "What really mattered," Tedder declared, "was the snapping of the enemy's life blood and stopping his ability to live." Indications were that the Germans left many planes on their fields for lack of fuel, since there was no other apparent reason for abandoning them.

EN ROUTE TO THE WESTERN DESERT FRONT, LIBYA, November 17—I have seen the graveyard of Rommel's hopes to conquer North Africa and it is a terrible sight to see. Even this scene of death and destruction on the desert, however, is not as awesome as that of Britain's victorious Eighth Army giving chase to the retreating enemy who is not many miles ahead.

The roads to Poland, Belgium, France and Greece must have looked like those I saw today—except that this time it was the Germans who were on the run and the British who were advancing. The Italian radio said this morning that the Axis armies in North Africa were "advancing" to new positions. It was not funny, it was a rather pathetic thing to hear after seeing the tremendous number of British troops, tanks, guns and supplies moving up to the front in a line unbroken for miles and miles. Transports moving along the coast road looked like a great brown snake writhing across the desert floor through the littered wreckage of twisted, burned enemy tanks, planes, and trucks. As far as I could see dust swirled and billowed over the army on the move. The sight made you feel warm inside with the knowledge that this time the Allies were going for the knockout and that there was stuff going up to do the job.

I came into the desert looking for the advance R.A.F. unit to which I am to report. But as yet, I am unable to catch up with it. It is always just ahead. Planes move into airdromes right behind the enemy withdrawal. That is how fast this advance is going right now. I left Cairo yesterday with only a vague idea of where I was headed. In fact, no one could say definitely where the advance units were. They had moved since the last reports.

The plane that brought me up was a Blenheim with a glass-enclosed front and so I had a grandstand seat over the battle area where Rommel's defense was broken. We were flying about an hour when the pilot turned the nose of the Blenheim down. I thought we were going to plow into the sand. Then we leveled off and skimmed over the desert in a ride I will remember as long as I live. We were not more than five feet off the ground at times, hurtling along at almost 200 miles an hour. I could almost have reached out and scooped up a handful of sand.

And then I saw why Pete had brought us down so low. Ahead were the gaunt, fire-blackened skeletons of what once had been Rommel's tanks. They littered the desert over an area known as "the Hill of Evil Men." Many of them must have been funeral pyres for their crews. Many were knocked out by American-made Sherman tanks which broke through the minefields behind the nighttime bayonet attacks of the infantry.

Sometimes it seemed that we were going to crash into a wrecked tank, but Pete would touch the controls, hop over, then grin like a devil. There was plenty of evidence that the Germans and Italians had dug in to hold the El Alamein line. Trenches, gun emplacements, dugouts and the remains of fortified positions were thick. I could almost identify abandoned articles of clothing and small equipment, we were flying so low. Pete is a marvel at this sort of flying which, I was told, is the safest way for a slow plane to escape detection by the enemy. He learned it doing low-level bombing over enemy-occupied channel ports. Although Pete is only 20, he has been flying almost three years with the R.A.F.

Over to the right of us were the blue Mediterranean and the coast road along which we were streaming transports. There were truck-borne Sherman tanks, guns of all kinds and hundreds and hundreds of vehicles rolling along without even a sign of interference from Jerry. On either side of the road were destroyed trucks and vehicles shot up by the R.A.F. and American fliers as the enemy fled in panic westward.

A few minutes after passing the tank battleground we roared low over the airport of El Daba, which a short while ago was one of Rommel's major advance bases. Here the scene was almost the same as the one we had left except that the sand was strewn with wrecked planes instead of tanks. It looked almost like 100 on that field alone. Skimming the dunes and dipping into depressions, we roared over the pens of German and

Italian prisoners. Some of them instinctively started to run. Others stared. They did not shake their fists or wave. They just stared, then ducked before we passed. We were so near I could see their tired, drawn, sun-blackened faces.

Once Pete climbed to 500 feet and then a couple of Hurricanes patrolling the road moved in to look us over. They were like a couple of hawks diving on a fat goose—but they saw our markings and veered off to keep watch over the brown column which had no end.

It was shortly after noon when Pete landed on an airfield pitted with bomb craters, cluttered with wrecked German and Italian planes and dozens of fifty and 250-pound bombs the Germans left behind in their haste. I left the plane at this field. My outfit was supposed to be there but it was not. So I hitched a ride on a truck. We merged with a transport column in a choking cloud of dust. At one point we passed a large space filled with British trucks. A sign on the roadside said: "parken verboten"—"no parking." We drove for ninety minutes, then turned off into the desert where headquarters was supposed to be. But my R.A.F. had just moved on.

Perhaps tomorrow I will be able to catch up with this war.

BIR EL ZIRDAN, TRIPOLITANIA, December 28—Chasing Marshal Erwin Rommel toward Tripoli has become a will o' the wisp hunt across the western desert with the Germans refusing battle at obvious strong points.

It is a puzzling game with the British Eighth Army approaching natural strong points expecting a fight only to find the enemy vanished or else a weak rear guard.

Despite Rommel's failure so far to take full advantage of positions, the desert terrain has checked the speed of the British drive.

There is no positive indication that Rommel is digging in anywhere between here and Tripoli or that he is massing forces to make a real bid to turn back the British. The most obvious places for a stand between Sirte and Tripoli were Wadi Bei El Chebir and Wadi Zemzem, both south of Misurata.

These depressions stretching from the coast inland offer barriers of sand which are rough traveling even for tanks and armored vehicles, much more so for supply transports.

The British expected Rommel to put up a fight at Wadi Bei El Chebir, some twenty-five miles west of Sirte and 180 miles short of Tripoli. The enemy was there yesterday but there was no sign of him today.

I rode with an advanced armored column across the wild country south of the coastal road. An armored car did catch a Panzer lieutenant, a former professor of languages at Heidelberg University, but he was the only enemy we encountered. The captive was in a staff car when he was trapped and brought in.

Our column left a desert camp southwest of Sirte with armored cars and tanks protecting the flanks of a convoy.

Jeeps buzzed about like terriers nipping at the heels of those getting out of position. We churned across the flat table land and then plowed through soft sands.

Wadi Bei El Chebir, 180 miles east of Tripoli, was like a great valley carved in the desert by some long forgotten stream. At the point we crossed, it was more than two miles wide. Machine guns on the escarpment could have caused a great deal of damage but Rommel had left no guns to cover this broad expanse and the column roared through the depression with its pennants flying.

Somewhere a short distance ahead of us tonight is the enemy.

His next strong point is Wadi Zemzem but no one yet knows whether he intends to fight.

[Editor's note: The following story was cowritten with George Tucker.]

TRIPOLI, January 23—Seeing people liberated from virtual bondage and watching their emotional outbursts form the most graphic impressions we have of the occupation of Tripoli.

Only a few hours ago British troops and advance units of the Royal Air Force rolled into this city and the official surrender to Gen. Sir Bernard L. Montgomery wrote the last chapter in the fall of Mussolini's African empire.

Touring the city, we visited Tripoli's ancient ghetto where some 16,000 Jews were crowded into a labyrinth of houses and cellars.

We walked through an arched gate guarded by military police and as soon as the people recognized us as Americans, the emotional outburst was almost riotous.

Some threw themselves at our feet, offering gifts of not only wine and tobacco but money as well.

Men threw their arms about our necks and kissed our cheeks. Women kissed our hands. Children clung to our legs and kissed our dusty shoes.

They showed us photographs of President Roosevelt and Prime Minister Churchill with cries of "Viva America! Viva Inglesi!"

They told us that a few hours before the troops entered the city, some leading Jewish merchants had been dragged from their shops and shot, but they expressed no surprise at this because, they said, it was the kind of thing that had been going on since the days when this city was the seat of Mediterranean piracy.

The Turks, the Arabs, the Germanic vandals, the Genoese and Florentines, the Maltese, Greeks and Spaniards all tried to superimpose their influence and culture on Tripolitania, and succeeded in a measure.

But in this city of 102,000, only 35,000 are Italians, mostly newcomers. There are 16,000 Jews and the remainder are Arabs.

You simply cannot grasp the effects that this victory had on the people until you try to wade through the street with little children clinging to your feet and beseeching you not for material things but for a word or a smile of comfort.

The first the populace knew of Tripoli's fall was when British armored cars and tanks rumbled through the streets this morning.

General Montgomery gave the civilian populace his assurance they had nothing to fear when he was greeted at the city's gate for the official surrender.

A U.S. FIGHTER BASE IN SOUTHERN TUNISIA, March 1—

Apparently in desperation, German pursuit pilots have changed their combat tactics since the battle of El Alamein and are engaging more frequently in dogfights with Allied fighters sweeping over the Mareth Line on strafing and bombing missions.

This is the report from United States fighter pilots who battled the Luftwaffe from El Alamein into Tunisia.

In addition, pilots return from missions with reports that German anti-aircraft fire from Gabès south is the heaviest they have ever encountered.

Lieut. Col. Arthur Salisbury, of Sedalia, Mo., returned from one strafing mission today with six planes in his flight punctured by bullets and shrapnel.

American fliers believe the German airmen, driven into the Tunisian corner, have orders from the high command to fight back instead of using hit-run tactics.

Gil Wymond of Louisville, Ky., a member of the Fighting Cock Squadron, said in discussing German tactics after returning from a mission over the Mareth Line: "The Jerries' tactics are entirely different now. At El Alamein they came at us out of the sun, diving in a column, and usually made one pass. If they didn't hit us in the first burst the chances are they'd hightail away. Sometimes they'd climb and dive a second time, but not often.

"Now they come at us from all sides and beneath. And they mix it with us. They're more progressive. I'm inclined to think we've got 'em cornered and they know it—so there is nothing left for them to do but stand up and fight."

WITH THE BRITISH EIGHTH ARMY WEST OF GABÈS, March 28—In his biggest gamble of the entire African campaign, General Sir Bernard L. Montgomery has outfoxed the "Fox of the Desert" by one of the boldest and most daring maneuvers accomplished by the British Eighth Army in its campaign to drive Field Marshal Erwin Rommel out of North Africa.

Strong elements of British troops outflanked the Mareth Line through a wild, sandy, dust-blown fringe of the Sahara desert across country that seemed impossible for an army to move over.

I know because I have just come across this waterless wasteland, which Marshal Rommel apparently thought could never be crossed by armor. Never in the almost 2,000-mile advance from El Alamein, Egypt, have I seen country which punishes men and machines more than this land.

But the Eighth Army accomplished the final phase of the move in a spectactular dash at almost unbelievable speed. It wasn't a case of playing safe and taking no chances—not this move. It was the greatest gamble General Montgomery had taken—a cool, calculated gamble that forced Marshal Rommel to divide his army into two parts in Southern Tunisia.

Three weeks ago a force went around the Matmata Hills and then toward Gabès, pioneering the wasteland. When the Germans repulsed the break-through in the Mareth Line on March 23, Montgomery made a quick decision.

Part of the armor and infantry was ordered to move swiftly from their Mareth positions. The move began at night on March 23 so that enemy observers in the Matmata Hills could not see the columns of transports, tanks and guns swarming south toward Foum Tatahouine and around the flank of the mountains forming part of the Mareth Line.

And, on March 26, when the armor arrived here, the battle plan was already made and the tanks were sent in to attack the Germans and Italians holding Melab Gap, twenty miles south of El Hamma and thirty miles from the sea.

After crossing some 200 miles of the desert along the trail of the ancient camel caravans, the armor went into the attack. Within forty-eight hours it had taken at least 3,000 prisoners. The sudden move threatened to cut Marshal Rommel's army in half and isolate the enemy forces holding the Mareth Line from those around Gabès.

With one British and one Australian correspondent, I arrived at this front amazed that an army could travel so swiftly across the desert. The trip took us three hard, jolting days of rough riding that ended with our battered car being towed into advance headquarters and the four of us wondering if we were going to have to follow the rest of this campaign at the end of a tow rope.

We left Medenine three days ago and drove south through Foum Tatahouine, a picturesque little Arab-French village hugging the hills. The village was like something out of a Biblical scene, with caravans of camels plodding down the roads, heavily-laden asses trotting in processions and robed Arabs coming out of the hills to market. At night the British armor moved during a curfew enforced in the village so that inquisitive eyes could not watch the columns.

South of Medenine, we turned into the desert along the route once taken by camel caravans. On either side rose curiously shaped barren hills, some looking like inverted wash basins, others like a giant tabletop hewn by hand.

And then the Khamseen began to blow—steady, monotonous, nerve-rasping winds that fog the air with sand and fill your eyes, nostrils, ears and hair with fine powdered dust.

We knew that water would be one of the most difficult problems, so water was rationed strictly with three mugs of tea each daily, and half a mug for shaving and washing. With half a mug you could at least get the worst of the sand from your face and get an illusion of cleanliness if you did not look in a mirror.

We camped in a gulch the first night, with the wind still blowing. In the morning fine sand had sifted over the beds and our faces, and the Khamseen had not slackened. Sand gritted in your teeth with every bite of food and rasped the eyeballs each time you blinked your eyes.

And again we set out in the brown dust clouds that swirled across the tracks made by the army and blotted out the horizon—an endless, jolting, bouncing, looking into nothingness.

We began passing trucks loaded with Italian and German prisoners. During the day I counted seventy-one trucks with at least twenty prisoners each.

In a sandstorm we lost the truck carrying our food, water and bedding. Immediately we developed a burning thirst, made worse when we had to get out and push our car bogged down in the soft sand.

But late in the day we caught up with the truck. It was a beautiful sight.

And beside the truck we saw a youth in the flying suit of an American airman, a blond pilot whose face was familiar.

"Hello," he said, "remember me?"

"Sure," I said. He was Dale R. Deniston of Akron, Ohio, whom I had met a few weeks ago when visiting American fighter squadrons operating in Southern Tunisia.

"What are you doing out here?"

"I just got shot down," Deniston said calmly.

He had set out earlier in the day leading a flight of Americans on a bombing-strafing mission near Gabès. While he was strafing enemy gun positions, antiaircraft had riddled the wings of his plane and damaged the fuselage controls. Denny had belly-landed the plane behind British lines and jumped out without so much as a bruise.

"I am hitch-hiking back to my landing ground to rejoin my squadron," Denny said.

We gave him blankets for the night and after breakfast the next morning he started the long trip back.

The Khamseen was still blowing as we resumed our trip. And then we stripped the gears on our car trying to pull out of the soft sand. We were taken in tow. But at least we managed to catch up with the army.

The way the troops and armor moved across that punishing route was so fast as to be almost unbelievable. It was one of the finest pieces of desert maneuvering in this war.

Notes

EDITOR'S NOTE AND ACKNOWLEDGMENTS

1. My father, Captain George C. Romeiser, First Armored Division, wrote in a similar vein to his parents while on duty in Tunisia: "This letter was just interrupted by about a dozen Stukas and some Messerschmitts that came over and bombed several miles north of here. They're not as brave as they used to be before someone threw something back at them. They come in high, do a very short dive, then get the devil home. Their bombing is usually very poor and ineffective. Those just a little while ago were all out in a field away from everyone. The morale effect is the most important and they don't bother us much anymore. We're still anxiously awaiting the time when we can see some Spitfires tangle with the Stukas. They really knock them down like ducks and the Spitfires like that kind of work." (April 1, 1943)

INTRODUCTION

1. See John B. Romeiser, *Beachhead Don: Reporting the War from the European Theater, 1942–1945* (New York: Fordham University Press, 2004), 348–50.

PART I

FROM MANHATTAN TO CAIRO, SEPTEMBER–OCTOBER 1942

1. Marie Whitehead, Don Whitehead's wife. She died in 1979, two years before her husband.
2. Alan J. Gould, executive assistant at the Associated Press.
3. Thoburn (Toby) Hughes Wiant (1911–63), born at Lagro, Indiana, was a World War II correspondent for the Associated Press. His daughter, Sue Wiant, has written an unpublished book on her father's career, *Between the Lines: A Father's Legacy*, with a foreword by Walter Cronkite. Her manuscript includes many of Wiant's letters and news stories. On September 12, 1942, Wiant wrote his parents as follows: "It now seems that Don Whitehead, one of our finest young reporters, will go with me to Cairo. He's a grand guy, in every way, and I hope it works out. We probably will fly to Natal, Brazil; cross the Atlantic; cut across the North-Central part of Africa; then swing up to Cairo. Of course, I won't be able to disclose the exact route or the exact time of departure."
4. Ed Kennedy, Associated Press bureau chief initially in the Middle East, then in the Mediterranean, and finally for the entire Western Front. He was known as moody and difficult. A veteran newsman in Europe since 1935, he defied press censorship in May 1945 to scoop

his peers on the German surrender, a move that wrecked his own career at AP, which he left in 1946.

5. *Harlan Daily Enterprise*, the newspaper that Don Whitehead worked for as a young man. Whitehead spent his early years in Harlan, Kentucky.

6. Ruth Whitehead, Don Whitehead's daughter, who died in 2003.

7. Like Whitehead, I have been unable to confirm this bit of local lore.

PART 2

CAIRO JOURNAL, OCTOBER–NOVEMBER 1942

1. See appendix for October 12, 1942, AP story ("America's armed forces are shoving aside . . .").

2. See appendix for October 13, 1942, AP story ("Incredible Cairo is living in the valley of the shadow of war . . .").

3. Shortly before U.S. entry into World War II, Brigadier General Russell L. Maxwell was sent to North Africa as head of the U.S. Military North African Mission. He was the Lend Lease coordinator in the area. Maxwell became the Commanding General of U.S. Army Forces in the Middle East (USAFIME), which consisted largely of Army Air Forces units. On November 4, 1942, Lieutenant General Frank M. Andrews replaced Maxwell as commander of USAFIME.

4. The Churchill story, while definitely a yarn that made the rounds, did underline the Russians' determination (and the Americans', especially George Marshall) for the Allies to open a new front in Northern Europe.

5. In September 1943, a group of battle-hardened Eighth Army soldiers refused orders in Salerno, Italy, and were tried for the biggest mutiny in British military history. They had been led to believe that they would be joining their old units in Sicily but later learned at sea that their destination was Salerno, where they would fight alongside the American 5th Army. They were dismayed to be joining new units and by the disorganization they encountered on the beaches.

6. The Desert Air Task Force (DATF) was established with Brigadier General Auby C. Strickland as Commanding General. This new organization, with HQ at Tripoli, Libya, supervised operationally and administratively all Ninth Air Force units west of, and including, Marble Arch. In addition, General Strickland was commander of U.S. troops in the area.

7. See appendix for November 10, 1942, AP story ("Given bases along the entire coast of North Africa . . .").

8. See appendix for November 17, 1942, AP story ("I have seen the graveyard of Rommel's hopes to conquer North Africa. . . .").

PART 3

IN PURSUIT OF ROMMEL (LIBYA), NOVEMBER 1942–FEBRUARY 1943

1. A political-religious organization in Libya and Sudan founded in Mecca in 1837 by Muhammad bin Ali al-Sanusi (1791–1859), known as the Grand Sanusi. The Sanusi unsuccessfully fought (1902–13) French expansion in the Sahara, and in 1911, the Italian invasion of

Libya forced them to concentrate there. During World War I they attacked British-occupied Egypt.

2. Rodolfo Graziani (1882–1955) became Italy's youngest colonel during World War I and enjoyed a prominent postwar military political career up to and during World War II, after which he was convicted of high treason.

3. Italo Balbo (1896–1940), Italian aviator, blackshirt leader and possible successor to Mussolini. Killed June 28, 1940, when he was returning from a patrol flight in Tobruk, Libya. His plane was shot down by an Italian antiaircraft gun from an Italian cruiser. The government in Rome maintained that the incident was an accident due to friendly fire, but Balbo's widow, Emanuela Florio, believed that it was an intentional assassination on Mussolini's orders.

4. See appendix for December 28, 1942, AP story ("Chasing Marshal Erwin Rommel toward Tripoli has become a will o' the wisp hunt across the western desert. . . .").

5. Major General Allen Francis Harding, Commander of the British Seventh Armored Division, the famous Desert Rats.

6. See appendix for January 23, 1943, AP story ("Seeing people liberated from virtual bondage and watching their emotional outbursts . . .").

7. Harry Crockett was the first AP reporter to die in World War II. Five AP correspondents were killed during World War II either due to hostile fire in combat or execution once captured. A total of sixty-eight journalists were killed during the war.

8. Larry Allen, 1941 Pulitzer Prize winner for outstanding foreign correspondence and AP writer. Allen was captured by the Italians at Tobruk on September 13, 1942, and taken to a prisoner of war camp in Italy. He was later transferred to a camp in Germany.

9. British General Harold Alexander, commander of the Middle Eastern theater.

10. Whitehead got as close as he could to the actual fighting. In World War II, reporters were free to move around without significant restriction. He remembered that he had not gone that close to the front lines in the early weeks in Egypt, but then he met *Time* magazine correspondent Jack Belden, who was also with the British Eighth Army. Whitehead said that Belden would disappear from time to time, and the other correspondents wondered where he was and what was going on. One day Whitehead asked him where he had been, and Belden replied that he had been up front with the troops. Whitehead realized that he "had not been covering the war as it should have been covered." "From that time on," he recalled, "I decided I would use the Belden approach to reporting and get as close as I possibly could to the fighting," despite the dangers. See Romeiser, *Beachhead Don*, xxvi.

11. See appendix for March 1, 1943, AP story ("Apparently in desperation, German pursuit pilots have changed their combat tactics. . . .").

PART 4

VICTORY IN TUNISIA, MARCH–APRIL 1943

1. Democratic Party chairman in the 1930s and one of President Franklin Delano Roosevelt's closest political advisors, James (Jim) Farley (1888–1973) was dedicated to the New Deal and to getting legislative support for Roosevelt's programs.

2. See appendix for March 28, 1943, AP story ("In his biggest gamble of the entire African campaign . . .").

AFTERWORD

1. See John B. Romeiser, *Beachhead Don: Reporting the War from the European Theater, 1942–1945* (New York: Fordham University Press, 2004), xxiv.

2. See Romeiser, *Beachhead Don*, 20–23.

Index

WORLD WAR II: THE GLOBAL, HUMAN, AND ETHICAL DIMENSION
G. Kurt Piehler, series editor

1. Lawrence Cane, David E. Cane, Judy Barrett Litoff, and David C. Smith, eds.,
Fighting Fascism in Europe: The World War II Letters of an American Veteran of the Spanish Civil War.

2. Angelo M. Spinelli and Lewis H. Carlson,
Life Behind Barbed Wire: The Secret World War II Photographs of Prisoner of War Angelo M. Spinelli.

3. Don Whitehead and John B. Romeiser,
"Beachhead Don": Reporting the War from the European Theater, 1942–1945.

4. Scott H. Bennett, ed.,
Army GI, Pacifist CO: The World War II Letters of Frank and Albert Dietrich.

5. Alexander Jefferson with Lewis H. Carlson,
Red Tail Captured, Red Tail Free: Memoirs of a Tuskegee Airman and POW.

6. Jonathan G. Utley,
Going to War with Japan, 1937–1941.

7. Grant K. Goodman,
America's Japan: The First Year, 1945–1946.

8. Patricia Kollander, with John O'Sullivan,
"I Must Be a Part of This War": One Man's Fight Against Hitler and Nazism.

9. Judy Barrett Litoff,
An American Heroine in the French Resistance: The Diary and Memoir of Virginia d'Albert-Lake.

10. Thomas R. Christofferson and Michael S. Christofferson,
France during World War II: From Defeat to Liberation.

11. Valdis O. Lumans,
Latvia in World War II.

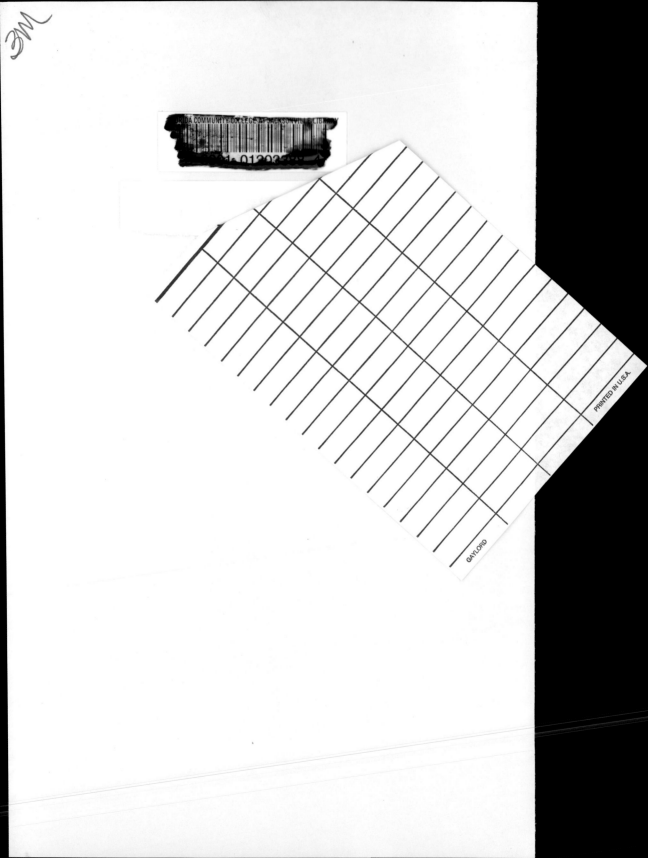